Mastering Ext JS

Learn how to build powerful and professional applications by mastering the Ext JS framework

Loiane Groner

[PACKT] PUBLISHING open source community experience distilled

BIRMINGHAM - MUMBAI

Mastering Ext JS

First published: July 2013

Production Reference: 1010713

Published by Packt Publishing Ltd.
Livery Place
35 Livery Street
Birmingham B3 2PB, UK..

ISBN 978-1-78216-400-5

`www.packtpub.com`

Cover Image by Asher Wishkerman (`a.wishkerman@mpic.de`)

Credits

Author
Loiane Groner

Reviewers
Aafrin
Vincenzo Ampolo
Yiyu Jia
Joel Watson

Acquisition Editor
Edward Gordon

Lead Technical Editor
Anila Vincent

Technical Editors
Arvind Koul
Worrell Lewis
Vaibhav Pawar
Amit Ramadas

Project Coordinator
Hardik Patel

Proofreader
Chris Smith

Indexer
Hemangini Bari

Graphics
Abhinash Sahu

Production Coordinator
Shantanu Zagade

Cover Work
Shantanu Zagade

About the Author

Loiane Groner lives in São Paulo, Brazil and has over eight years of software development experience. While at university, she demonstrated great interest in IT. She worked as an assistant teacher for two and a half years, teaching algorithms, data structures, and computing theory. She represented her university at the ACM International Collegiate Programming Contest - Brazilian Finals (South America Regionals) and also worked as Student Delegate of SBC (Brazilian Computing Society) for two years. She won a merit award in her senior year for being one of the top three students with better GPAs in the Computer Science department and also graduated with honors.

She has worked at multinational companies such as IBM. Her areas of expertise include Java SE, Java EE, and also Sencha technologies (Ext JS and Sencha Touch). She is now working as Software Development Manager at a financial institution, where she manages overseas solutions. She also works as an independent Sencha consultant and coach.

Loiane is also the author of *Ext JS 4 First Look* and *Sencha Architect App Development, Packt Publishing*.

She is passionate about Sencha and Java, and is the leader of CampinasJUG/SouJava Campinas (Campinas Java Users Group) and coordinator of ESJUG (Espirito Santo Java Users Group) , both Brazilian JUGs.

She also contributes to the software development community through her blogs: `http://loianegroner.com` (English) and `http://loiane.com` (Portuguese-BR), where she writes about IT careers, Ext JS, Sencha Touch, Sencha Architect, Java, and general development notes and also publishes screencasts.

If you want to keep in touch, you can find Loiane on Facebook (`https://www.facebook.com/loianegroner`) and Twitter (`@loiane`).

Acknowledgement

I would like to thank my parents for giving me education, guidance, and advice, through all these years, and helping me be a better human being and professional. A very special thank you to my husband, for being patient and supportive and giving me encouragement. Also a big thanks to my friends and readers for all the support.

About the Reviewers

Aafrin is a self-taught programmer who has a cyber security and digital forensic background. He has been actively developing and prototyping web applications since 2003. He codes in various programming languages including C++, Java, PHP, ASP, VB, VB.net, and has also worked with frameworks such as EXTJS, CakePHP, CodeIgniter, and Yii. In his free time, he blogs at `www.aafrin.com` and researches on the computer security/computer forensic field.

Vincenzo Ampolo has a Master's degree in Computer Systems Engineering at Politecnico di Milano, Italy. He has been a freelancer for over six years. His passion for technology started when he was nine, when he assembled his first computer. By 12 he learned the BASIC language. At 15 he learned C, then Python and Javascript. He is a free software evangelist and has been using the GNU/Linux system from the age of 14. He created the first usermode bootsplash system for Linux systems when he was 17. He moved to the silicon valley a year ago.

He is a philanthropist and believes in the power of software communities and has helped in organizing many FOSS-related conferences such as Linux day and the Ubuntu release party.

To all the people who believed in me.

Yiyu Jia has been developing web applications since 1996. He worked as a technical leader and solution architect on various projects with Java and PHP as the major backend languages. He also has professional experience on interactive TV, middleware, and home gateway projects. He is especially interested in designing multichannel web applications.

He is also the main founder of the novel data mining research topic—Promotional Subspace Mining (PSM), which aims at finding out useful information from subspaces on a very large data set. He is now working on Big Data technologies.

He can be reached at his blog and website. They are `http://yiyujia.blogspot.com` and `http://www.idatamining.org` respectively.

Joel Watson is a web enthusiast, working for the past eight years in website design and development. He loves exploring web technologies of all sorts, and particularly enjoys creating web experiences that leverage the newest features of HTML5 and its related technologies.

When he's not coding, Joel enjoys spending time with his wife and two daughters, playing guitar, and watching cheesy sci-fi and anime.

www.PacktPub.com

Support files, eBooks, discount offers and more

You might want to visit www.PacktPub.com for support files and downloads related to your book.

Did you know that Packt offers eBook versions of every book published, with PDF and ePub files available? You can upgrade to the eBook version at www.PacktPub.com and as a print book customer, you are entitled to a discount on the eBook copy. Get in touch with us at service@packtpub.com for more details.

At www.PacktPub.com, you can also read a collection of free technical articles, sign up for a range of free newsletters and receive exclusive discounts and offers on Packt books and eBooks.

http://PacktLib.PacktPub.com

Do you need instant solutions to your IT questions? PacktLib is Packt's online digital book library. Here, you can access, read and search across Packt's entire library of books.

Why Subscribe?

- Fully searchable across every book published by Packt
- Copy and paste, print and bookmark content
- On demand and accessible via web browser

Free Access for Packt account holders

If you have an account with Packt at www.PacktPub.com, you can use this to access PacktLib today and view nine entirely free books. Simply use your login credentials for immediate access.

Table of Contents

Preface **1**
Chapter 1: Getting Started **7**
Installing the required software **8**
Presenting the application and its capabilities **10**
The splash screen 10
The login screen 11
The main screen 11
User control management 13
MySQL table management 13
Content management control 14
The e-mail client module 16
Creating the structure of the application using MVC **17**
A quick word about MVC 17
Creating the application 18
Creating the loading page **25**
Summary **32**
Chapter 2: The Login Page **33**
The Login screen **33**
Creating the Login screen **34**
Client-side validations 38
Creating custom VTypes 40
Adding the toolbar with buttons 40
Running the code 42
Using itemId versus id – Ext.Cmp is bad! 43
Creating the login controller **44**
Adding the controller to app.js 45
Listening to the button click event 46
Cancel button listener implementation 51

Submit button listener implementation 52
Creating the User and Groups tables 56
Handling the login page on the server 57
Connecting to the database 57
login.php 58
Handling the return of the server – logged in or not? 60
Success versus failure 60
Enhancing the Login screen 64
Applying a loading mask on the form while authenticating 65
Form submit on Enter 65
The Caps Lock warning message 66
Summary 71
Chapter 3: Logout and Multilingual 73
The base of the application 74
The logout capability 78
Refactoring the login and logout code 79
Handling the logout capability on the server 82
The client-side activity monitor 82
The multilingual capability 84
Creating the change language component 84
Creating the translation files 87
Applying the translation on the application's components 88
HTML5 local storage 89
Handling the language change in real-time 90
Locale – translating Ext JS 93
Summary 94
Chapter 4: Advanced Dynamic Menu 95
Creating the dynamic menu 96
The database model – groups, menus, and permissions 97
Creating the menu models – hasMany association 99
Creating the store – loading the menu from the server 102
Handling the dynamic menu on the server 102
Creating the menu with Accordion panel and Tree panel 106
Replacing the central container on the viewport 107
Creating the menu controller-side 108
Rendering the menu from nested JSON (hasMany association) 109
Opening a menu item dynamically 111
Changing app.js 112
Summary 113

Chapter 5: User Identification and Security **115**
Managing users **115**
Listing all the users – simple Grid panel **117**
User model 117
Users store 118
Users Grid panel 119
Users controller 123
Adding and editing a new user **124**
Creating the edit view – a form within a window 125
The group model 129
The groups store 130
The controller – listening to the add button 131
The controller – listening to the edit button 132
The controller – saving a user 133
The controller – listening to the cancel button 135
Previewing a file before uploading it 135
Deleting a user **138**
Summary **140**
Chapter 6: MySQL Table Management **141**
Presenting the tables **142**
Creating the models **143**
Abstract model 144
Specific models 145
Creating the stores **146**
The Abstract Store 147
The Abstract Proxy 148
Specific stores 152
Creating the menu items **153**
Creating an abstract Grid panel for reuse **156**
Handling the action column in the MVC architecture 161
Setting iconCls instead of icon on the action column 161
The Live Search plugin versus the Filter plugin 162
Specific Grid panels for each table 164
A generic controller for all tables **166**
Loading the Grid panel store when the grid is rendered 167
Adding a new record on the Grid panel 168
Editing an existing record 169
Deleting – handling the action column on the controller 170
Saving the changes 171
autoSync configuration 172
Canceling the changes 172

Clearing the filter 173
Listening to store events on the controller 173
Summary 174
Chapter 7: Content Management 175
Managing information – films, clients, and rentals 175
Displaying the Film data grid 180
The Film model 180
Films store 181
Film data grid (with paging) 183
Handling paging on the server side 188
Creating the controller 191
Editing in the Film grid panel 192
Packt.view.sakila.WindowForm 198
Film categories 200
Store 200
Edit view 201
Search categories – MultiSelect 203
Film actors 206
Store 206
Edit view 207
Searching for actors – live search combobox 208
The films controller 212
Loading the existing film information within the Edit form 212
Getting the MultiSelect values 214
Getting the selected actor from live search 215
Summary 216
Chapter 8: Adding Extra Capabilities 217
Exporting the Grid panel to PDF and Excel 217
Exporting to PDF 219
Generating the PDF file on the server (PHP) 221
Exporting to Excel 221
Printing Grid panel content with the Grid printer plugin 221
Creating the Sales by Film Category chart 223
Pie chart 225
Column chart 227
The chart panel 230
Changing the chart type 233
Exporting charts to images (PNG and SVG) 233
Exporting charts to PDF 235
Summary 238

Chapter 9: The E-mail Client Module 239
Creating the inbox – list of e-mails 240
The mail message model 240
The mail messages store 241
The mail list view 242
The preview mail panel 246
The mail menu (tree menu) 248
The mail menu tree store 248
Creating the mail menu view 249
The mail container – organizing the e-mail client 250
The controller 252
Previewing an e-mail 254
Organizing e-mails – drag-and-drop 255
Creating a new message 258
Dynamically displaying Cc and Bcc fields 261
Adding the file upload fields dynamically 262
Summary 263
Chapter 10: Preparing for Production 265
Before we start 265
Customizing a theme 266
Packaging the application for production 273
What to deploy in production 277
Benefits 278
From web to desktop – Sencha Desktop Packager 279
Installation 280
Mac OS and Linux 280
Windows 281
Packaging the application 285
Required changes on the server side 288
Ajax versus JSONP versus CORS 291
Summary 292
Chapter 11: Building a WordPress Theme 293
Before we start 293
A brief introduction to WordPress themes 296
Structuring our theme 296
Building the Header 300
Creating the Ext JS code 302
Building the Footer 305
Building the Main page 306
Building the Sidebar 309
Building the single post page 314

Building the single page 316
Summary 316
Chapter 12: Debugging and Testing 317
Debugging Ext JS applications 318
Testing Ext JS applications 320
Generating the "test" build with Sencha command 321
Installing Siesta and creating test cases 323
Helpful tools 327
From Ext JS to mobile 329
Third-party components and plugins 331
Summary 331
Index 333

Preface

If you are an Ext JS developer, it probably took you a while to learn the framework. We know that the Ext JS learning curve is not short. After we have learned the basics, and we need to use Ext JS in our daily jobs, a lot of questions pop up: how can one component talk to another? What are the best practices? Is it really worth using this approach and not any other? Is there any other way I can implement the same feature? This is normal.

This book was written keeping these developers in mind. How do we put everything together and create really nice applications with Ext JS?

So this is what this book is about. We are going to create a complete application together, from the mockup of the screens until we are able to put it into production. We are going to create the application structure, a splash screen, a login screen, multilingual capability, activity monitor, a dynamic menu that depends on users' permission, and modules to manage database information (simple and complex information). Then, we will learn how to build the application for production, as a native desktop application, to debug and test it. As an extra chapter, we will learn how to build a WordPress theme using Ext JS features.

We will use real-world examples and see how we can implement them using Ext JS components. Throughout the book we'll see a lot of tips, do this and do not do that, and best practices to help you boost your Ext JS knowledge and take you to the next level.

What this book covers

Chapter 1, Getting Started, introduces the application that is going to be implemented throughout the book and its features, the mockup of each screen and module (each chapter covers a different module) and also demonstrates how to create the structure of the application using the MVC architecture and how to create a splash screen.

Chapter 2, The Login Page, explains how to create a login page with Ext JS, how to handle it on the server side and also shows some extra capabilities such as adding a *Caps Lock* warning message, submitting the login page when pressing the *Enter* key, and also encrypting the password before sending to the server.

Chapter 3, Logout and Multilingual, covers how to create the logout capability and also the client-side activity monitor timeout, which is in case the user does not use the mouse or press any key on the keyboard the system will end the session automatically and it will logout. This chapter also provides a multilingual capability example and how to create a component that the user can use to change the system's language and locale settings.

Chapter 4, Advanced Dynamic Menu, is about how to create a dynamic menu that depends on user's permission. The options of the menu are rendered according to the user, if he has permission or not; if not, the option will not be displayed.

Chapter 5, User Identification and Security, explains how to create a screen to list all the users that already have access to the system and also how to create a screen to create/edit or delete an existing user and change this user's permission.

Chapter 6, MySQL Table Management, covers how to implement a module where the user will be able to edit information as if they were editing information directly from a MySQL table. This chapter also explores some capabilities such as live search, filter, inline editing (using the Cell Editing and Row Editing plugins) and also, we start exploring real-world issues when we develop big applications with Ext JS, such as reuse of components throughout the application.

Chapter 7, Content Management, explores further the complexity of managing information from a table of the database and all its relationships with other tables. So we will cover how to manage complex information, and how to handle associations within data grids and form panels.

Chapter 8, Adding Extra Capabilities, covers how to add features such as printing, export to PDF, and Excel that are not supported natively by Ext JS. This chapter also covers charts and how to export them to image and PDF and also how to use third-party plugins.

Chapter 9, The E-mail Client Module, explores how to create a screen that is based on the look and feel of Outlook, a very popular e-mail client from Microsoft. This chapter only covers how to create the screen using Ext JS; it does not cover loading or sending e-mails using any e-mail library.

Chapter 10, Preparing for Production, covers very briefly how to customize a theme using Ext JS 4.2. It also explores what are the steps, the benefits of packaging the application for production, and also how to use Desktop Packager to create native desktop applications with Ext JS.

Chapter 11, Building a WordPress Theme, steps out of the main subject that we cover in the other chapters of the book by demonstrating how to create a WordPress theme using Ext JS. This is an extra chapter and demonstrates a different approach of using Ext JS.

Chapter 12, Debugging and Testing, is about debugging Ext JS applications, what we need to be careful about and why it is very important to know how to debug. It also covers a quick look at the Siesta framework, which is a framework that can be used for testing Ext JS applications. We also briefly talk about transforming Ext JS projects into mobile apps, some helpful tools that can help us in our developer daily basis work and also some recommendations on where to find extra and open source plugins to use in Ext JS projects.

What you need for this book

Following is a list of the software you will need to have installed beforehand to execute the examples of the book. The following is a list of the software used to implement and execute the examples of this book, but you can use any similar software that you already have installed that has the same features.

A browser with a debugger tool:

- Firefox with Firebug: `https://www.mozilla.org/firefox/` and `http://getfirebug.com/`
- Google Chrome: `http://www.google.com/chrome`

Web server with PHP support:

- Xampp: `http://www.apachefriends.org/en/xampp.html`

Database:

- MySQL: `http://dev.mysql.com/downloads/mysql/`
- MySQL Workbench: `http://dev.mysql.com/downloads/tools/workbench/`
- MySQL Sakila sample database: `http://dev.mysql.com/doc/index-other.html` and `http://dev.mysql.com/doc/sakila/en/index.html`

Sencha command and required tools:

- Sencha Cmd: `http://www.sencha.com/products/sencha-cmd/download`
- Ruby: `http://www.ruby-lang.org/en/downloads/`
- Sass: `http://sass-lang.com/`
- Compass: `http://compass-style.org/`
- Java JDK: `http://www.oracle.com/technetwork/java/javase/downloads/index.html`
- Java environment variables: `http://docs.oracle.com/javase/tutorial/essential/environment/paths.html`
- And of course, Ext JS: `http://www.sencha.com/products/extjs/`

We will use Ext JS 4.2 on this book.

Who this book is for

This book is for developers who are familiar with using Ext JS and who want to augment their skills to create even better web applications. This book will not teach you the basics of Ext JS.

Conventions

In this book, you will find a number of styles of text that distinguish between different kinds of information. Here are some examples of these styles, and an explanation of their meaning.

Code words in text are shown as follows: "We will be adding a new CSS style to the loading `DIV` tag."

A block of code is set as follows:

```
Ext.application({ // #1
    name: 'Packt', // #2
    launch: function() { // #3
        console.log('launch');   // #4
    }
});
```

When we wish to draw your attention to a particular part of a code block, the relevant lines or items are set in bold:

```
controllers: [
    'Login',
    'TranslationManager',
    'Menu'
]
```

Any command-line input or output is written as follows:

```
sencha generate theme masteringextjs-theme
```

New terms and **important words** are shown in bold. Words that you see on the screen, in menus or dialog boxes for example, appear in the text like this: "After the application is fully loaded, the first screen the user will see is the **Login** screen."

> Warnings or important notes appear in a box like this.

> Tips and tricks appear like this.

Reader feedback

Feedback from our readers is always welcome. Let us know what you think about this book—what you liked or may have disliked. Reader feedback is important for us to develop titles that you really get the most out of.

To send us general feedback, simply send an e-mail to `feedback@packtpub.com`, and mention the book title via the subject of your message.

If there is a topic that you have expertise in and you are interested in either writing or contributing to a book, see our author guide on `www.packtpub.com/authors`.

Customer support

Now that you are the proud owner of a Packt book, we have a number of things to help you to get the most from your purchase.

Errata

Although we have taken every care to ensure the accuracy of our content, mistakes do happen. If you find a mistake in one of our books—maybe a mistake in the text or the code—we would be grateful if you would report this to us. By doing so, you can save other readers from frustration and help us improve subsequent versions of this book. If you find any errata, please report them by visiting `http://www.packtpub.com/submit-errata`, selecting your book, clicking on the **errata submission form** link, and entering the details of your errata. Once your errata are verified, your submission will be accepted and the errata will be uploaded on our website, or added to any list of existing errata, under the Errata section of that title. Any existing errata can be viewed by selecting your title from `http://www.packtpub.com/support`.

Piracy

Piracy of copyright material on the Internet is an ongoing problem across all media. At Packt, we take the protection of our copyright and licenses very seriously. If you come across any illegal copies of our works, in any form, on the Internet, please provide us with the location address or website name immediately so that we can pursue a remedy.

Please contact us at `copyright@packtpub.com` with a link to the suspected pirated material.

We appreciate your help in protecting our authors, and our ability to bring you valuable content.

Questions

You can contact us at `questions@packtpub.com` if you are having a problem with any aspect of the book, and we will do our best to address it.

1
Getting Started

Ext JS is a great cross-browser **RIA** (**Rich Internet Application**) framework used to build very rich and user-friendly frontend interfaces. When you explore the examples that come within the Ext JS SDK, you can see examples of how to use some components, such as Grid, Tree, Form, and Chart. There are also examples of how to use the **MVC** (**Model-View-Controller**) architecture. But most of these examples are standalone versions and it can be a little tricky when we try to put all of them together into a single application. Also, when we are developing an application, there are a few things that we can do to reuse a great part of the source code, making the code easy to maintain.

In this book, we are going to dive into the Sencha Ext JS world and explore real case examples, and we will also build a complete application from scratch from the prototype phase until the deployment in production.

In this chapter, we will learn about the application we are going to develop and we will also learn how to organize the files of the application that is going to be built throughout the chapters of this book. This chapter will also present the mockup of the application and how to start organizing the screens (which is a very important step and some developers forget to do it). In this chapter, we will cover:

- Installation of the required software
- Presenting the application and its capabilities
- Creating mockups of each screen
- Creating the structure of the app using MVC
- Creating the loading page

Installing the required software

The application that we are going to develop has a very simple architecture. We are going to use Ext JS on the frontend, which is going to communicate with a server-side module, which will then communicate with a database as shown in the following diagram:

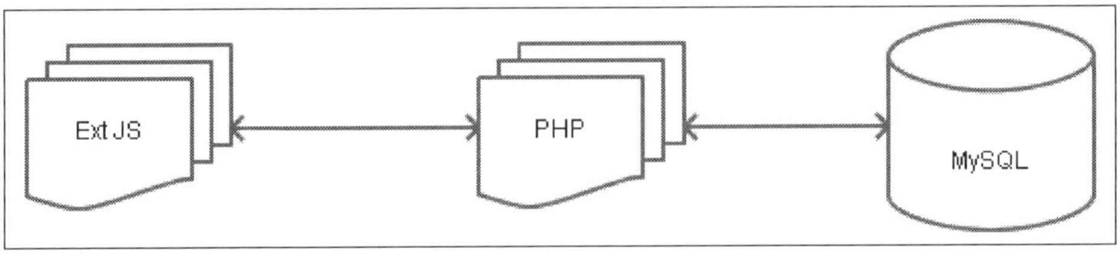

The server-side module will be developed using PHP. Do not worry if you do not know PHP. We are going to use a very basic code and we are going to focus on the programming logic that needs to be implemented on the server side. This way you can apply the same logic using any other programming language such as Java, ASP .NET, Ruby, Python, or any other one that has support to exchange data in JSON or XML format as this is the communication format used by Ext JS.

And for the database we will use MySQL. We will also use the Sakila sample schema, which is perfect to demonstrate how to work with **CRUD** (**Create**, **Read**, **Update**, and **Delete/Destroy**) operations on a database table and also use more complex operations, such as views and stored procedures (we will learn how to handle all this information with Ext JS).

After we have finished implementing the application, we will customize the theme, and because of this we will need to install Ruby and the Sass and Compass gems. Also, we will need to install Sencha Command to customize the theme and also make the production build. To have Sencha Command working properly, we will also need to have the Java SDK installed and configured.

To deploy the application, we need a web server. If you do not have any web server installed on your computer yet, do not worry. In this book we will use XAMPP as the default web server.

We will also need a browser to run our application in. The recommended ones are Firefox (with Firebug) or Google Chrome.

So to summarize all the tools and software we need to have installed prior starting the fun, here is a list with the links where you can download them and find installation instructions:

- A browser with a debugger tool:
    - Firefox with Firebug: `https://www.mozilla.org/firefox/` and `http://getfirebug.com/`
    - Google Chrome: `www.google.com/chrome`
- A web server:
    - XAMPP: `http://www.apachefriends.org/en/xampp.html`
- A database:
    - MySQL: `http://dev.mysql.com/downloads/mysql/`
    - MySQL Workbench: `http://dev.mysql.com/downloads/tools/workbench/`
    - MySQL Sakila sample database: `http://dev.mysql.com/doc/index-other.html` and `http://dev.mysql.com/doc/sakila/en/index.html`
- Sencha Command and required tools
    - Sencha Command: `http://dev.mysql.com/doc/sakila/en/index.html`
    - Ruby: `http://www.ruby-lang.org/en/downloads/`
    - Sass: `http://sass-lang.com/`
    - Compass: `http://compass-style.org/`
    - Java JDK: `http://www.oracle.com/technetwork/java/javase/downloads/index.html`
    - Java environment variables: `http://docs.oracle.com/javase/tutorial/essential/environment/paths.html`

And of course Ext JS: `http://www.sencha.com/products/extjs/`; we will use Ext JS 4.2 in this book.

Presenting the application and its capabilities

The application that we are going to develop throughout this book is very common to other web systems that you are probably used to implementing. We will implement a Video Manager Store (that is why the use of the Sakila sample database). Some of the features of the application are the security management (able to manage users and their permissions within the application), manage Actors, Films, Inventory, and Rental Information.

Ext JS will help us to achieve our goal. Ext JS provides beautiful components, which make the final user's eye shine when looking at a beautiful application with components that are intuitive and user friendly, and for us developers it provides a complete architecture, the possibility to reuse components (and decrease our work), and a very complete data package that makes easier to make connections to the server side and send and retrieve information.

We will divide the application in modules, and each module will be responsible for some features of the application. In each chapter of this book, we will implement one of the modules.

The application is composed of:

- A splash screen (so the user does not need to see a blank screen while the application is still launching)
- A login screen
- A main screen
- User control management
- MySQL table management (for categories and combobox values)
- Content management control
- An e-mail client module

For each of the modules and screens mentioned above, we will create mockups so we can plan how the application will work (for example, will it have a menu, will we open the menu items in a window or center of the screen or use a tab panel?).

The splash screen

When we first load the application, it can take some time until the application has everything that is required loaded prior its execution. If we do not do anything, the user will see a blank page, which is a little bit boring.

Our application will have a splash screen so the user does not need to see a blank page while the application is still loading the required files and classes prior its initialization.

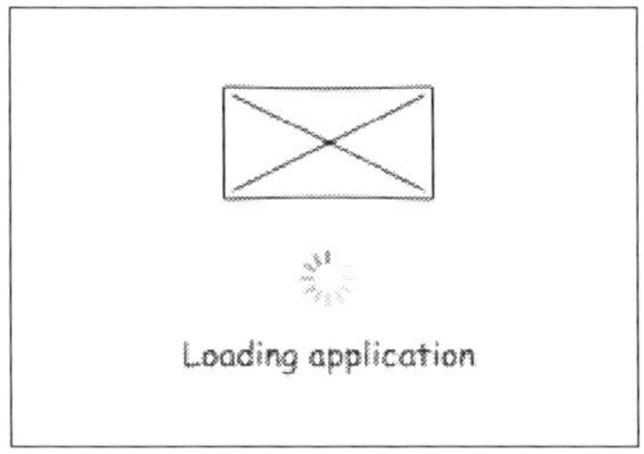

The login screen

After the application is fully loaded, the first screen the user will see is the **Login** screen. The user will be able to enter the **UserName** and **Password**. There is also a multilingual combobox where the user can choose the language of the system. Then, we have the **Cancel** and **Submit** buttons:

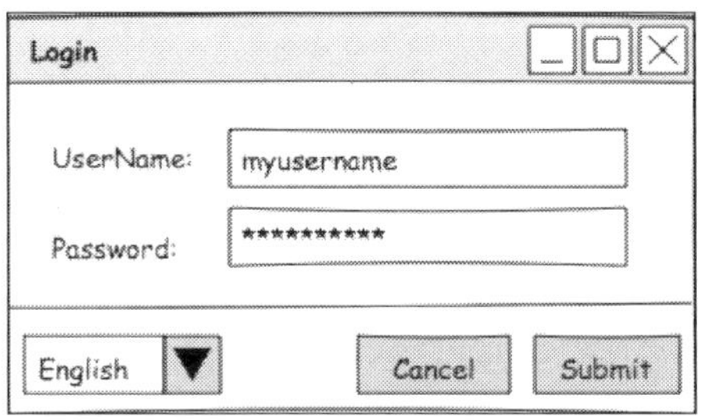

The main screen

The general idea of the application is to have a main screen that will be organized using the border layout. In the center region, we will have a tab panel, and each tab will represent a screen of the application (each screen will have its own layout); only the first tab item will not be closable (the Home tab). On the north region we will have a header with the name of the application (Video Store Manager), the multi lingual combobox (in case the user wants to change the current language of the application), and a Logout button. On the south region we will have the footer with a copyright message (or it can be the name of the company or developer that implemented the project). And on the east region we will have a dynamic menu (we will have user control management). The menu will be implemented using accordion panels (for each module) and in each panel we will use a tree to list the menu options of each module.

The main screen will look something like the following mockup:

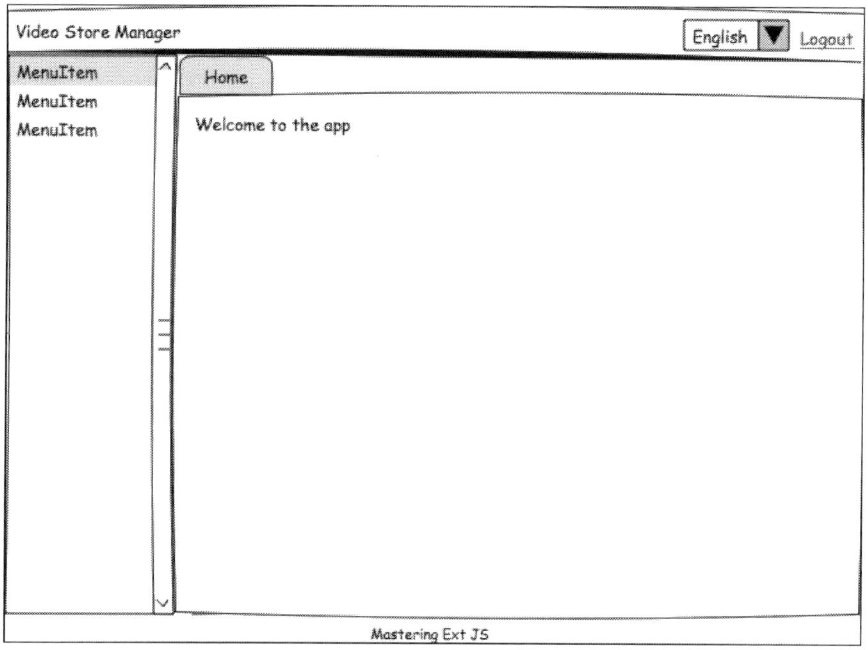

If we try to translate into the previous mockup everything that we explained in the beginning of this topic, we will see the following diagram with the layout regions that we will use in the main screen:

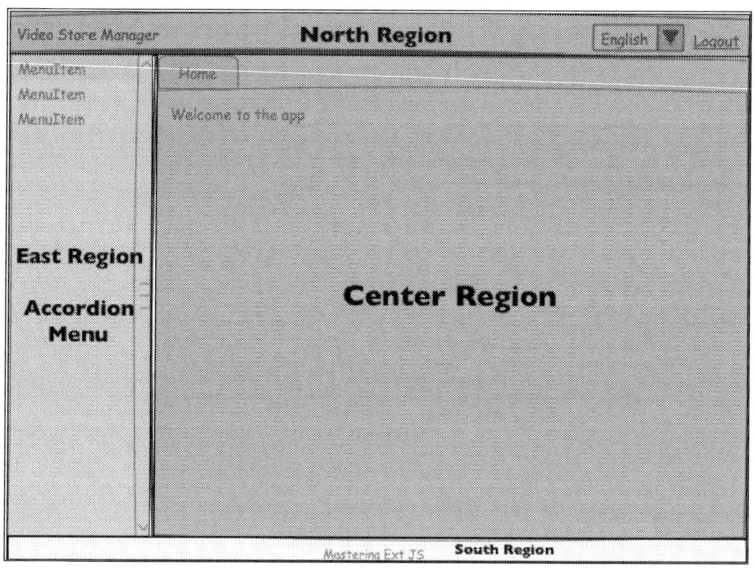

User control management

In user control management, the user will have access to create new users, new groups, and assign new roles to users. The user will be able to control the system permissions (which user can see which modules in the system).

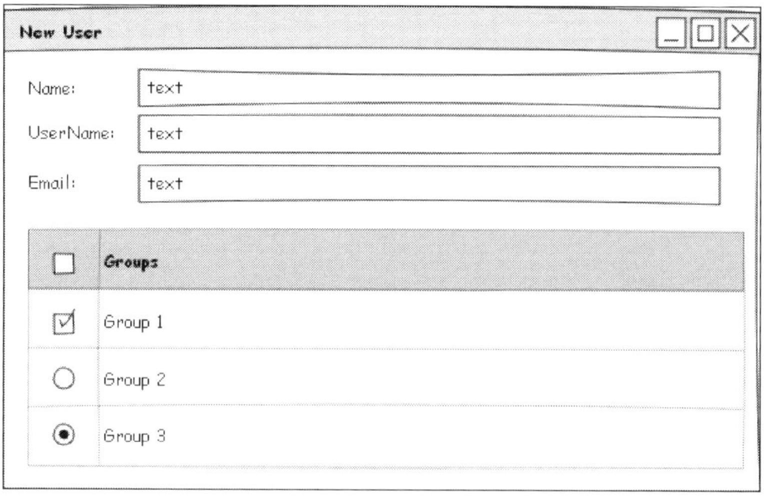

MySQL table management

Every system has options that fit into the **Categories** category, such as film categories, film language, combobox options, and so on. For these tables, we need to provide all CRUD options and also filter options. The screens from this module will be very similar to the **Edit table data** option from MySQL Workbench.

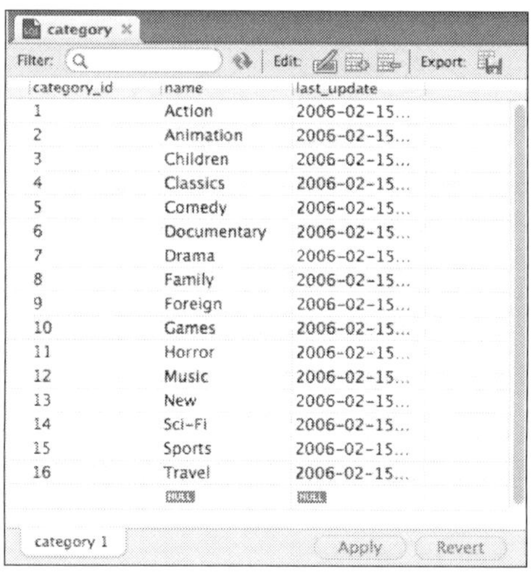

The user will be able to edit the data in the rows of the grid.

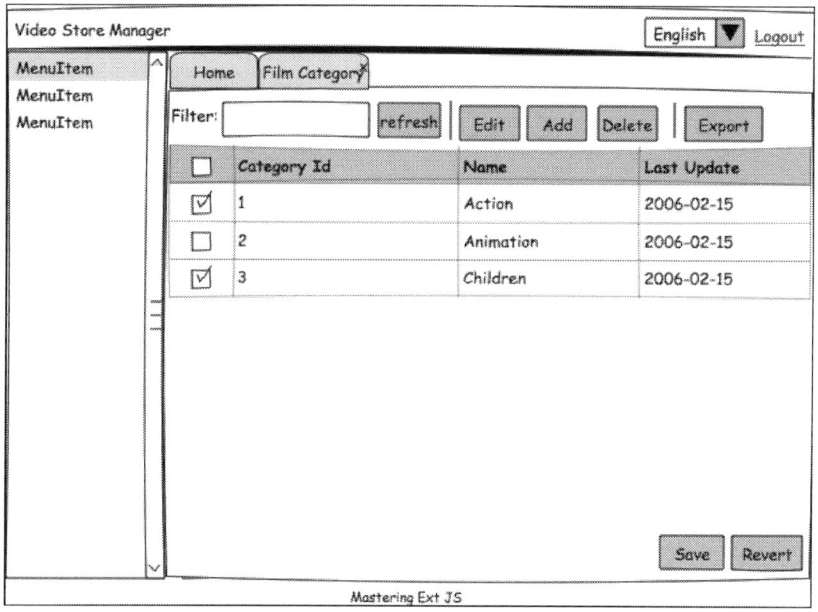

Content management control

In this module the user will be able to see and edit the core information from the system. As most of the database tables we will be handling in this module have relationship with other tables, the editing of the information will be more complex involving master-detail information. Usually, we will present the information to the user in a Grid panel and the editing of the information will be made in a Form panel that is inside a window.

It is also very important to remember that most of the screens from a module will have similar capabilities, and as we are going to build an application with a lot of screens, it is important to design the system to be able to reuse as much code as possible With this you can easily maintain and add features and capabilities to the system.

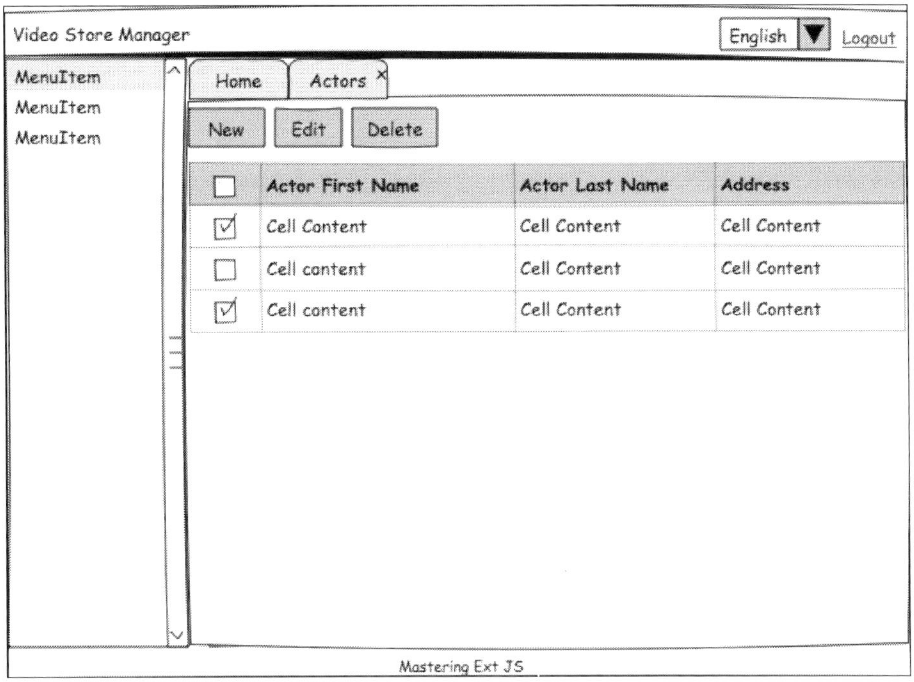

When you click on **New** or **Edit**, a new window will open to edit the information as shown in the following screenshot:

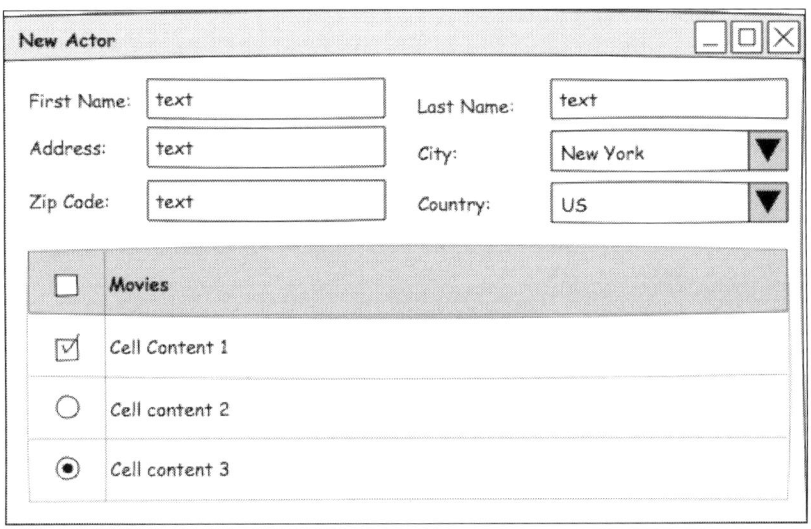

The e-mail client module

In this module we will design an e-mail client built with Ext JS. This is important because it demonstrates that we can build anything with Ext JS, not only CRUD screens. In this module we will implement on the client-side part of an e-mail client, meaning only the screens. We will not implement the sending/receiving e-mail code (which would be the server-side code).

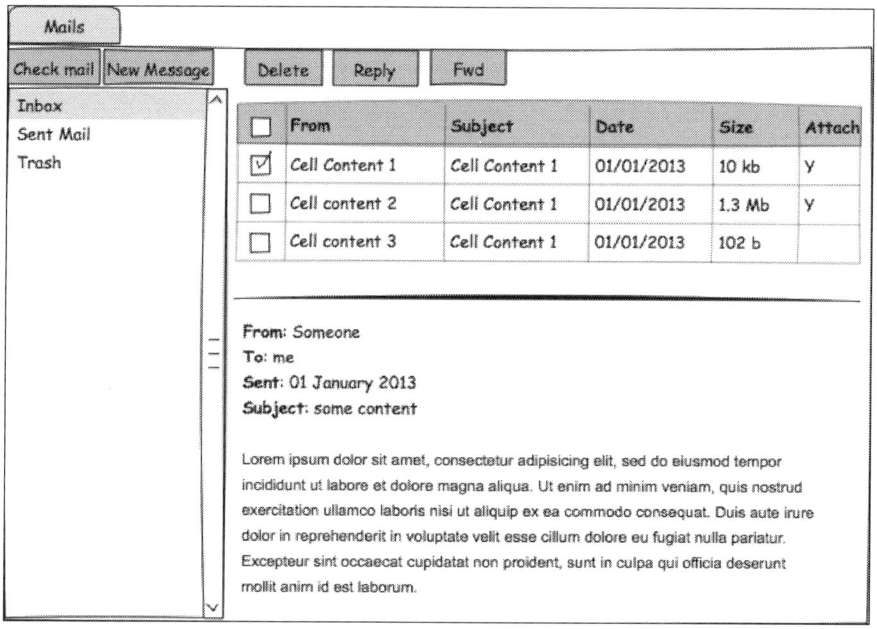

Creating the structure of the application using MVC

Let's get started and get our hands on the code. The first thing we are going to do is to create the application using the MVC structure. **Sencha Command** (**Sencha Cmd**) provides us the capability of creating the application automatically. And creating the application with Sencha Cmd is helpful because it already creates the structure of the application according to the MVC architecture, and it also provides all the files we need to build the application for production and customizing the theme (we will learn how to do it later on this book).

A quick word about MVC

MVC stands for **Model-View-Controller**. It is a software architecture pattern that separates the representation of the information from the user's interaction with it. The **Model** represents the application data, the **View** represents the output of the representation of the data (**Form**, **Grid**, **Chart**), and the **Controller** mediates the input converting it to commands for the **Model** or **View**.

Ext JS uses **MVCS**, which is a **Model-View-Controller-Store** pattern. The Model is a representation of the data we want to manipulate in our application, a representation of a table from the database. The Views are all the components and screens we create to manage the information of a Model. As Ext JS is event-driven, all the Views fire events when the user interacts with them, and the Controller will capture these events and will do something, redirecting the command to the Model (or Store) or the View. The Store in Ext JS is very similar to the **DAO** (**Data Access Object**) pattern used on the server side.

For a quick example, let's say we have a WidgetA which is a **Grid panel** that displays all the records from a table A. This table is represented by ModelA. StoreA is responsible for retrieving the information (collection of ModelA from the server). When the user clicks on a record from WidgetA, a window will be opened (called WidgetB) displaying information from a table B (represented by ModelB). And of course, StoreB will be responsible for retrieving the collection of ModelB from the server. In this case, we will have ControllerA to capture the click event from WidgetA and do all the required logic to display WidgetB and load all the ModelB information. If we try to put this in a quick reference diagram, it would be something like the following diagram:

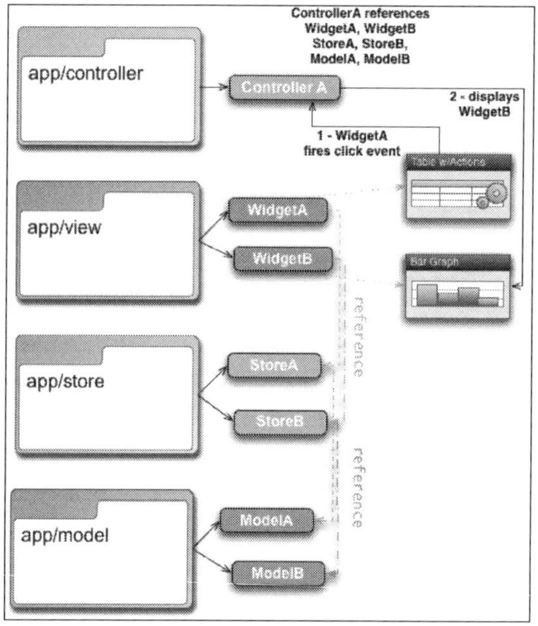

Creating the application

We are going to create the application inside the `htdocs` folder of the `xampp` directory and our application will be named `masteringExtjs`.

Before we start, let's take a look how the `htdocs` folder looks like.

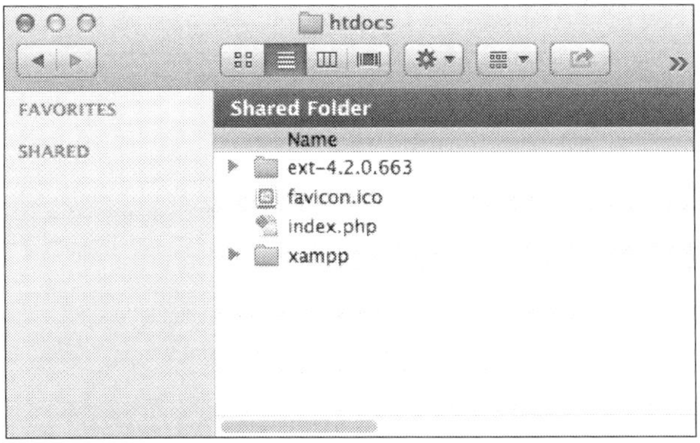

We have the XAMPP files inside it and the Ext JS 4.2 folder.

The next step is to use the Sencha Cmd to create the application for us. To do so, we need to open the terminal application that comes with the operating system we use. For Linux and Mac OS users, it is the terminal application, and for Windows users, the command prompt application.

Here are the steps we are going to execute: first we need to change the current directory to Ext JS directory (`htdocs/ext-4.2.0.663` directory in this case), and then we will use the following command:

```
sencha generate app Packt ../masteringextjs
```

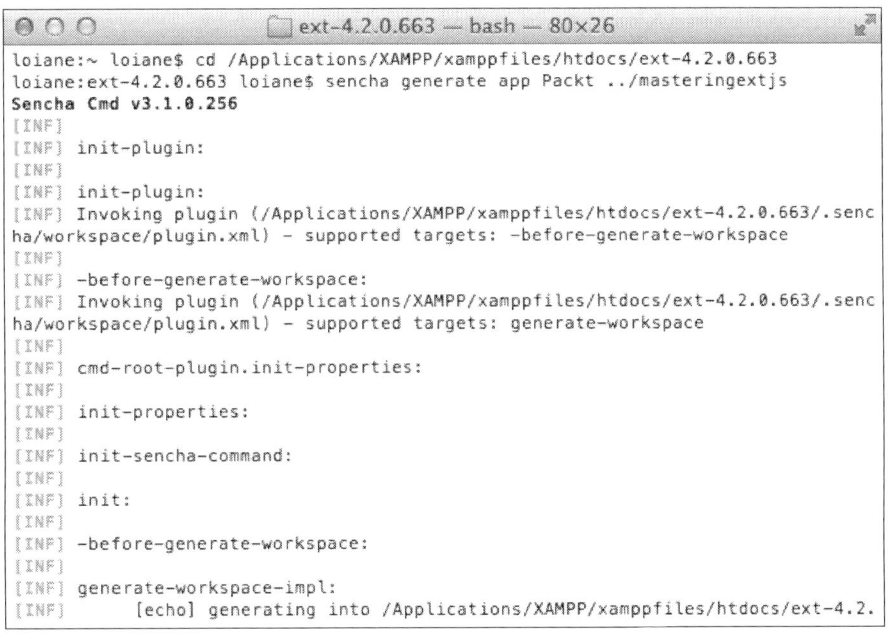

The `sencha generate app` command will create the `masteringextjs` directory inside the `htdocs` folder with necessary file structure required by the MVC architecture. `Packt` is the name of the namespace of our application, meaning that every class we create is going to start with `Packt`, as for example: `Packt.model.Actor`, `Pack.view.Login`, and so on. And the last argument passed to the command is the directory where the application will be created. In this case it is inside a folder named `masteringextjs`, which is located inside the `htdocs` folder.

After the command finishes its execution, we will have something like the following:

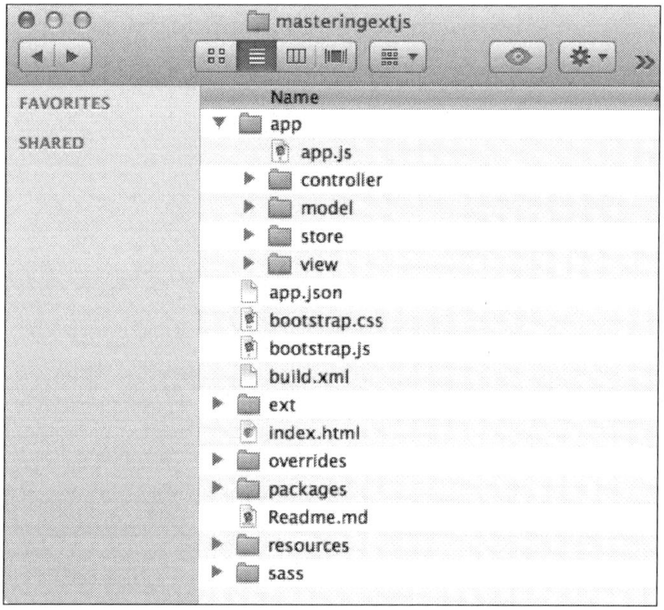

But why do we need to create a project structure like this one? This is the structure used by Ext JS MVC applications.

> For more information about the `sencha generate app` command, please consult: `http://docs.sencha.com/extjs/4.2.0/#!/guide/command_app`.

Let's see what each folder does.

First, we have the `app` folder. This is where we will create all the code for our application. Inside the `app` folder we can find the following folders as well: `controller`, `model`, `store`, and `view`. We can also find the `app.js` file. Let's talk about each one:

- In the `model` folder we will create all files that represent a Model, which is an Ext JS class that represents a set of fields, meaning an Object that our application manages (Actor, Country, Film). It is similar to a class on the server side with only the attributes of the class plus getter and setter methods used to represent a table from the database.
- In the `store` folder we will create all the store classes, which is a cache of a collection of Models. They are very similar to **DAO** (**Data Access Object**); classes used on server-side languages to perform CRUD operations on the database. And as Ext JS does not communicate directly with databases, the store classes are used to communicate with the server side or a local storage used with a proxy (Proxies are used by Stores to handle the loading and saving of the Model data).
- In the `view` folder we will create all view classes, also known as the **UI Components** (**User Interface Components**), such as the Grid panel, the Tree panel, the Menu, the Form panel, the Window, and so on. In these classes we will only code what the user will see on the screen; we will not handle the events fired by a component (the Grid panel, the Tree panel, the Menu, the Form panel, the Window are subclasses of the `Component` class).
- And finally, in the `controller` folder we will handle all the events fired by the components (events fired because of the life cycle of the component or because of some interaction of the user with a component). We always need to remember that Ext JS is event driven, and on the `Controller` classes we will control these events and update any Model, View, or Store (if needed).

We also have the `app.js` file. This is the entry point of the application. We will talk more about it in a few paragraphs.

Then, going back to the `masteringextjs` directory, we have a few more files and directories:

- `app.json`: This is a configuration file used by Sencha Cmd. If we open it, we will see only a `JSON` object with the name of the application (`Packt`).
- `bootstrap.css` and `bootstrap.js`: Both files are also created by Sencha Cmd and should not be edited. The CSS file contains the import of the theme used by the application (which is the blue classic theme) and the JS file contains some require directives, the custom `xtype` attributes and other meta-driven class system features.

- `build.xml`: Sencha Cmd uses Apache Ant (`http://ant.apache.org/`), which is a Java tool used to build Java projects. Ant uses a configuration file named `build.xml`, which contains all the required configurations and commands to build a project. Sencha Cmd uses Ant as engine to build an Ext JS application in the background (while we simply need to use a command). This is the reason why we need to have the Java SDK installed to use some of the Sencha Cmd features.
- `index.html`: This is the index file of our project. This is the file that will be rendered by the browser when we execute our application. Inside this file we will find the import of the bootstrap CSS and JS file, along with the import of the Ext JS framework file (`ext/ext-dev.js` and the `app/app.js` file).
- `ext`: Inside this folder we can find all the Ext JS framework files (`ext-all`, `ext-all-debug`, `ext-dev`) and also its source code.
- `overrides`: When we create the application it is empty. But inside this folder we should create any Ext JS overrides that we need to create for our project.
- `packages`: Inside this folder we can find all the packages managed by Sencha Cmd. A theme is a package. For more information about packages, please go to `http://docs.sencha.com/extjs/4.2.0/#!/guide/command_packages`.
- `resources`: Inside this folder, we will place all the CSS files we need to create for our application (with custom styles, CSS for icon images, and so on), and also all the static files (images).
- `sass`: Inside this folder we can find some Sass files used to create themes.

Let's start with the hands-on now!

First, we need to edit the `app.js` file. This is how the file looks like:

```
Ext.application({
    name: 'Packt',

    views: [
        'Main',
        'Viewport'
    ],

    controllers: [
        'Main'
    ],

    autoCreateViewport: true
});
```

We are going to change it so that it looks like the following:

```
Ext.application({ // #1

    name: 'Packt', // #2

    launch: function() { // #3
         console.log('launch');   // #4
    }
});
```

On first line of the previous code we have the `Ext.application` declaration (`#1`). This means that our application will have a single page and the parent container of the app will be the Viewport. The Viewport is a specialized container representing the viewable application area that is rendered inside the `body` tag of the HTML page (`<body></body>`). It also manages the application's size inside the browser and manages the window resizing.

Inside `Ext.application` we can also declare models, views, stores, and controllers used by the application. We will add this information to this file as we create new classes for our project.

We need to declare the name of the application which will be the namespace (`#2`).

We can also create a launch function inside `Ext.application` (`#3`). This function will be called after all the application's controllers are initialized and this means that the application is completely loaded. So this function is a good place to instantiate our main view. For now, we will only add `console.log` (`#4`), which just prints on the browser's JavaScript interpreter console to verify if the application was loaded successfully.

Do we need to use `Ext.onReady` when using `Ext.application`?

The answer is no. We only need to use one of the options. According to the Ext JS API documentation, `Ext.application` loads the `Ext.app.Application` class and starts it up with the given configuration after the page is ready and `Ext.onReady` adds a new listener to be executed when all required scripts are fully loaded. And if we take a look at the source code for `Ext.application` we have:

```
Ext.application = function(config) {
    Ext.require('Ext.app.Application');
    Ext.onReady(function() {
        new Ext.app.Application(config);
    });
};
```

This means that `Ext.application` is already calling `Ext.onReady`, so we do not need to do it twice. So use `Ext.onReady` when you have a few components to be displayed and they are not in the MVC architecture (similar to the jQuery `$(document).ready()` function) and use `Ext.application` when you are developing an Ext JS MVC application.

To execute this application on the browser, we can access `http://localhost/masteringextjs`, and we will get the following output:

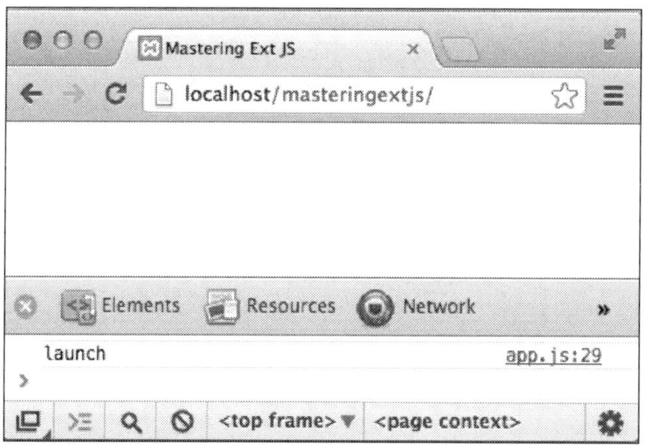

Now we need to start building the application.

Creating the loading page

When working with large Ext JS applications, it is normal to have a small delay when loading the application. This happens because Ext JS is loading all the required classes to have the application up and running and meanwhile, all the users see is a blank screen, which can be annoying for them. A very common solution to this problem is to have a loading page, also known as a splash screen.

So let's add a splash screen to our application that looks like the following:

First we need to understand how this splash screen will work. At the moment the user loads the application and the loading screen will be displayed. The application will show the splash screen while it loads all the required classes and code so the application can be used.

We already know that the application calls the launch function when it is ready to be used. So we know that we will need to remove the splash screen from the launch method. The question now is where inside `Ext.application` can we call the splash screen? The answer is inside the `init` function. The `init` function is called when the application boots so it gives some time for all required code to be loaded and after that the launch function is called.

Now that we know how the splash screen will work, let's implement it.

Inside `Ext.application`, we will implement a function called `init`:

```
init: function() {
     splashscreen = Ext.getBody().mask('Loading application',
     'splashscreen');
},
```

All we need to do is apply a mask into the HTML body of the application (`Ext.getBody()`), and that is why we are calling the `mask` method passing the loading message ("Loading Application") and applying a CSS, which will be loading gif and is already part of the Ext JS CSS ("splashscreen"). The mask method will return `Ext.dom.Element`, which we will need to manipulate later (remove the mask from the HTML body) and for this reason, we need to keep a reference to `Ext.dom.Element` and we will store this reference inside an attribute of `Ext.application`:

```
splashscreen: {},
```

With the code of the `init` method only, we will have a loading screen as the following:

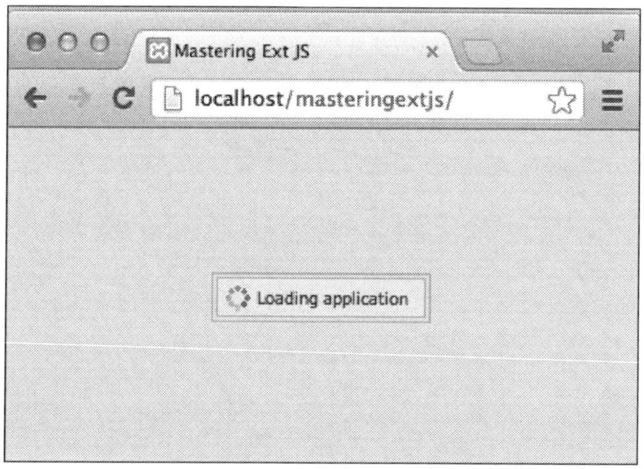

If this is all you need that is OK. But let's go a little bit further and customize the loading screen adding a logo image so it can look like the first image of this topic, which is our final output.

First, we need to create a CSS file which will contain all the CSS for our application. We will name it `app.css` and we will also create it inside a `resources` folder:

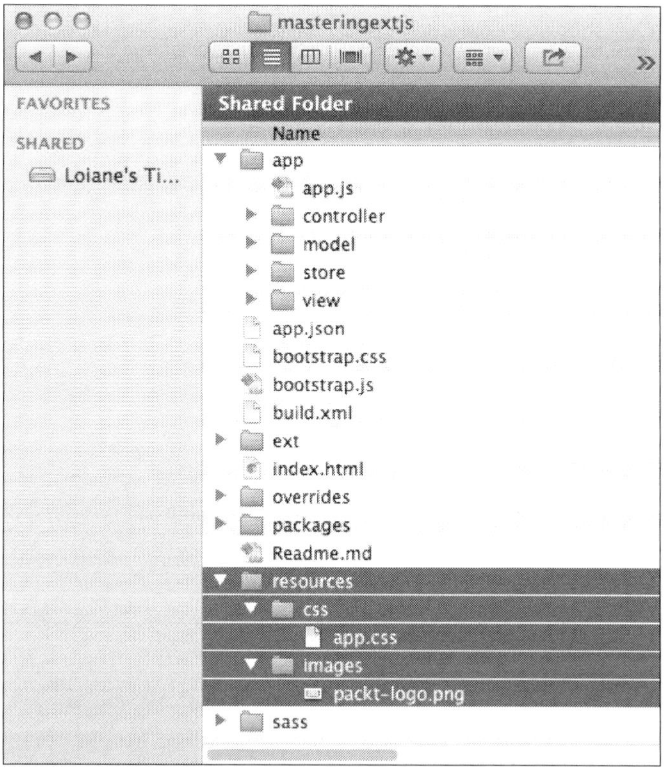

Inside `resources` we will also create an `images` folder with the Packt logo image.

We also must not forget to add the new CSS file into `index.html`:

```
<link rel="stylesheet" href="resources/css/app.css">

And the app.css file will look like the following: .x-mask.
splashscreen {
    background-color: white;
    opacity: 1;
}

.x-mask-msg.splashscreen,
.x-mask-msg.splashscreen div {
    font-size: 16px;
    font-weight: bold;
    padding: 30px 5px 5px 5px;
```

```
        border: none;
        background-color: transparent;
        background-position: top center;
    }

    .x-message-box .x-window-body .x-box-inner {
        min-height: 110px !important;
    }

    .x-splash-icon {
        background-image: url('../images/packt-logo.png') !important;
        margin-top: -30px;
        margin-bottom: 15px;
        height: 100px;
    }
```

Now let's go back to the `app.js` file and continue to add some code to the `init` function.

If we add the following code after the code we already have:

```
splashscreen.addCls('splashscreen');
```

We will be adding a new CSS style to the loading `DIV` tag. Note that the following styles from our `app.css` file will be applied: `.x-mask.splashscreen` and `.x-mask-msg.splashscreen div`. This will make the background white instead of gray and it is also going to change the font of the "Loading Application" message.

This is how the generated HTML will be:

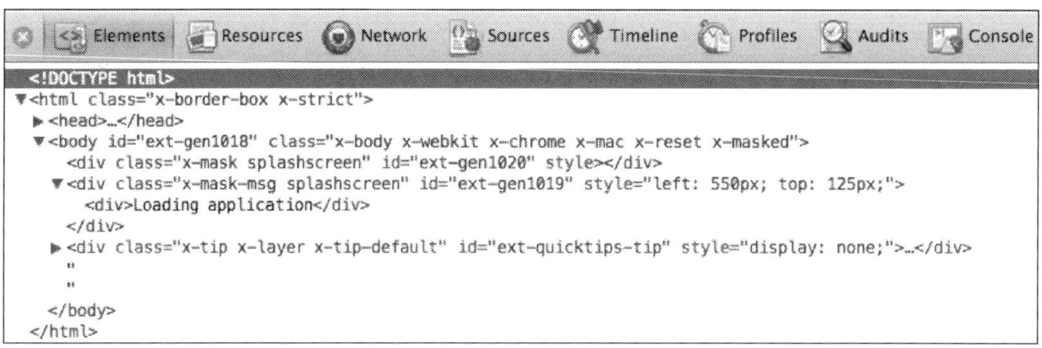

Now we will add the following code in the `init` function:

```
Ext.DomHelper.insertFirst(Ext.query('.x-mask-msg')[0], {
      cls: 'x-splash-icon'
});
```

The previous code will search for the first `DIV` tag that contains the `.x-mask-msg` class (`Ext.query('.x-mask-msg')[0]`) and will add a new `DIV` tag as child with the class `x-splash-icon` that will be responsible for adding the logo image above the loading message.

And this is how the generated HTML will be:

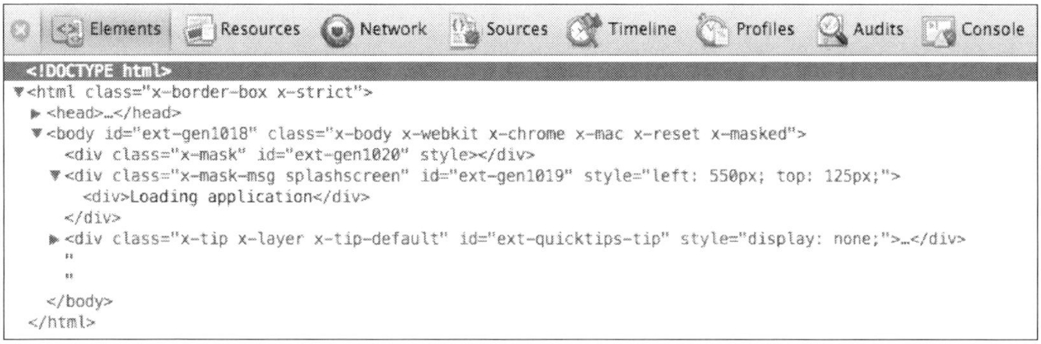

After we execute the previous code, we will have an output exactly as the image we showed at the beginning of this topic.

Now we already have the splash screen being displayed. We need to work on the launch function to remove the splash screen after all the code the application needs is loaded, otherwise the loading message will be there indefinitely!

To remove the splash screen the only code we need to add to the `launch` function is the following one, which is removing the mask from the HTML body:

```
Ext.getBody().unmask();
```

However, removing the mask abruptly is not nice because the user cannot even see the loading message. Instead of only removing the mask, let's give the user 2 seconds to see the loading message after the application is ready:

```
var task = new Ext.util.DelayedTask(function() { // #1
     Ext.getBody().unmask(); // #2
});

task.delay(2000); // #3
```

To do so, we are going to use the `DelayedTask` class (`#1`), which is a class that provides a chance of a function to be executed after the given timeout in milliseconds (`#3`). So in the case of the task, we are removing the mask from the HTML body (`#2`) after two seconds of timeout (2,000 milliseconds).

If we test the output right now, it works, but it is still not nice for the user. It would be even better if we can add an animation to the masking. So we will add a fade out animation (which animates the opacity of an element from opaque to transparent) and after the animation we will remove the masking (inside the `Ext.util.DelayedTask` function).

```
splashscreen.fadeOut({
    duration: 1000,
    remove:true
});
```

After we execute this code, notice that the loading message is still being displayed. We need to analyze the generated HTML to find out why.

Before we call the `fadeOut` function, the following screenshot is the HTML of the loading message:

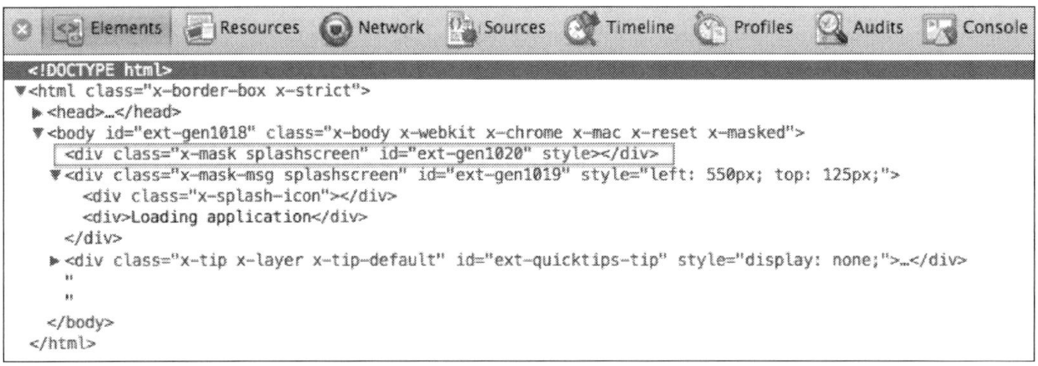

After we call the fadeout function, the HTML will be the following:

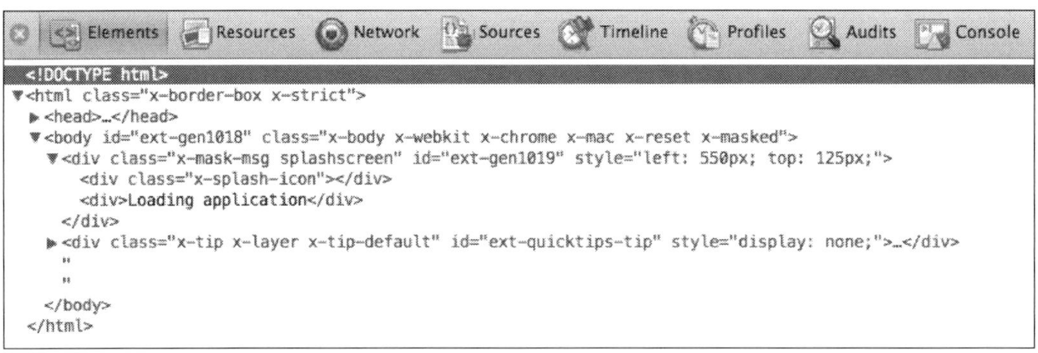

Only the first DIV tag with the class splashscreen was faded out. We need to also fade out the DIV tag with class x-mask-msg splashscreen that contains the logo and the loading message.

```
splashscreen.next().fadeOut({
    duration: 1000,
    remove:true
});
```

The output will be a pleasant animation that is shown to the user. Also note that the splashscreen DIV tag is removed from the generated HTML:

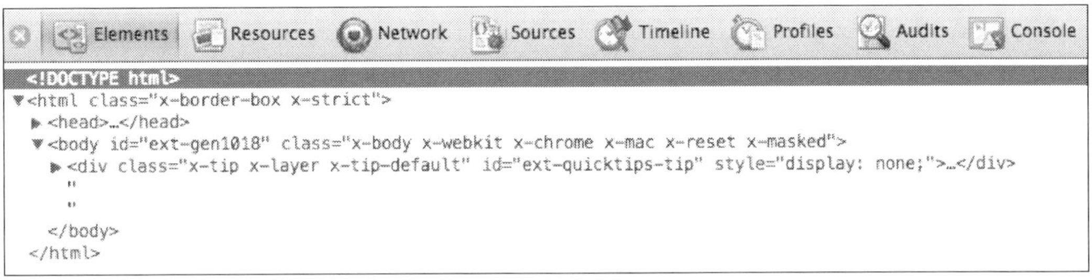

After the loading mask is removed, we need to display the initial component of our application. We will be showing a login screen that we will implement in the next chapter. For now, we will add a console message (#1) just to know where we need to call the initial component. The complete code for the launch function will be the following:

```
launch: function() {
    var task = new Ext.util.DelayedTask(function() {

        splashscreen.fadeOut({
            duration: 1000,
            remove:true
        });

        splashscreen.next().fadeOut({
            duration: 1000,
            remove:true
        });

        console.log('launch'); // #1
    });

    task.delay(2000);
}
```

> Note that all the code we used to display the loading message mask and remove it is part of the `Ext.dom.Element` class. This class encapsulates a **DOM** (**Document Object Model**) element where we can manage using the class's methods. This class is part of the `Ext Core` library, which is part of the foundation of Ext JS framework.

Summary

In this chapter, we have covered the details in high level about the application we will implement throughout the chapters of this book. We have also covered all the requirements to create the development environment for this application. We learned how to create the initial structure of an Ext JS MVC application.

And we also learned, through examples, how to create a splash screen (also known as the loading screen) manipulating DOM using the `Ext.dom.Element` class. We learned the difference between using `Ext.onReady` and `Ext.application` and also the difference between the `init` and `launch` methods from `Ext.application`. We left the `app.js` file ready to display its first screen, which will be a login screen, which we will learn how to implement in the next chapter.

2
The Login Page

It is very common to have a login page for an application, which we can use to control access to the system by identifying and authenticating the user through the credentials presented by him/her. Once the user is logged in, we can track the actions performed by the user. We can also restrain access of some features and screens of the system that we do not want a particular user or even a specific group of users to have access to.

In this chapter, we will cover:

- Creating the login page
- Handling the login page on the server
- Adding the Caps Lock warning message in the **Password** field
- Submitting the form by pressing the *Enter* key
- Encrypting the password before sending to the server

The Login screen

The **Login** window will be the first view we are going to implement in this project. We are going to build it step by step and it will have the following capabilities:

- User will enter the username and password to log in
- Client-side validation (username and password required to log in)
- Submit the **Login** form by pressing *Enter*
- Encrypt the password before sending to the server
- Password Caps Lock warning (similar to Windows OS)
- Multilingual capability

Except for the multilingual capability, which we are going to implement in the next chapter, we will implement all the other features throughout this topic. So at the end of the implementation, we will have a **Login** window that looks like the following:

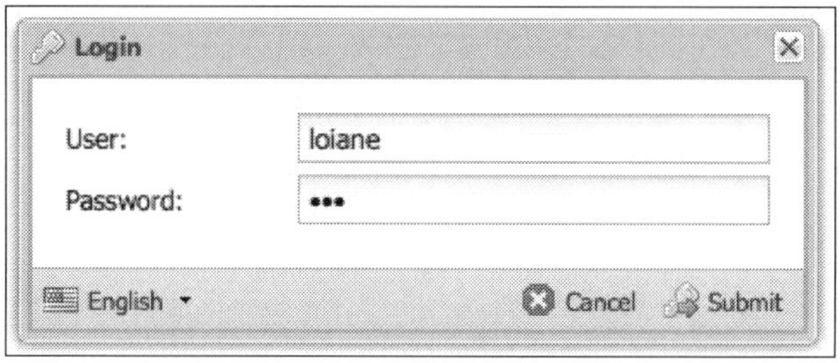

So let's get started!

Creating the Login screen

Under the `app/view` directory, we will create a new file named `Login.js`. In this file, we will implement all the code that the user is going to see on the screen.

Inside the `Login.js` file, we will implement the following code:

```
Ext.define('Packt.view.Login', { // #1
    extend: 'Ext.window.Window', // #2
    alias: 'widget.login',       // #3

    autoShow: true,              // #4
    height: 170,                 // #5
    width: 360,                  // #6
    layout: {
        type: 'fit'              // #7
    },
    iconCls: 'key',              // #8
    title: "Login",              // #9
    closeAction: 'hide',         // #10
    closable: false              // #11
});
```

On the first line (`#1`) we have the definition of the class. To define a class we use `Ext.define`, followed by parentheses (`()`), and inside the parentheses we first declare the name of the class, followed by a comma (") and curly brackets ({ }), and at the end a semicolon. All the configurations and properties (`#2` to `#11`) go inside curly brackets.

We also need to pay attention to the name of the class. This is the formula suggested by Sencha in Ext JS MVC projects: App Namespace + package name + name of the JS file. In the previous chapter, we defined the namespace as `Packt` (configuration name inside the `app.js` file). We are creating a View for this project, so we will create the JS file under the `view` package/directory. And then, the name of the file we created is `Login.js`; therefore, we will lose the `.js` part and use only Login as the name of the View. Putting all together, we have `Packt.view.Login` and this will be the name of our class.

Then, we are saying that the `Login` class will extend from the `Window` class (`#2`), because we want it to be displayed inside a window, and not on any other component.

We are also assigning this class an `alias` (`#3`). The `alias` for a class that extends from a component always starts with `widget.`, followed by the `alias` we want to assign. The naming convention for an `alias` is *lowercase*. It is also important to remember that the `alias` must be unique in an application. In this case we want to assign `login` as `alias` to this class so later we can instantiate this same class using its `alias` (that is the same as `xtype`). For example, we can instantiate the `Login` class using four different options:

- Using the complete name of the class, which is the most used one:
  ```
  Ext.create('Packt.view.Login');
  ```
- Using the alias in the `Ext.create` method:
  ```
  Ext.create('widget.login');
  ```
- Using the `Ext.widget`, which is a shorthand way of using `Ext.ClassManager.instantiateByAlias`:
  ```
  Ext.widget('login');
  ```
- Using the `xtype` as an item of another component:
  ```
  items: [
    {
      xtype: 'login'
    }
  ]
  ```

In this book we will use the first, third, and fourth options most of the time.

Then we have `autoShow` configured to `true` (`#4`). What happens with the window is that instantiating the component is not enough for displaying it. When we instantiate the window we will have its reference, but it will not be displayed on the screen. If we want it to be displayed we need to call the method `show()` manually. Another option is to have the `autoShow` configuration set to `true`. This way the window will be automatically displayed when we instantiate it.

We also have `height` (`#5`) and `width` (`#6`) of the window. We set the layout as `fit` (`#7`) because we want to add a form inside this window that will contain the `username` and `password` fields. And using the fit layout the form will occupy all the body space of the window. Remember that when using the fit layout we can only have one item as a child component.

We are setting an `iconCls` (`#8`) property to the window; this way we will have an icon of a key in the header of the window. We can also give a title for the window (`#9`), and in this case we chose `Login`. Following is the declaration of the key style used by the `iconCls` property:

```
.key {
  background-image:url('../icons/key.png') !important;
}
```

All the styles we will create to use as `iconCls` have a format like the preceding one.

And at last we have the `closeAction` (`#10`) and `closable` (`#11`) configurations. The `closeAction` configuration will tell if we want to destroy the window when we close it. In this case, we do not want to destroy it; we only want to hide it. The `closable` configuration tells if we want to display the X icon on the top-right corner of the window. As this is a **Login** window, we do not want to give this option for the user.

If you would like to, you can also add the `resizable` and `draggable` options as `false`. This will prevent the user to drag the **Login** window around and also to resize it.

So far, this will be the output we have. A single window with an icon at the top-left corner with a title **Login**:

The next step is to add the form with the `username` and `password` fields. We are going to add the following code to the `Login` class:

```
items: [
    {
        xtype: 'form',          // #12
        frame: false,           // #13
        bodyPadding: 15,        // #14
        defaults: {               // #15
            xtype: 'textfield', // #16
            anchor: '100%',       // #17
            labelWidth: 60      // #18
        },
        items: [
            {
                name: 'user',
                fieldLabel: "User"
            },
            {
                inputType: 'password', // #19
                name: 'password',
                fieldLabel: "Password"
            }
        ]
    }
]
```

As we are using the fit layout, we can only declare one child `item` in this class. So we are going to add a form (`#12`) and to make the form to look prettier, we are going to remove the `frame` property (`#13`) and also add `padding` to the form body (`#14`). The form's `frame` property is by default set to `false`. But by default, there is a blue border that appears if we to do not explicitly add this property set to `false`.

As we are going to add two fields to the form, we probably want to avoid repeating some code. That is why we are going to declare some field configurations inside the `defaults` configuration of the form (`#15`); this way the configuration we declare inside `defaults` will be applied to all items of the form, and we will need to declare only the configurations we want to customize. As we are going to declare two fields, both of them will be of type `textfield`. The default layout of the form is the anchor layout, so we do not need to make this declaration explicit. However, we want both fields can occupy all the horizontal available space of the body of the form. That is why we are declaring `anchor` as `100%` (`#17`). By default, the width attribute of the label of the `TextField` class is 100 pixels. It is too much space for a label `User` and `Password`, so we are going to decrease this value to `60` pixels (`#18`).

And finally, we have the `user` text field and the `password` text field. The configuration name is what we are going to use to identify each field when we submit the form to the server. But there is only one detail missing: when the user types the password into the field the system cannot display its value, we need to mask it somehow. That is why `inputType` is `'password'` (`#19`) for the `password` field, as we want to display bullets instead of the original value, and the user will not be able to see the password value.

Now we have improved our **Login** window a little more. This is the output so far:

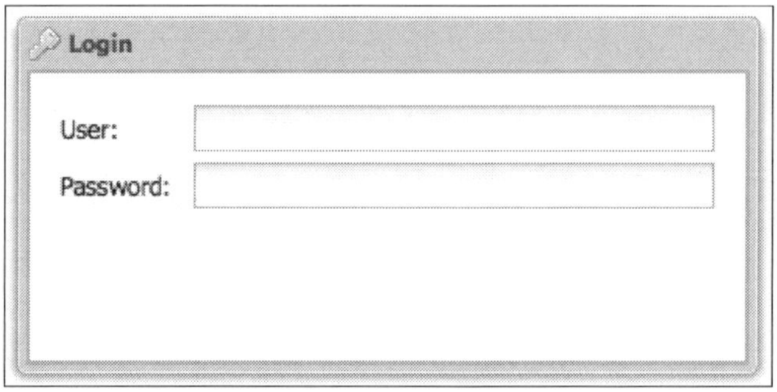

Client-side validations

The field component in Ext JS provides some client-side validation capability. This can save time and also bandwidth (the system will only make a server request when it is sure the information has passed the basic validation). It also helps to point out to the user where they have gone wrong in filling out the form. Of course, it is also good to validate the information again on the server side for security reasons, but for now we will focus on the validations we can apply to the form of our **Login** window.

Let's brainstorm some validations we can apply to the username and password fields:

- The username and password must be mandatory—how are going to authenticate the user without a username and password?
- The user can only enter alphanumeric characters (A-Z, a-z, and 0-9) in both the fields.
- The user can only type between 3 and 25 chars in the username field.
- The user can only type between 3 and 15 chars in the password field.

So let's add into the code the ones that are common to both fields:

```
allowBlank: false, // #20
vtype: 'alphanum', // #21
minLength: 3,      // #22
msgTarget: 'under' // #23
```

We are going to add the preceding configurations inside the `defaults` configuration of the form, as they all apply to both the fields we have. First, both need to be mandatory (`#20`), we can only allow to enter alphanumeric characters (`#21`) and the minimum number of characters the user needs to input is three (`#22`). Then, a last common configuration is that we want to display any validation error message under the field (`#23`).

And the only validation customized for each field is that we can enter a maximum of 25 characters in the User field:

```
name: 'user',
fieldLabel: "User",
maxLength: 25
```

And a maximum of 15 characters in the Password field:

```
inputType: 'password',
name: 'password',
fieldLabel: "Password",
maxLength: 15
```

After we apply the client validations, we will have the following output in case the user went wrong in filling out the **Login** window:

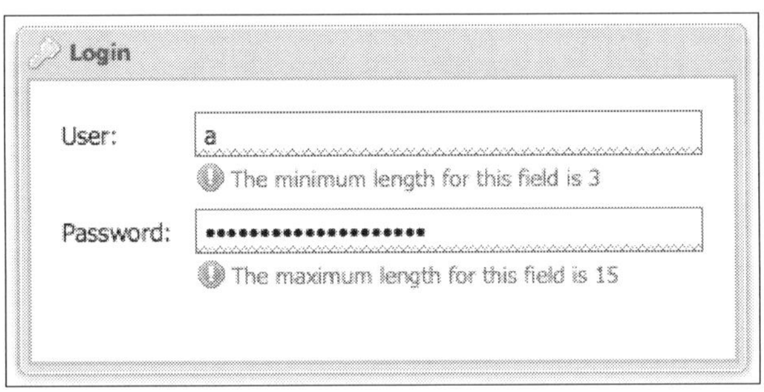

If you do not like it, we can change the place where the error message appears. We just need to change the `msgTarget` value. The available options are: `title`, `under`, `side`, and `none`. We can also show the error message as a tooltip (`qtip`) or display it in a specific target (inner HTML of a specific component).

Creating custom VTypes

Many systems have a special format for passwords. Let's say we need the password to have at least one digit (0-9), one letter lowercase, one letter uppercase, one special character (@, #, $, %, and so on) and its length between 6 and 20 characters.

We can create a regular expression to validate that the password is entering into the app. And to do this, we can create a custom **VType** to do the validation for us. Creating a custom VType is simple. For our case, we can create a custom VType called `passRegex`:

```
Ext.apply(Ext.form.field.VTypes, {
    customPass: function(val, field) {
        return /^((?=.*\d)(?=.*[a-z])(?=.*[A-Z])(?=.*[@#$%]).{6,20})/.
test(val);
    },
    customPassText: 'Not a valid password.  Length must be at least
6 characters and maximum of 20Password must contain one digit, one
letter lowercase, one letter uppercase, onse special symbol @#$% and
between 6 and 20 characters.',
});
```

`customPass` is the name of our custom VType, and we need to declare a function that will validate our regular expression. `customPassText` is the message that will be displayed to the user in case the incorrect password format is entered.

The preceding code can be added anywhere on the code, inside the `init` function of a controller, inside the `launch` function of the `app.js`, or even in a separate JavaScript file (recommended) where you can put all your custom VTypes.

To use it, we simply need to add `vtype: 'customPass'` to our `Password` field.

> To learn more about regular expressions, please visit `http://www.regular-expressions.info/`.

Adding the toolbar with buttons

So far we have created the **Login** window, which contains a form with two fields and it is already being validated as well. The only thing missing is to add the two buttons: **cancel** and **submit**.

We are going to add the buttons as items of a toolbar and the toolbar will be added on the form as a docked item. The docked items can be docked to either on the top, right, left, or bottom of a panel (both form and window components are subclasses of panel). In this case we will dock the toolbar to the bottom of the form. Add the following code right after the items configuration of the form:

```
dockedItems: [
    {
        xtype: 'toolbar',
        dock: 'bottom',
        items: [
            {
                xtype: 'tbfill' //#24
            },
            {
                xtype: 'button', // #25
                itemId: 'cancel',
                iconCls: 'cancel',
                text: 'Cancel'
            },
            {
                xtype: 'button', // #26
                itemId: 'submit',
                formBind: true,  // #27
                iconCls: 'key-go',
                text: "Submit"
            }
        ]
    }
]
```

If we take a look back to the screenshot of the **Login** screen we first presented at the beginning of this chapter, we will notice that there is a component for the translation/multilingual capability. And after this component there is a space and then we have the **Cancel** and **Submit** buttons. As we do not have the multilingual component yet, we can only implement the two buttons, but they need to be at the right end of the form and we need to leave that space. That is why we first need to add a toolbar fill component (`#24`), which is going to instruct the toolbar's layout to begin using the right-justified button container.

Then we will add the **Cancel** button (`#25`) and then the **Submit** button (`#26`). We are going to add icons to both buttons (`iconCls`) and later, when we implement the controller class, we will need a way to identify the buttons. This is why we assigned `itemId` to both of them.

We already have the client validations, but even with the validations, the user can click on the **Submit** button and we want to avoid this behavior. That is why we are binding the **Submit** button to the form (#27); this way the button will only be enabled if the form has no error from the client validation.

In the following screenshot, we can see the current output of the **Login** form (after we added the toolbar) and also verify the behavior of the **Submit** button:

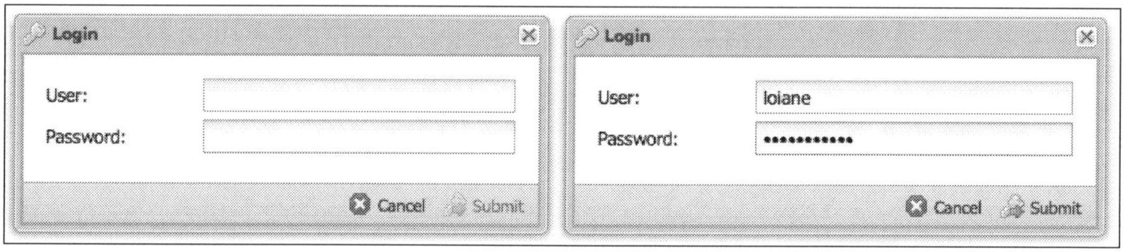

Running the code

To execute the code we have created so far, we need to make a few changes in the `app.js` file.

First, we need to declare `views` we are using (only one in this case). Also, as we are going to instantiate using the `Login` class' `xtype`, we need to declare this class in the `requires` declaration:

```
requires: [
    'Packt.view.Login'
],

views: [
    'Login'
],
```

And the last change is inside the launch function. In the previous chapter, we left a `console.log` message where we needed to instantiate our initial view; now we only need to replace the `console.log` message with the `Login` instance (#1):

```
splashscreen.next().fadeOut({
    duration: 1000,
    remove:true,
    listeners: {
        afteranimate: function(el, startTime, eOpts ){
            Ext.widget('login'); // #1
        }
    }
});
```

Now the `app.js` is OK and we can execute what we have implemented so far!

Using itemId versus id – Ext.Cmp is bad!

Before we create the controller, we will need to have some knowledge about `Ext.ComponentQuery` selectors. And in this topic we will discuss a subject to help us to understand better why we took some decisions while creating the **Login** window and why we are going to take some other decisions on the controller topic.

Whenever we can, we will always try to use the `itemId` configuration instead of `id` to uniquely identify a component. And here comes the question, why?

When using `id`, we need to make sure that `id` is unique, and none of all the other components of the application has the same `id`. Now imagine the situation where you are working with other developers of the same team and it is a big application. How can you make sure that `id` is going to be unique? Pretty difficult, don't you think? And this can be a hard task to achieve.

Components created with an `id` may be accessed globally using `Ext.getCmp`, which is a short-hand reference for `Ext.ComponentManager.get`.

Just to mention one example, when using `Ext.getCmp` to retrieve a component by its `id`, it is going to return the last component declared with the given `id`. And if the `id` is not unique, it can return the component that you are not expecting and this can lead into an error of the application.

Do not panic! There is an elegant solution, which is using `itemId` instead of `id`.

The `itemId` can be used as an alternative way to get a reference of a component. The `itemId` is an index to the container's internal `MixedCollection`, and that is why the `itemId` is scoped locally to the container. This is the biggest advantage of the `itemId`.

For example, we can have a class named `MyWindow1`, extending from window and inside this class we can have a button with item ID `submit`. Then we can have another class named `MyWindow2`, also extending from window, and also with a button with item ID `submit`.

Having two item IDs with the same value is not an issue. We only need to be careful when we use `Ext.ComponentQuery` to retrieve the component we want. For example, if we have a **Login** window whose alias is `login` and another screen called the **Registration** window whose alias is `registration`. Both the windows have a button **Save** whose `itemId` is `save`. If we simply use `Ext.ComponentQuery.query('button#save')`, the result will be an array with two results. However, if we narrow down the selector even more, let's say we want the **Login** window's **Save** button, and not the **Registration** window's **Save** button, we need to use `Ext.ComponentQuery.query('login button#save')`, and the result will be a single item, which is exactly we expect.

You will notice that we will not use `Ext.getCmp` in the code of our project. Because it is not a good practice; especially for Ext JS 4 and also because we can use `itemId` and `Ext.ComponentQuery` instead. We will understand `Ext.ComponentQuery` better during the next topic.

Creating the login controller

We have created the view for the **Login** screen so far. As we are following the MVC architecture, we are not implementing the user interaction on the `View` class. If we click on the buttons on the Login class, nothing will happen because we have not yet implemented this logic. We are going to implement this logic now on the controller class.

Under the `app/controller` directory, we will create a new file named `Login.js`. In this file we will implement all the code related to the events management of the **Login** screen.

Inside the `Login.js` file we will implement the following code, which is only a base of the `controller` class we are going to implement:

```
Ext.define('Packt.controller.Login', { // #1
    extend: 'Ext.app.Controller',      // #2

    views: [
        'Login'                        // #3
    ],

    init: function(application) {      // #4
        this.control({                 // #5

        });
    }
});
```

As usual, on the first line of the class we have its name (#1). Following the same formula we used for the view/Login.js we will have Packt (app namespace) + controller (name of the package) + Login (which is the name of the file), resulting in Packt.controller.Login.

> Note that that the controller JS file (controller/Login.js) has the same name as view/Login.js, but that is OK because they are in a different package. It is good to use a similar name for the views, models, stores and controllers because it is going to be easier to maintain the project later. For example, let's say that after the project is in production, we need to add a new button on the Login screen. With only this information (and a little bit of MVC concept knowledge) we know we will need to add the button code on the view/Login.js file and listen to any events that might be fired by this button on the controller/Login.js. Easier maintainability is also a great pro of using the MVC architecture.

The controller classes need to extend from Ext.app.Controller (#2), so we will always use this parent class for our controllers.

Then we have the views declaration (#3), which is where we are going to declare all the views that this controller will care about. In this case, we only have the Login view so far. We will add more views later on this chapter.

Next, we have the init method declaration (#4). The init method is called before the application boots, before the launch function of Ext.application (app.js). The controller will also load the views, models, and stores declared inside its class.

Then we have the control method configured (#5). This is where we are going to listen to all events we want the controller to react. And as we are coding the events fired by the **Login** window and its child components, this will be our scope in this controller.

Adding the controller to app.js

Now that we already have a base of the login controller, we need to add it to the app.js file.

We can remove this code, since the controller will be responsible for loading the view/Login.js file for us:

```
requires: [
    'Packt.view.Login'
],
```

```
views: [
    'Login'
],
And add the controllers declaration:
controllers: [
    'Login'
],
```

And as our project is only starting, declaring the views on the controller classes will help us to have a code more organized, as we do not need to declare all the application's `views` in the `app.js` file.

Listening to the button click event

Our next step now is to start listening to the **Login** window events. First, we are going to listen to the **Submit** and **Cancel** buttons.

We already know that we are going to add the listeners inside the `this.control` declaration. The format that we need to use is the following:

```
'Ext.ComponentQuery selector': {
  eventWeWantToListenTo: functionOrMethodWeWantToExecute
}
```

First, we need to pass the selector that is going to be used by the `Ext.ComponentQuery` class to find the component. Then we need to list the event that we want to listen to. And then, we need to declare the function that is going to be executed when the event we are listening to is fired, or declare the name of the `controller` method that is going to be executed when the event is fired. In our case, we are going to declare the method only for code organization purposes.

Now let's focus on finding the correct selector for the **Submit** and **Cancel** buttons. According to `Ext.ComponentQuery` API documentation, we can retrieve components by using their `xtype` (if you are already familiar with jQuery, you will notice that `Ext.ComponentQuery` selectors are very similar to jQuery selectors' behavior). Well, we are trying to retrieve two buttons, and their `xtype` is button. We try then the selector `button`. But before we start coding, let's make sure that this is the correct selector to avoid us to change the code all the time when trying to figure out the correct selector. There is one very useful tip we can try: open the browser console (command editor), type the following command, and click on **Run**:

```
Ext.ComponentQuery.query('button');
```

As we can see in the screenshot, it returned an array of the buttons that were found by the selector we used, and the array contains six buttons; too many buttons and it is not what we want. We want to narrow down to the **Submit** and **Cancel** buttons.

Let's try to draw a path of the **Login** window using the components `xtype` we used:

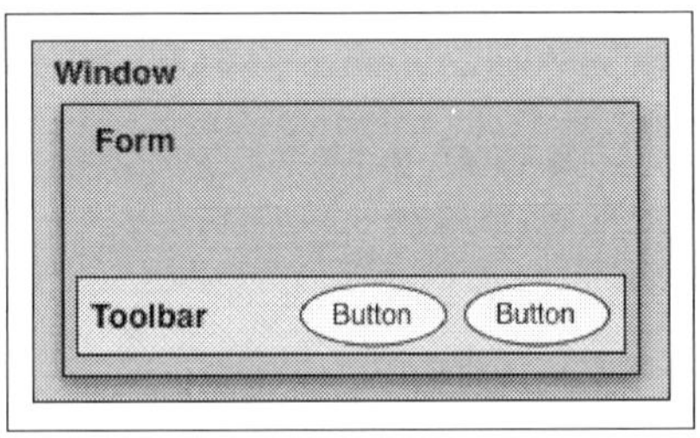

We have a **Login** window (`xtype`: `login` or `window`), inside the window we have a form (`xtype`: `form`), inside the form we have a toolbar (`xtype`: `toolbar`), and inside the toolbar we have two buttons (`xtype`: `button`). Therefore, we have `login-form-toolbar-button`. However, if we use `login-form-button` we will have the same result, because we do not have any other buttons inside the form. So we can try the following command:

```
Ext.ComponentQuery.query('login form button');
```

So let's try this last selector on the command editor:

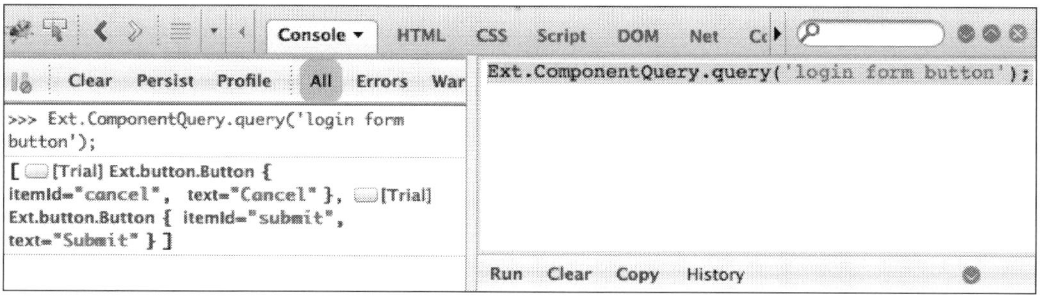

Now the result is an array of two buttons and these are the buttons that we are looking for! There is still one detail missing: if we use the `login form button` selector, it will listen to the click event (which is the event we want to listen to) of both buttons. When we click on the **Cancel** button one thing should happen (reset the form) and when we click on the **Submit** button, another thing should happen (submit the form to the server to validate the login). So we still want to narrow down the selector even more, until it returns the **Cancel** button and another selector that will return the **Submit** button.

Going back to the `view/Login` code, notice that we declared a configuration named `itemId` to both buttons. We can use these `itemId` configurations to identify the buttons in a unique way. According to the `Ext.ComponentQuery` API docs, we can use `#` as a prefix of `itemId`. So let's try the following command on the command editor to get the **Submit** button reference:

```
Ext.ComponentQuery.query('login form button#submit');
```

The output will be only one button as we expect:

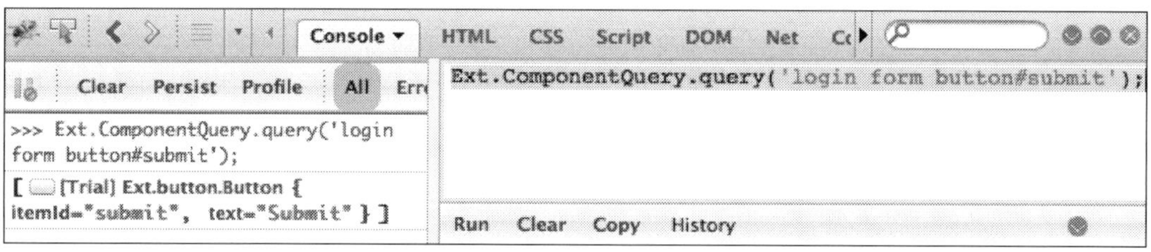

Now let's try the following command to retrieve the **Cancel** button reference:

```
Ext.ComponentQuery.query('login form button#cancel');
```

The output will be only one button as we expect:

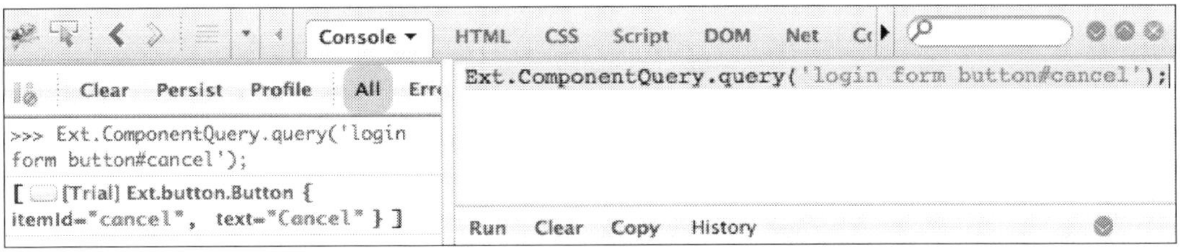

So now we have the selectors that we were looking for! Console command editor is a great tool and using it can save us a lot of time when trying to find the exact selector that we want, instead of coding, testing, not the selector we want, code again, test again, and so on.

Could we use only `button#submit` or `button#cancel` as selectors? Yes, we could use a shorter selector. However, it would work perfectly for now. As the application grows and we declare many more classes and buttons, the event would be fired for all buttons that have the `itemId` named `submit` or `cancel` and this could lead to an error in the application. We always need to remember that `itemId` is scoped locally to the container. By using `login form button` as the selector, we make sure that the event will come from the button from the **Login** window.

So let's implement the code inside the `controller` class:

```
init: function(application) {
    this.control({
        "login form button#submit": {        // #1
            click: this.onButtonClickSubmit // #2
        },
        "login form button#cancel": {        // #3
            click: this.onButtonClickCancel // #4
        }
    });
},

onButtonClickSubmit: function(button, e, options) {
    console.log('login submit');            // #5
},

onButtonClickCancel: function(button, e, options) {
    console.log('login cancel');           // #6
}
```

In the preceding code, we have first the listener to the **Submit** button (`#1`), and on the following line we say that we want to listen to the `click` event, and then, when the `click` event of the **Submit** button is fired, the `onButtonClickSubmit` method should be executed (`#2`).

Then we have the same for the **Cancel** button: we have the listener to the **Cancel** button (`#3`), and on the following line we say that we want to listen to the `click` event, and then, when the `click` event of the **Cancel** button is fired, the `onButtonClickCancel` method should be executed (`#4`).

Next, we have the declaration of the methods `onButtonClickSubmit` and `onButtonClickCancel`. For now, we are only going to output a message on the console to make sure that our code is working. So we are going to output `login submit` (`#5`) in case the user clicks on the **Submit** button, and `login cancel` (`#6`) in case the user clicks on the **Cancel** button.

But how do you know which are the parameters the event method can receive? You can find the answer to this question in the documentation. If we take a look at the `click` event in the documentation, this is what we will find:

click(`Ext.button.Button this, Event e, Object eOpts`)

Fires when this button is clicked, before the configured handler is invoked. ...

This is exactly what we declared. For all the other event listeners, we will go to the docs and see which are the parameters the event accepts, and then list them as parameters in our code. This is also a very good practice. We should always list out all the arguments from the docs, even if we are only interested in the first one. This way we always know that we have the full collection of the parameters, and this can come very handy when we are doing maintenance of the application.

Let's go ahead and try it. Click on the **Cancel** button and then on the **Submit** button. This should be the output:

Cancel button listener implementation

Let's remove the `console.log` messages and add the code we actually want the methods to execute. First, let's work on the `onButtonClickCancel` method. When we execute this method, we want it to reset the form.

So this is the logic sequence we want to program:

1. Get the **Login** form reference.
2. Call the method `getForm`, which is going to return the form basic class.
3. Call the `reset` method to reset the form.

> The form basic class provides input field management, validation, submission, and form loading services. The `Ext.form.Panel` class (`xtype: form`) works as the container, and it is automatically hooked up with an instance of `Ext.form.Basic`. That is why we need to get the form basic reference to call the `reset` method.

If we take a look at the parameters we have available on the `onButtonClickCancel` method, we have: `button`, `e`, and `options`, and none of them provides us the form reference.

So what can we do about it? We can use the up method from the `Button` class (inherited from the `AbstractComponent` class). With this method, we can use a selector to try to retrieve the form. The `up` method navigates up the component hierarchy, searching from an ancestor container that matches the passed selector.

As the button is inside a toolbar that is inside the form we are looking for, if we use `button.up('form')`, it will retrieve exactly what we want. Ext JS will see what is the first ancestor in the hierarchy of the button and will find a toolbar. Not what we are looking for. So it goes up again and it will find a form, which is what we are looking for.

So this is the code that we are going to implement inside the `onButtonClickCancel` method:

```
button.up('form').getForm().reset();
```

> Some people like to implement the toolbar inside the window instead of the form. No problem at all, it is only a matter of how you like to implement it. In this case, if the toolbar that contains the **Submit** button is inside the `Window` class we can use:
>
> ```
> button.up('window').down('form').getForm().reset()
> ```
>
> And we will have the same result!

Submit button listener implementation

Now we need to implement the `onButtonClickSubmit` method. Inside this method, we want to program the logic to send the username and password values to the server so that the user can be authenticated.

We can implement two programming logics inside this method: the first one is to use the `submit` method that is provided by the form basic class and the second one is to use an **Ajax** call to submit the values to the server. Either way we will achieve what we want to do. However, there is one detail that we need to know prior to making this decision: if using the `submit` method of the form basic class, we will not be able to encrypt the password before we send it to the server, and if we take a look at the parameters sent to the server, the password will be a plain text, and this is not good. Using the Ajax request will result the same; however, we can encrypt the password value before sending to the server. So apparently, the second option seems better and that is the one that we will implement.

So to summarize, following are the steps we need to perform in this method:

- Get the **Login** form reference
- Get the **Login** window reference (so that we can close it once the user has been authenticated)
- Get the username and password values from the form
- Encrypt the password
- Send login information to the server
- Handle the server response
    - If user is authenticated display application
    - If not, display an error message

First, let's get the references that we need:

```
var formPanel = button.up('form'),
    login = button.up('login'),
    user = formPanel.down('textfield[name=user]').getValue(),
    pass = formPanel.down('textfield[name=password]').getValue();
```

To get the form reference, we can use the `button.up('form')` code that we already used in the `onButtonClickCancel` method; to get the **Login** window reference we can do the same thing, only changing the selector to `login` or `window`. Then to get the values from the **User** and **Password** fields we can use the `down` method, but this time the scope will start from the form reference. For the selector we will use the text field `xtype`, and to make sure we are retrieving the text field we want, we can create an `itemId` attribute, but there is no need for it. We can use the `name` attribute since the `user` and `password` fields have different names and they are unique within the `Login` window. To use attributes within a selector we must wrap it in brackets.

The next step is to submit the values to the server:

```
if (formPanel.getForm().isValid()) {
    Ext.Ajax.request({
        url: 'php/login.php',
        params: {
            user: user,
            password: pass
        }
    });
}
```

If we try to run this code, the application will send the request to the server, but we will get an error as the response because we do not have the `login.php` page implemented yet. That's OK because we are interested in other details right now.

With **Firebug** or **Chrome Developer Tools** enabled, open the **Net** tab and filter by the **XHR** requests. Make sure to enter a username and password (any valid value so that we can click on the **Submit** button). This will be the output:

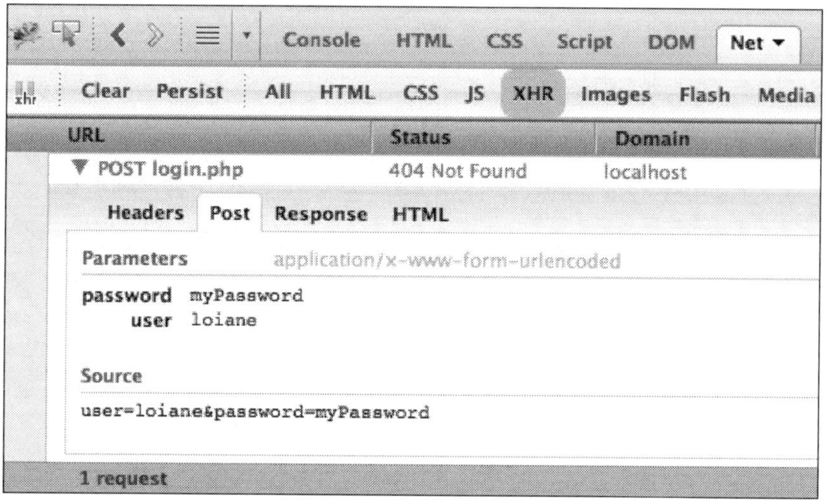

We still do not have the password encrypted. The original value is still being displayed and this is not good. We need to encrypt the password.

Under the `app` directory, we will create a new folder named `util` where we are going to create all the utility classes. We will also create a new file named `MD5.js`; therefore, we will have a new class named `Packt.util.MD5`. This class contains a static method called `encode` and this method encodes the given value using the **MD5** algorithm. To understand more about the **MD5** algorithm go to `http://en.wikipedia.org/wiki/MD5`. As `Packt.util.MD5` is big, we will not list its code here, but you can download the source code of this book from `http://www.packtpub.com/mastering-ext-javascript/book` or get the latest version at `https://github.com/loiane/masteringextjs`).

> If you would like to make it even more secure, you can also use SSL and ask for a random salt string from the server, salt the password and hash it. You can learn more about it at one the following URLs: `http://en.wikipedia.org/wiki/Transport_Layer_Security` and `http://en.wikipedia.org/wiki/Salt_(cryptography)`.

A static method does not require an instance of the class to be able to be called. In Ext JS, we can declare static attributes and methods inside the static configuration. As the `encode` method from `Packt.util.MD5` class is static, we can call it like `Packt.util.MD5.encode(value);`.

So before `Ext.Ajax.request`, we will add the following code:

```
pass = Packt.util.MD5.encode(pass);
```

We must not forget to add the `Packt.util.MD5` class on the controller's `requires` declaration (the `requires` declaration is right after the `extend` declaration):

```
requires: [
    'Packt.util.MD5'
],
```

Now, if we try to run the code again, and check the **XHR** requests on the **Net** tab, we will have the following output:

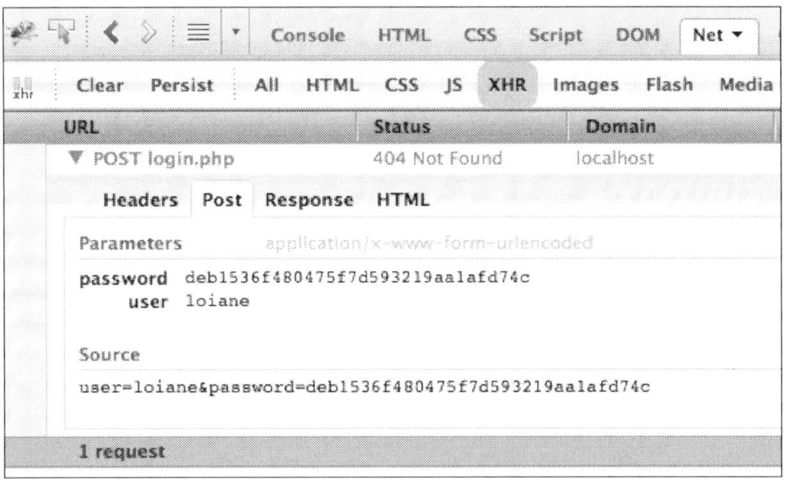

The password is encrypted and it is much safer now.

Creating the User and Groups tables

Before we start coding the `login.php` page, we need to add two tables to the `sakila` database. These two tables are going to represent the users and also the groups that the users can belong to. In our project, a user can belong to only one group, as shown in the following screenshot:

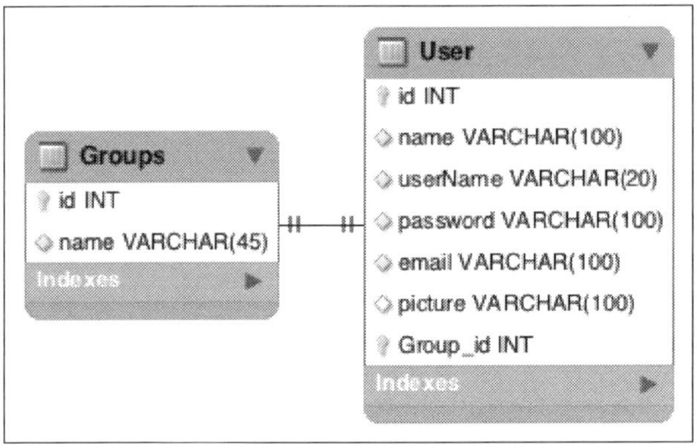

First, we are going to create the `Groups` table:

```
CREATE  TABLE IF NOT EXISTS `sakila`.`Groups` (
  `id` INT NOT NULL AUTO_INCREMENT ,
  `name` VARCHAR(45) NOT NULL ,
  PRIMARY KEY (`id`) )
ENGINE = InnoDB;
```

Then, we are going to create the `User` table containing the indexes, and will also create the foreign key to the `Groups` table:

```
CREATE  TABLE IF NOT EXISTS `sakila`.`User` (
  `id` INT NOT NULL AUTO_INCREMENT ,
  `name` VARCHAR(100) NOT NULL ,
  `userName` VARCHAR(20) NOT NULL ,
  `password` VARCHAR(35) NOT NULL ,
  `email` VARCHAR(100) NOT NULL ,
  `picture` VARCHAR(100) NULL ,
  `Group_id` INT NOT NULL ,
  PRIMARY KEY (`id`, `Group_id`) ,
  UNIQUE INDEX `userName_UNIQUE` (`userName` ASC) ,
  INDEX `fk_User_Group1_idx` (`Group_id` ASC) ,
  CONSTRAINT `fk_User_Group1`
    FOREIGN KEY (`Group_id` )
    REFERENCES `sakila`.`Groups` (`id` )
```

```
    ON DELETE NO ACTION
    ON UPDATE NO ACTION)
ENGINE = InnoDB;
```

The next step is to insert some data into these tables:

```
INSERT INTO `sakila`.`Groups` (`name`) VALUES ('admin');
INSERT INTO `sakila`.`User` (`name`, `userName`, `password`, `email`,
`Group_id`)
VALUES ('Loiane Groner', 'loiane', 'e10adc3949ba59abbe56e057f20f883e',
'me@loiane.com', '1');
```

As the password will be encrypted and saved in the database, the value `e10adc3949ba59abbe56e057f20f883e` corresponds to the value `123456`.

Now we are ready to start developing the `login.php` page.

Handling the login page on the server

Since we have part of the Ext JS code to send the login information to the server, we can implement the server-side code. As mentioned in *Chapter 1, Getting Started*, we are going to use PHP to implement the server-side code. But if you do not know PHP, do not worry because the code is not going to be complicated and we are going to use pure PHP as well. The goal is to focus on the programming logic we need to use on the server side; this way we can apply the same programming logic to any other server-side language that you like to use (Java, .NET, Ruby, Python, and so on).

Connecting to the database

The first step is to create the file that is going to be responsible to connect to the database. We are going to reuse this file in almost every PHP page that we are going to develop.

Create a new folder named `php` under the project's root folder, and under `php` create a new folder named `db`. Then, create a new file named `db.php`:

```
<?php
$server = "127.0.0.1";
$user = "root";
$pass = "root";
$dbName = "sakila";

$mysqli = new mysqli($server, $user, $pass, $dbName);

/* check connection */
```

```
    if ($mysqli->connect_errno) {
        printf("Connect failed: %s\n", mysqli_connect_error());
        exit();
    }
    ?>
```

The connection is pretty straightforward. We simply need to inform the server (which is going to be localhost), the database username and password, and also the database name that we want to connect to. And at last, we can check if the connection has happened successfully or has any error occurred.

> To learn more about mysqli, please go to `http://php.net/manual/en/book.mysqli.php`.

login.php

Finally, we can create the `login.php` file under the `php` folder. So let's start implementing it:

```
require("db/db.php"); // #1

session_start(); // #2

$userName = $_POST['user']; // #3
$pass = $_POST['password']; // #4

$userName = stripslashes($userName); // #5
$pass = stripslashes($pass);         // #6

$userName = $mysqli->real_escape_string($userName); // #7
$pass = $mysqli->real_escape_string($pass);         // #8
$sql = "SELECT * FROM USER WHERE userName='$userName' and
password='$pass'"; // #9
```

First, we need to require the `db.php` file to connect to the database (`#1`). Then, we start a session (`#2`) where we are going to store the username on the session later.

The next step is to retrieve the `user` and `password` values sent by the `Ext.Ajax.request` (`#3` and `#4`).

The `stripslashes` function removes the backslashes from the given string (`#5` and `#6`). For example, if the user value is `Loiane\'s`, the return of the `stripslashes` function will be `Loiane's`.

Then, we prepare the $username and $pass variables for the SQL statement by using the function real_escape_string (#7 and #8), which escapes special characters in a string for use in an SQL statement.

Next, we prepare the SQL query that is going to be executed (#9). It is a simple SELECT statement that is going to return a result matching the given username and password.

Let's continue with the next part of the code:

```
$result = array(); // #10

if ($resultdb = $mysqli->query($sql)) { // #11

  $count = $resultdb->num_rows; // #12

  if($count==1){

    $_SESSION['authenticated'] = "yes"; // #13
        $_SESSION['username'] = $userName;  // #14

    $result['success'] = true; // #15
    $result['msg'] = 'User authenticated!'; // #16

  } else {

    $result['success'] = false; // #17
    $result['msg'] = 'Incorrect user or password.'; // #18
  }

  $resultdb->close(); // #19
}
```

In this second part of the login.php code, we first need to create a result variable (#10) that is going to store the result information that we are going to send back to Ext JS.

Next, we need to execute the SQL query and we are going to store the result set into the resultdb variable (#11). Then, we are going to store if the result set returned any rows within the result set (#12).

Now comes the most important part of the code. We are going to verify if the result set returned any rows. As we passed the username and password, if the username and password match with the information we have on the database, the number of rows returned within the result set must be exactly 1. So if the number of rows is equal to 1, we are going to store the username of the authenticated user (#13) in the session, and also store the information that the user is authenticated (#14).

We also need to prepare the result that we are going to return to Ext JS. We are going to send back two pieces of information: the first one is if the user is authenticated (`#15`)—in this case true—and we can also send back a message (`#16`).

If the username and password do not match (number of rows returned within the result set is different from `1`), we are also going to send back a message to Ext JS saying the username or password informed by the user is incorrect (`#18`). Therefore, the `success` information will be `false`. Then, we need to close the result set (`#19`).

Now, the third and last part of the code of `login.php`:

```
$mysqli->close(); // #20

echo json_encode($result); // #21
```

We need to close the database connection (#20) and we are going to encode the result that we are going to send back to Ext JS in the **JSON (JavaScript Object Notation)** format (`#21`).

And now the `login.php` code is complete. However, we should not forget to wrap the preceding code within `<?php` and `?>`.

Handling the return of the server – logged in or not?

We already took care of the server-side code. Now we need to go back to the Ext JS code and handle the response from the server.

But first, we need to understand a very important concept that usually confuses most of the Ext JS developers.

Success versus failure

The `Ext.Ajax` class performs all Ajax requests done by Ext JS. If we look at the documentation, this class has three events, namely `beforerequest`, `requestcomplete`, and `requestexception`.

The event `beforerequest` is fired before the request. The `requestcomplete` event is fired when Ext JS is able to get a response from the server and the `requestexception` event is fired when an HTTP error status is returned from the server.

Now, let's go back to the `Ext.Ajax.request` call. We can pass some options to the request, including the URL we want to connect to, parameters, and other options, including the success and failure functions. Now this is where the misunderstanding happens. Some developers understand that if the actions happened successfully on the server we usually return `success = true` from the server. If something went wrong, we return `success = false`. Then, on the success function the `success = true` is handled and on the failure function the `success = false` is handled. This is *wrong* and it is not how Ext JS works.

For Ext JS, success is when the server returns a response (`success = true` or `success = false` does not matter) and failure is when the server returns an HTTP error status. This means that if the server was able to return a response, we will handle this response on the `success` function (and we will need to handle if the `success` information is `true` or `false`); on the `failure` message we need to inform the user that something went wrong and the user should contact the system administrator.

We will implement the `failure` function first. So inside the `Ext.Ajax.request` call, we will add the following code:

```
failure: function(conn, response, options, eOpts) {
  Ext.Msg.show({
        title:'Error!',
        msg: conn.responseText,
        icon: Ext.Msg.ERROR,
        buttons: Ext.Msg.OK
    });
}
```

We are going to display an alert to the user with an error icon and an **OK** button with the HTTP status error information.

To reproduce an error so that the requestexception event can be fired, we can rename the `login.php` file to something else (for example, `login_.php`) only for testing purposes. Then, we can execute the code and have the following output:

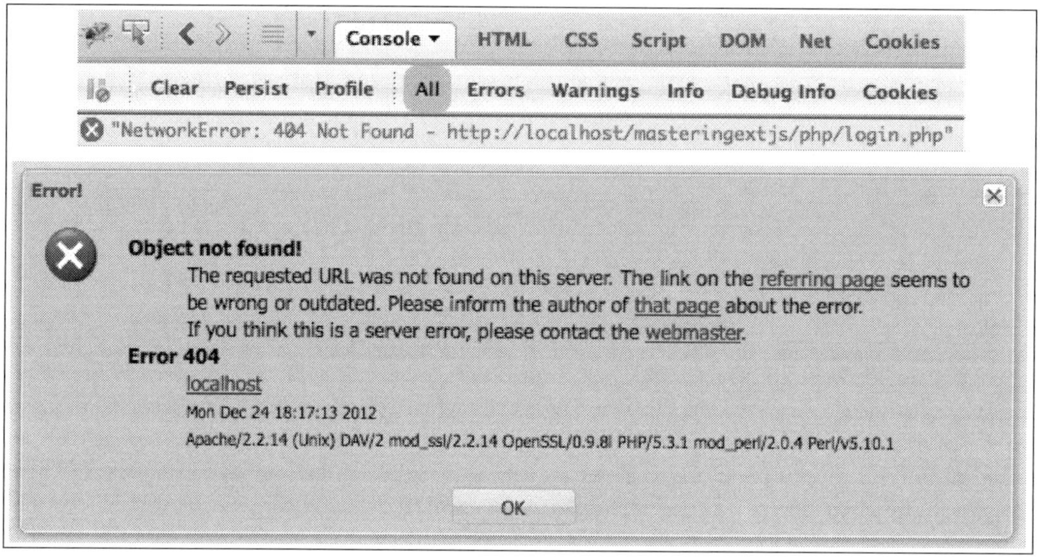

And this is all we need for the `failure` function. We can reuse this code in all failure functions for all `Ext.Ajax.request` calls in our project.

Now, let's focus on the `success` function:

```
success: function(conn, response, options, eOpts) {

    var result = Ext.JSON.decode(conn.responseText, true); // #1

    if (!result){ // #2
        result = {};
        result.success = false;
        result.msg = conn.responseText;
    }

    if (result.success) { // #3

        login.close(); // #4
        Ext.create('Packt.view.MyViewport'); // #5

    } else {
        Ext.Msg.show({
```

```
                title:'Fail!',
                msg: result.msg, // #6
                icon: Ext.Msg.ERROR,
                buttons: Ext.Msg.OK
            });
        }
    },
```

The first thing we need to do is to decode the JSON message (`#1`) that we received from the server. If we log the `conn` parameter sent to the `success` function (`console.log(conn)`), this will be the output we will get on the console:

▶ request	Object { id=1, headers={...}, options={...}, more... }
requestId	1
▼ responseText	"{"success":false,"msg":"Incorrect user or password."}"
responseXML	*null*
status	200
statusText	"OK"
getAllResponseHeaders	function()
getResponseHeader	function()

So when we decode `conn.responseText`, which is where the information we want to retrieve is, we will be able to access `result.success` and `result.msg`. We also need to be careful about one detail: we do not know what is going to be returned from the server, we always hope that is our `success` and `msg` information; however, we cannot be sure of it. If any other MySQL error is returned, it is going to be returned inside `conn.responseText` as well, and it cannot have the JSON format we are expecting. If this happens, the `Ext.JSON.decode` function will fail and it will throw an exception. We can silence the exception (passing `true` as the second parameter to the `Ext.JSON.decode` function, and the `result` variable will have value `null`), but we still need to handle it. And that is what we are doing when checking if the `result` variable is `null` (`#2`). If it is null, we are instantiating the `result` variable and assigning some values (the `msg` will receive the error sent by the server). If we do not handle this, the user will click on the **Submit** button and nothing will happen.

If `success` is `true` (`#3`), meaning the user was authenticated on the server, we can do something such as closing the **Login** window (`#4`) and then displaying the application (`#5`). As we do not have the `Packt.view.MyViewport` class created yet, we will comment it, so that later when we have the class implemented, we can come here and remove the comment. In this class (`Packt.view.MyViewport`) we will display the menu, header, footer, and the central panel of the application, which is where we are going to display the screens.

On the other hand, when `success` is `false`, meaning the username or password do not match with the information we have on the database, we will display an error message to the user with the message sent by the server (`#6`), in this case **Incorrect user or password**.

In case any other error happens on the server side, this error will be returned to Ext JS as we already described on line `#2`. To exemplify, let's say that we entered a wrong password for the database connection. If we try to login, we will get the following error:

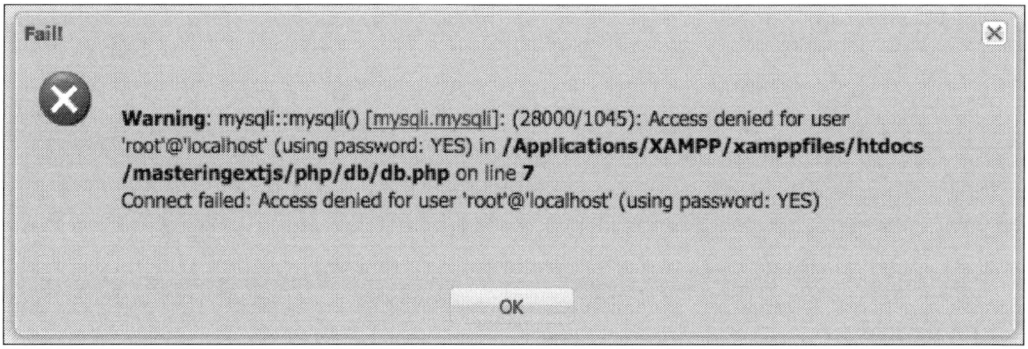

This way we can handle all kinds of server responses, the ones we are waiting for and also any exception!

Enhancing the Login screen

Our **Login** screen is done. However, there are some enhancements we can apply to it to make it even better and also offer a better experience to the user.

Following are the enhancements that we are going to apply in our **Login** screen:

- Applying a loading mask while authenticating
- Submitting the form when a user presses *Enter*
- Displaying a Caps Lock warning message

Applying a loading mask on the form while authenticating

Sometimes, when the user clicks on the **Submit** button, there can be some delay while waiting for the server to send back the response. Some users will be patient, some will not be. The ones that are not very patient will click on the **Submit** button again; this means making another request to the server. We can avoid this behavior by applying a loading mask to the **Login** window while awaiting the response.

First, we need to add the following code right before the `Ext.Ajax.request` call:

```
Ext.get(login.getEl()).mask("Authenticating... Please wait...",
'loading');
```

This will apply the mask to the **Login** window.

Then, on the first line inside the `success` and `failure` functions, we need to add the following line of code:

```
Ext.get(login.getEl()).unmask();
```

This will remove the mask from the `Login` window.

If we try to execute the code, we will have the following output:

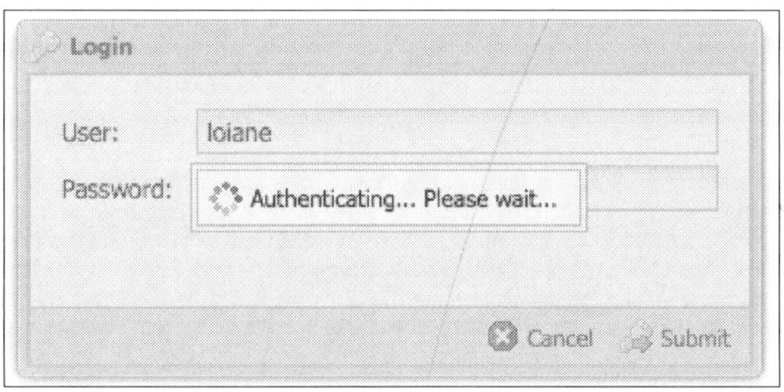

Notice that all the buttons are not reachable and the user cannot click on them again until the server sends back a response.

Form submit on Enter

For some forms, especially for the **Login** form, it is very natural for people to hit *Enter* when they are ready. This behavior is not automatic for Ext JS; therefore, we have to implement it.

The `textfield` component has an event to handle special keys such as *Enter*. This event is called `specialkey` and it is the one that we are going to listen to in our login controller. First, we need to add the event to the `this.control` declaration:

```
"login form textfield": {
    specialkey: this. onTextfieldSpecialKey
}
```

The selector that we are going to use is `login form textfield` because this selector will retrieve all the text fields from the **Login** form, which are `user` and `password`. The user can hit *Enter* while typing at any text field of the form.

Next, we need to implement the `onTextfieldSpecialKey` method inside the controller as well:

```
onTextfieldSpecialKey: function(field, e, options) {
    if (e.getKey() == e.ENTER){
        var submitBtn = field.up('form').down('button#submit');
        submitBtn.fireEvent('click', submitBtn, e, options);
    }
}
```

First, we are going to verify if the key pressed by the user is *Enter*. Then, we will get the reference for the **Submit** button: we need first to get the form reference, and then retrieve the **Submit** button that is below the form in the component's hierarchy. And at last, we will fire the click event of the **Submit** button manually. This way the `onButtonClickSubmit` method will be called automatically. As we also verify if the form is valid inside the `onButtonClickSubmit` method, we can be sure that the request will not be made even if the client validations fail.

The Caps Lock warning message

The last enhancement we will apply to the form is the **Caps Lock** message. Sometimes the *Caps Lock* key is active and when we input the password, we may input the correct password and yet have the system term it incorrect because it is case sensitive. And warning the user about this is a nice thing to do.

The following screenshot presents the final result of the Caps Lock warning implementation:

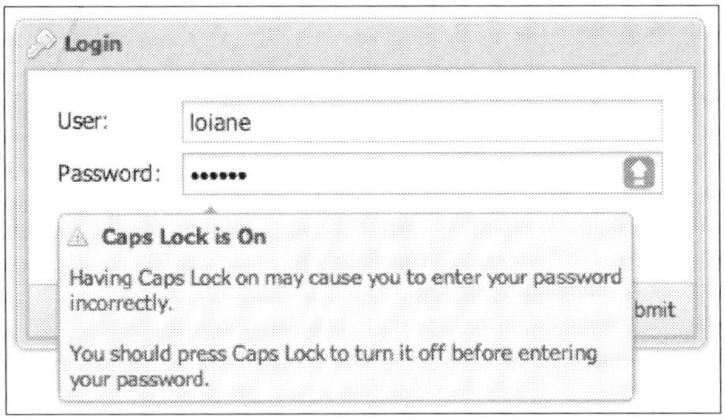

As you can see in the preceding screenshot, we will display the warning as a tooltip. So the first thing we need to do is go back to the `app.js` launch function and on the first line we need to add the following code:

```
Ext.tip.QuickTipManager.init();
```

Without the preceding line of code, the tooltips will not work.

Another option is to set `enableQuickTips` to `true` inside `Ext.application` (`app.js`).

The event that we are going to listen to is the `keypress` event, and we are only going to listen to this event fired by the `password` field. By default, the `textfield` components do not fire this event because it is a little bit heavy with regards to the performance. As we want to listen to this event, we need to add a configuration to the `password` field (inside `Login.js` file):

```
name: 'password',
fieldLabel: "Password",
enableKeyEvents: true,
id: 'password'
```

We also need to add `id` to this field. And yes, as we discussed using `id` instead of `itemId` is bad, but in this case, there is nothing we can do about it. This is because when creating the tooltip, we need to set a target (in this case, the `password` field), and this target only accepts `id` of the component, and not `itemId`.

Before we add the code to the controller, we need to create the tooltip. We are going to create a new view called `Packt.view.authentication.CapsLockTooltip`. So we need to create a file named `CapsLockTooltip.js` under the `app/view/authentication` directory.

```
Ext.define('Packt.view.authentication.CapsLockTooltip', {
    extend: 'Ext.tip.QuickTip',
    alias: 'widget.capslocktooltip',

    target: 'password',
    anchor: 'top',
    anchorOffset: 60,
    width: 300,
    dismissDelay: 0,
    autoHide: false,
    title: '<div class="capslock">Caps Lock is On</div>',
    html: '<div>Having Caps Lock on may cause you to enter your 
password</div>' +
        '<div>incorrectly.</div><br/>' +
        '<div>You should press Caps Lock to turn it off before 
entering</div>' +
        '<div>your password.</div>'
});
```

In the `Packt.view.authentication.CapsLockTooltip` view we declared some configurations that are going to set the behavior of the tooltip. For example, we have the following:

- `target`: This has the `id` value of the password fields.
- `anchor`: This indicates that the tip should be anchored to a particular side of the target element (the password `id` field), with an arrow pointing back at the target.
- `achorOffset`: This is a numeric value (in pixels) used to offset the default position of the anchor arrow. In this case, the arrow will be displayed 60 pixels after the starting point of the tooltip box.
- `width`: This is the numeric value (in pixels) to represent the width of the tooltip box.
- `dismissDelay`: This is the delay value (in milliseconds) before the tooltip automatically hides. As we do not want tooltip to be automatically hidden, we set the value to `0` (zero) to disable it.
- `autoHide`: This is set to `true` to automatically hide the tooltip after the mouse exits the target element. If we do not want this, we set it to `false`.

- `title`: This is the title text to be used as the title of the tooltip.
- `html`: This is the HTML fragment that will be displayed in the tooltip body.

We also need to add the CSS code into `app.css` related to the `capslock` class:

```
.capslock{
    background:url('../icons/bullet_error.png') no-repeat center left;
    padding:2px;
    padding-left:20px;
    font-weight:700;
}
```

And at last, we need to make some changes in the login controller. First, in the `views` declaration, we will add the `CapsLockTooltip` class. As we created a subfolder inside the `view` folder, the controller will not understand if we simply add `CapsLockTooltip` as a view. So, we need to add `authentication.CapsLockTooltip` and the controller will understand that the class is inside the `view/authentication` folder:

```
views: [
    'Login',
    'authentication.CapsLockTooltip'
],
```

We can have as many subfolders as we need under the `app/model`, `store`, `view`, and `controller` folders. This can help us to organize the code better, especially when we work with big applications. In the `views`, `controllers`, `stores`, and `models` declarations we also need to add the name of the subfolder as we did with `authentication.CapsLockTooltip`.

The next step is to listen to the `keypress` event inside the `this.control` declaration:

```
"login form textfield[name=password]": {
    keypress: this.onTextfieldKeyPress
}
```

The selector that we are going to use is the `login form textfield[name=password]`. As we have two text fields on the form, we need a way of finding the `password` field; we can use the `name` attribute for this.

Then, we need to implement the `onTextfieldKeyPress` method inside the controller:

```
onTextfieldKeyPress: function(field, e, options) {
    var charCode = e.getCharCode(); // #1

    if((e.shiftKey && charCode >= 97 && charCode <= 122) || // #2
```

```
            (!e.shiftKey && charCode >= 65 && charCode <= 90)){

            if(this.getCapslockTooltip() === undefined){ // #3
                Ext.widget('capslocktooltip');           // #4
            }

            this.getCapslockTooltip().show(); // #5

        } else {

            if(this.getCapslockTooltip() !== undefined){ // #6
                this.getCapslockTooltip().hide();        // #7
            }
        }
    }
```

First, we need to get the code of the key that the user pressed (`#1`). Then, we need to verify if the *Shift* key is pressed and the user has pressed one of the lower alpha keys (a-z), or if the *Shift* key is not pressed and the user has pressed one of the capital alpha keys (A-Z) (`#2`). If the result of this verification is true, this means that the *Caps Lock* key is active. If you want to check the values of each key, you can go to `http://www.asciitable.com/`.

If *Caps Lock* is active, we will verify if there is a reference of the `CapsLockTooltip` class (`#3`). If there is not, we will create a reference using its `xtype` (`#4`).

If *Caps Lock* is not active, we need to verify if there is a reference of the `CapsLockTooltip` class (`#6`). If positive, we will hide the tooltip.

The last detail: we do not have the reference for `this.getCapslockTooltip()` inside the controller. That is why we need to create it as well:

```
    refs: [
        {
            ref: 'capslockTooltip',
            selector: 'capslocktooltip'
        }
    ]
```

`ref` (reference) is an alternative to locate a component. It also uses the `ComponentQuery` syntax. `ref` is very useful, especially if we need to get a reference of a component several times inside a controller. The controller will also generate a `get` method automatically for a `ref`. In this case, the controller generates the `getCapslockTooltip` method for us.

The Caps Lock warning code is now complete. We can save the project and test it.

Summary

In this chapter, we have covered the details of how to implement a login page step by step. We covered how to create the login view and controller and organized them according to the Ext JS MVC architecture. We applied client validations on the form to make sure that we are sending acceptable data to the server, and we also encrypted the password before sending it to the server. We covered how to do a basic login using PHP, and we covered important concepts of how to handle the data that the server is going to send back to Ext JS.

We learned about some enhancements that we can apply to the **Login** screen, such as submitting the form when the user hits *Enter*, and displaying a Caps Lock warning in the password field, and also learned how to apply a load mask on the form while it is sending data and waiting for information from the server.

In the next chapter, we will continue to work on the **Login** screen. We will learn how to add the multilingual capability and also implement the logout and session monitor capabilities.

3

Logout and Multilingual

In this chapter we are going to implement the multilingual capability of the system. This feature will allow the system to display the translation of the labels according to the language selected by the user (using some of the new HTML 5 features).

We will also learn how to implement the logout capability, so that the user can end the session, and also for security reasons we will learn how to implement a session timeout warning for the user in case of inactivity (not using the mouse or keyboard for a while).

Also, after the user is authenticated we need to display the application.
In this chapter we will learn how to implement the base of the application using a Viewport.

So in this chapter, we will cover:

- The base of the application
- The logout capability
- Activity monitoring and the session timeout warning
- Structuring the application to receive the multilingual capability
- Creating the change language component
- Handling the language change at runtime

The base of the application

When we implemented the `success` function in the **Submit** button listener on the Login Controller, we mentioned the `Packt.view.MyViewport` class. We are going to create this class now (as a new file named `MyViewport.js` under the `view` folder). Before we start, let's take a look at what is going to be the output:

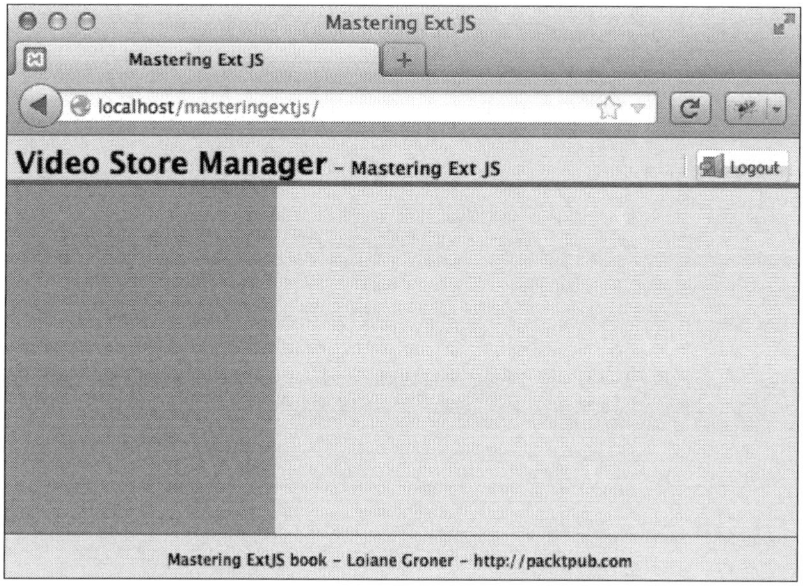

Now, let's a look at the code that is going to generate the previous output:

```
Ext.define('Packt.view.MyViewport', {
    extend: 'Ext.container.Viewport', // #1
    alias: 'widget.mainviewport',     // #2

    requires: [
        'Packt.view.Header'  // #3
    ],

    layout: {
        type: 'border' // #4
    },

    items: [
        {
            xtype: 'container', // #5
            width: 185,
```

```
                collapsible: true,
                region: 'west',
                style: 'background-color: #8FB488;'
            },
            {
                xtype: 'appheader', // #6
                region: 'north'
            },
            {
                xtype: 'container', // #7
                region: 'center'
            },
            {
                xtype: 'container', // #8
                region: 'south',
                height: 30,
                style: 'border-top: 1px solid #4c72a4;',
                html: '<div id="titleHeader"><center><span style="font-
    size:10px;">Mastering ExtJS book - Loiane Groner - http://packtpub.
    com</span></center></div>'
            }
        ]
    });
```

The `Packt.view.MyViewport` class will be a `Viewport` (`#1`), which is a specialized container representing the viewable application area (the browser viewport). The `Viewport` renders itself to the document body, and automatically sizes itself to the size of the browser viewport and manages window resizing. There may only be one `Viewport` created in a page. We will also create an alias for this class (`#2`).

`MyViewport` will use the `border` layout. The Border Layout divides the available in five regions: North, South, West, East, and Center. The central region is the only one that is mandatory to have in a container using the Border Layout. In this case, we will not use the east region (`#4`).

Then, in the items array, we will declare the four components in the four regions that we are going to use. The first one will be a container (`#5`) that is located in the west region. As it is in the west region we need to set a width. We can also make it collapsible, so the user can see the central area better. Later, we will replace this container with the dynamic menu that we are going to create. For now, we will apply a greenish background color to be able to see the region.

We have `appheader` (`#6`), which is the `xtype` for the `Packt.view.Header` class. In this class, we will implement all the header area, composed of the title of the application and also the **Logout** button. As we are using the `appheader xtype`, we need to add the `Packt.view.Header` class on the `requires` declaration of this class (`#3`).

Next we have the central container (`#7`). This is where we are going to display the screens of the application later. We will replace it with a Tab panel. And as last item we have another container that contains all the footer information (`#8`).

Now we need to implement the `Packt.view.Header` class. To do so, we need to create a new file named `Header.js` under the `app/view` folder:

```
Ext.define('Packt.view.Header', {
    extend: 'Ext.toolbar.Toolbar', // #1
    alias: 'widget.appheader',     // #2

    height: 30, // #3
    ui: 'footer', // #4
    style: 'border-bottom: 4px solid #4c72a4;', // #5

    items: [
        {
            xtype: 'label', // #6
            html: '<div id="titleHeader">Video Store Manager<span
style="font-size:12px;"> - Mastering Ext JS</span></div>'
        },
        {
            xtype: 'tbfill' // #7
        },
        {
            xtype: 'tbseparator' // #8
        },
        {
            xtype: 'button', // #9
            text: 'Logout',
            itemId: 'logout',
            iconCls: 'logout'
        }
    ]
});
```

The `Header` class extends from the `Toolbar` class (`#1`). We will also assign an alias to this class (`#2`), which we already used on the `MyViewport` class. Then, we will set a height of the toolbar (`#3`) and we will also apply a style to it. The `footer ui` (`#4`) makes the buttons pop up when looking at the toolbar; otherwise the toolbar and its buttons will have the same color. We will also apply a style to the toolbar adding a bottom border to it (`#5`).

Then we have its items: first we have a label representing the title of the application (`#6`). And as we want the **Logout** button aligned on the right of the toolbar, we will add the toolbar fill component (`#7`). Then we have a toolbar separator just to make the toolbar look prettier (`#8`). And at last we have the **Logout** button (`#9`).

For `#7` and `#8`, we can also use the short-hand version. So instead of using the following code:

```
{
    xtype: 'tbfill' // #7
},
{
    xtype: 'tbseparator' // #8
},
```

We can use the following code:

```
'->', // #7
'-', // #8
```

The result will be the same. It is only a matter of personal preference. For example, for experienced developers, it may be faster to declare the short-hand version of the `tbfill` and `tbseparator` components. But for a beginner who will do some maintenance on the code, it may require a little bit more experience to understand the short-hand version.

Finally, we need to add a new style to the `app.css` file:

```
#titleHeader {
    color:#000;
    font-size:20px;
    font-weight:bold;
    font-family:'Lucida Grande', Arial, Sans;
}
```

And now we have the base of our application. We will work on it in the upcoming chapters.

The logout capability

As the user has the option to log into the application, the user can also log out from it. The logout capability will be the last one that we will implement in the Login Controller.

First, we will add the `Header` class as one of the views of the controller:

```
views: [
    'Login',
    'Header',
    'authentication.CapsLockTooltip'
]
```

The next step is to add the click event listener from the **Logout** button inside the `this.control` declaration:

```
"appheader button#logout": {
    click: this.onButtonClickLogout
}
```

As the selector, we will use `appheader` because this is the `xtype` of the toolbar where the **Logout** button is located, `button` because **Logout** is a button (`xtype: button`), and `#logout` because this is its `itemId`. This way we make sure `ComponentQuery` will retrieve the button that we are looking for.

Then, we need to implement the `onButtonClickLogout` method inside the controller:

```
onButtonClickLogout: function(button, e, options) {

    Ext.Ajax.request({
        url: 'php/logout.php', // #1
        success: function(conn, response, options, eOpts){

            var result = Ext.JSON.decode(conn.responseText, true);

            if (!result){
                result = {};
                result.success = false;
                result.msg = conn.responseText;
            }

            if (result.success) { // #3

                button.up('mainviewport').destroy(); // #4
                window.location.reload();            // #5
```

```
            }
            else {
                Ext.Msg.show({          // #6
                    title:'Error!',
                    msg: result.msg,
                    icon: Ext.Msg.ERROR,
                    buttons: Ext.Msg.OK
                });
            }
        },
        failure: function(conn, response, options, eOpts) {

                Ext.Msg.show({        // #7
                    title:'Error!',
                    msg: conn.responseText,
                    icon: Ext.Msg.ERROR,
                    buttons: Ext.Msg.OK
                });
        }
    });
}
```

We will make an Ajax call (`#1`) to `php/logout.php` (we will create this file soon). As usual, we will handle the success and failure callbacks. On success, first we need to decode the response from the server. If any error, we will handle it creating a new instance of the result variable. If the result `success` information is `true` (`#3`), we will get the `mainviewport` reference (the `Packt.view.MyViewport` class) and will destroy it (it is good to release the browser memory), and this will destroy all the application's components (`#4`). And then, we will reload the application displaying the login screen again (`#5`).

If `success` is `false` (or any error occurred), we will display an error alert with the error message (`#6`).

In case of failure, we will also display an error message (`#7`).

Refactoring the login and logout code

If we take a closer look, we are reusing a lot of the code we used on the **Submit** button listener. Well, reuse is not the correct word; we are actually making copy of the code and this is not good. What if we need to maintain this code and make a simple change? We will need to change the code in all the places that we are using it, and this can be a boring task. We need to refactor this code and create it in such a way that we can really reuse the code.

So we need to create a new `Util` class inside the `util` folder: `Packt.util.Util`.

```
Ext.define('Packt.util.Util', {

    statics : { // #1

        decodeJSON : function (text) { // #2

            var result = Ext.JSON.decode(text, true);

            if (!result){
                result = {};
                result.success = false;
                result.msg = text;
            }

            return result;
        },

        showErrorMsg: function (text) { // #3

            Ext.Msg.show({
                title:'Error!',
                msg: text,
                icon: Ext.Msg.ERROR,
                buttons: Ext.Msg.OK
            });
        }
    }
});
```

All the methods/functions will be static (`#1`), to avoid creating an instance of this class.

The first method we are going to declare is the `decodeJSON` method (`#2`). In this method, we will add the `decode` call, and also handle if it was not possible to decode the response from the server because of an error. The second method that we will implement is `showErrorMsg` (`#3`), which is simply going to display an error alert with an **OK** button and an error icon.

Going back to the Login Controller, we need to add the `Packt.util.Util` class inside the `requires` declaration. After that, we can refactor the `onButtonClickLogout` method:

```
onButtonClickLogout: function(button, e, options) {

    Ext.Ajax.request({
        url: 'php/logout.php',
        success: function(conn, response, options, eOpts){

            var result =
            Packt.util.Util.decodeJSON(conn.responseText);

            if (result.success) {

                button.up('mainviewport').destroy();
                window.location.reload();
            }
            else {
                Packt.util.Util.showErrorMsg(conn.responseText);
            }
        },
        failure: function(conn, response, options, eOpts) {
            Packt.util.Util.showErrorMsg(conn.responseText);
        }
    });
}
```

Much cleaner and we only coded what really matters to the logout capability. We can optimize this code even more, but this is enough for now. We can also apply the same refactoring to the `onButtonClickSubmit` method.

> This refactoring may seem silly, but this is part of what it is called **minimizing the payload size**, which is one of the best practices while developing with JavaScript, and also a concern of the web development. To learn more about this, please visit `https://developers.google.com/speed/docs/best-practices/payload`.

Handling the logout capability on the server

To handle the logout capability on the server, we will create a new PHP page named `logout.php` under the `php` folder. The code is very simple:

```
<?php

session_start(); // #1

$_SESSION = array(); // #2

session_destroy(); // #3

$result = array(); // #4

$result['success'] = true;
$result['msg'] = 'logout';

echo json_encode($result); // #5

?>
```

First, we need to resume the current session (`#1`), then we need to unset all of the session variables (`#2`), and next we need to destroy the session (`#3`). Lastly, we need to send back the information to Ext JS that the session has been destroyed (`#4` and `#5`).

And now we also have the logout capability implemented.

The client-side activity monitor

Let's enhance our application a little bit more. It is very important to let the users know that web applications have a timeout and they cannot leave it open all day for security reasons. Server-side languages also have timeout. Once the user is logged in, the server will not be available forever. This is for security reasons. That is why we need to add this capability to our application as well.

We are going to use a plugin do to this. The plugin is called `Packt.util.` SessionMonitor based on the Activity Monitor plugin from Sencha Market (`https://market.sencha.com/extensions/extjs-activity-monitor`). After an interval (default of 15 minutes of inactivity), the plugin will display a message to the user asking if the user wants to keep the session alive. If yes, it will send an Ajax request to the server to also keep the server session alive. If the user does not do anything after the message is displayed for 60 seconds, the application will logout automatically.

We can get the source code of this plugin from `https://github.com/loiane/masteringextjs/blob/master/app/util/SessionMonitor.js`.

If we would like to change the inactivity interval, we only need to change the `maxInactive` configuration.

To start monitoring the session, we only need to add this line of code inside the method, `onButtonClickSubmit`, of the Login Controller, right after we instantiate the `MyViewport` class:

```
Ext.create('Packt.view.MyViewport');
Packt.util.SessionMonitor.start();
```

On line 42 of the class `SessionMonitor.js`, there is a call for a file named `php/sessionAlive.php`. We need to create this file inside the `php` folder. Inside this file we will have the following code:

```
<?php
session_start();
?>
```

That is only to keep the server session alive and also to reset the session timer back to 15 minutes.

If we run this code and wait for the inactivity time (15 minutes), we will see a message like in the following screenshot:

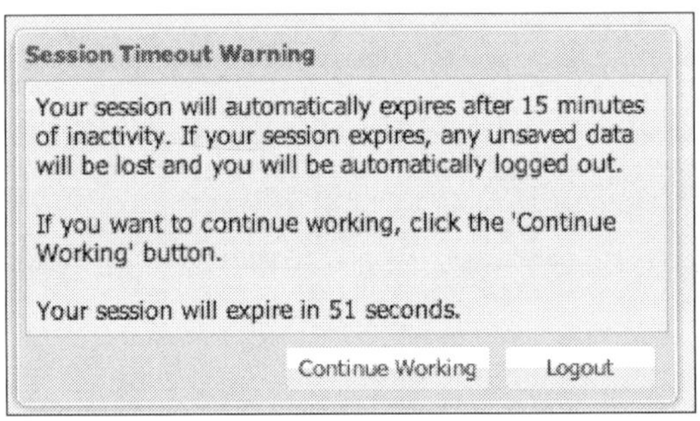

Ext JS does not provide this capability natively. But as we can see, it is very easy to implement and we can reuse this plugin for all Ext JS projects that we work on.

The multilingual capability

Sometimes you want to ship the project or product that you are working on overseas, and having a translation capability is very important, after all, not everyone understands or speaks the same language that you do. And this is what we are going to implement in this topic: a multilingual component that we can use to translate the labels of this project. So at the end of this topic, the following is going to be our output:

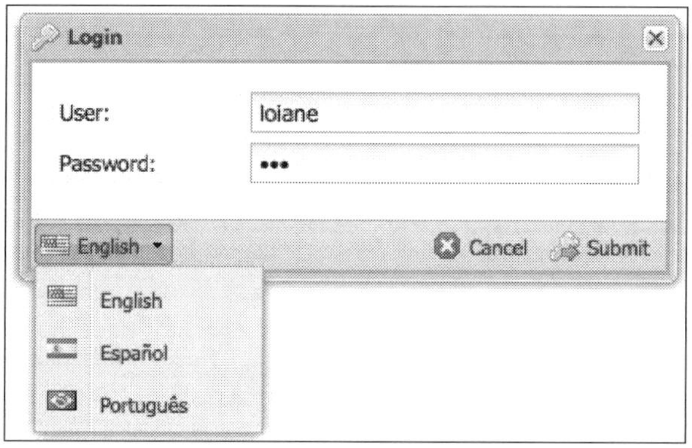

The idea is to store the user language preference locally, so the next time the user loads the application, the preferred language will be automatically set. And when the user changes the language, the application needs to be reloaded so that the new translations can be loaded into the memory.

Creating the change language component

If we take a look at the screenshot we showed at the beginning of this topic, we can notice that the multilingual component is a button and when we click on the arrow, a menu pops up with the available languages.

The button with the arrow is a Split button component and it has a Menu, and each language option is a menu item of the menu. So let's go ahead and create a new class named `Packt.view.Translation` containing the characteristics we described. We need to create a new file named `Translatation.js` under the `app/view` folder:

```
Ext.define('Packt.view.Translation', {
    extend: 'Ext.button.Split',  // #2
    alias: 'widget.translation', // #1
    menu: Ext.create('Ext.menu.Menu', { // #3
        items: [
            {
```

```
                xtype: 'menuitem',   // #4
                iconCls: 'en',
                text: 'English'
            },
            {
                xtype: 'menuitem',   // #5
                iconCls: 'es',
                text: 'Español'
            },
            {
                xtype: 'menuitem',   // #6
                iconCls: 'pt_BR',
                text: 'Português'
            }
        ]
    })
});
```

So the class that we created is extending from the `Split` button class (`#1`). A Split button is a class that provides a built-in drop-down arrow that can fire an event separately from the default click event of the button. Typically this would be used to display a drop-down menu that provides additional options to the primary button action. And we are also assigning an alias to this class (`#2`).

Then, on the menu configuration we need to create an instance of the `Menu` class (`#3`), followed by the menu items that are going to represent each translate option. So we have: an option to translate to English (`#4`), and it will also show an American flag; an option to translate to Spanish (`#5`), and it will also show the Spanish flag; and also an option to translate to Portuguese (`#6`), and it will also display the Brazilian flag.

We can add as many options as we need to. For each translation option, we only need to add a new menu item.

The next step now is to add the CSS for `iconCls` we used in this component in the `app.css` file:

```
.pt_BR {
  background-image:url('../flags/br.png') !important;
}

.en {
  background-image:url('../flags/us.png') !important;
}

.es {
  background-image:url('../flags/es.png') !important;
}
```

And the component is ready (only what is going to be displayed to the user). We are going to use the translation component in two places of our project: on the login screen and also before the **Logout** button on the header toolbar.

First, we will add it to the login screen. Open the `Packt.view.Login` class again. On the toolbar, we will add it as the first item so it can look exactly as we showed in the screenshot at the beginning of this topic:

```
items: [
  {
    xtype: 'translation'
  },
  {
    xtype: 'tbfill'
  },
  //
]
```

We must not forget to add the class to the requires declaration of the login screen class:

```
requires: [
    'Packt.view.Translation'
],
```

Now we will do the same for the `Packt.view.Header` class. We will add the translation component right after the toolbar fill component:

```
{
    xtype: 'tbfill'
},
{
    xtype: 'translation'
},
{
    xtype: 'tbseparator'
},
```

And if we run the application now we will see the login screen with the translation component and after we login, the translation component will be located on the left-hand side of the **Logout** button:

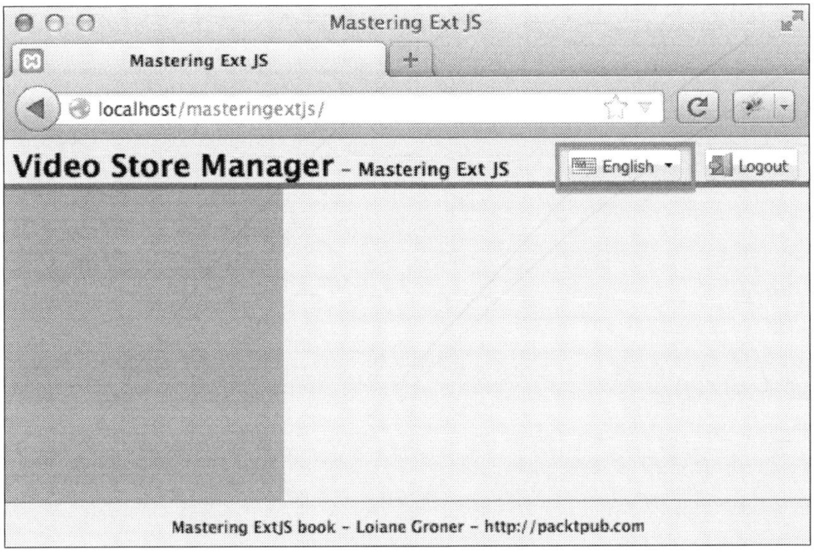

Creating the translation files

We need to store the translations somewhere in our project. We are going to store the translations for each language in a JavaScript file inside the `translations` folder. And as we are going to use iconCls as the code to load the translation files, we need to create three files: `en.js`, `es.js`, and `pt_BR.js`. Inside each file, we will create a JavaScript object named `translations` and each attribute in this object will be a translation. All translation files must be the same; the only thing that will be different is the value of each attribute that will contain the translation.

For example, the following code is for the `en.js` file:

```
translations = {
  login: "Please Login",
  user: "User",
  password: "Password",

  cancel: "Cancel",
  submit: "Submit",
  logout: 'Logout',

  capsLockTitle: 'Caps Lock is On',
  capsLockMsg1: 'Having Caps Lock on may cause you to enter your
  password',
  capsLockMsg2: 'incorrectly.',
```

```
    capsLockMsg3: 'You should press Caps Lock to turn it off before
    entering',
    capsLockMsg4: 'your password.'
  }
```

And the following code is for `pt_BR.js`, which contains the Portuguese translations:

```
  translations = {
    login: "Faça o Login",
    user: "Usuário",
    password: "Senha",

    cancel: "Cancelar",
    submit: "Enviar",
    logout: 'Logout',

    capsLockTitle: 'Caps Lock está ativada',
    capsLockMsg1: 'Se Caps lock estiver ativado, isso pode fazer com
    que você',
    capsLockMsg2: 'digite a senha incorretamente.',
    capsLockMsg3: 'Você deve pressionar a tecla Caps lock para
    desativá-la',
    capsLockMsg4: 'antes de digitar a senha.'
  }
```

As we can see, the files are the same; however, the translation is different. As the application grows, we will add more translations to it, and it is a good practice to maintain the files organized in the same way, to facilitate maintenance if we need to change any translation in the future.

Applying the translation on the application's components

To apply the translations on the components that we have developed so far is very simple; we need to use `translation.property` instead of the string that is going to represent the label.

For example, on the `Packt.view.Login` class we have the title of the window, `fieldLabel` of username and password, and the text of the **Cancel** and **Submit** buttons. The labels are hardcoded and we want to get the translation from the translation files.

So we need to replace the title of the login window with:

```
title: translations.login,
```

We need to replace `fieldLabel` of the username text field with:

```
fieldLabel: translations.user,
```

We need to replace the `fieldLabel` of the password text field with:

```
fieldLabel: translations.password,
```

We need to replace text of the **Cancel** button with:

```
text: translations.cancel
```

We need to replace text of the **Submit** button with:

```
text: translations.submit
```

And so on. We can also apply the translation for the **Logout** button and also to the `CapsLockTooltip` class.

HTML5 local storage

Our idea for the translate component is to store somewhere the language preference of the user. We could use cookies for this, but what we want is so simple, and cookies are included with every HTTP request. We want to store this information on a long-term, and also use something that can be persisted beyond a page refresh or the fact that the user closed the browser. And the perfect option is to use Local Storage, one of the new features of HTML5.

Ext JS has support for Local Storage, it can be used using the `LocalStorage` proxy, but we need something simpler and using the HTML5 feature itself in the code is simpler. And it also demonstrates that we can use other APIs along with Ext JS API.

The Local Storage is not supported by every browser; it is only supported by: IE 8.0+, Firefox 3.5+, Safari 4.0+, Chrome 4.0+, Opera 10.5+, iPhone 2.0+, and Android 2.0+. We will build a nice page warning the user to upgrade the browser later in this book. We will also use other HTML5 features along with Ext JS in other screens as well. So for now, we need to know that this code that we will implement now does not work on every browser.

For more information about HTML5 Storage, please visit `http://diveintohtml5.info/storage.html`.

We will create a new file named `locale.js` inside the `translations` folder. The following is what we need to implement inside this file:

```
var lang = localStorage ? (localStorage.getItem('user-lang') || 'en')
: 'en';
var file = 'translations/' + lang + '.js';

document.write('<script type="text/javascript" src="' + file + '"></
script>');
```

So first, we are going to verify if the `localStorage` proxy is available. If it is available, we are going to check if there an item named `user-lang` stored on `localStorage`; if not, English will be the default language. If `localStorage` is not available, English will also be set as the default language.

Then, we are creating a variable named `file` that is going to receive the path of the translation file that must be loaded by the application.

And at last, we are going to add the selected translation file into the `index.html` page. So we need to go to the `index.html` file and add the following code:

```
<script src="translations/locale.js"></script>
```

It is adding the JavaScript file we just created. This code will be executed when the `index.html` file is being loaded by the browser. By the time our application is loaded, we will have all the translations available.

Handling the language change in real-time

Now comes the final part of the code of the translation component. When the user selects a different language, we need to reload the application so the `translations/locale.js` file can be executed again and load the new language translations chosen by the user.

To do so, we will create a new controller in our application just to handle the translation component. So we need to create a new class named `Packt.controller.TranslationManager`, and to create this class, we need to create a new file named `TranslationManager.js` under the `app/controller` folder.

In this controller, we will need to listen to two events: one fired by the translation component itself and the other one fired by the menu items.

```
Ext.define('Packt.controller.TranslationManager', {
    extend: 'Ext.app.Controller',

    views: [
```

```
        'Translation' // #1
    ],

    refs: [
        {
            ref: 'translation', // #2
            selector: 'translation'
        }
    ],

    init: function(application) {
        this.control({
            "translation menuitem": { // #3
                click: this.onMenuitemClick
            },
            "translation": {          // #4
                beforerender: this.onSplitbuttonBeforeRender
            }
        });
    }
});
```

First, we will declare the translation component as a view (`#1`) of the controller because we want the controller to be responsible for all events fired from this component. Then, we will create a reference for the translation component, where `xtype` is `translation` and we will name `ref` as `translation` (`#2`). With this `ref` declared, the controller will automatically generate the `getTranslation` method for us to retrieve the reference of this component.

The next step is to start listening to the events that we are interested in. First, we want to listen to the `beforerender` (`#4`) event from the translation component, which is a **Split** button. The `beforerender` event is going to be fired before the **Split** button is rendered. What we want to happen is based on the language chosen by the user, we will set the icon and also the name of the language that was chosen. The second event that we want to listen to is the click of the menu item (`#3`). When the user clicks on one option of the menu, we need to set the new language on `localStorage`, change the icon and text of the **Split** button, and also reload the application.

So let's take a look at the `onSplitbuttonBeforeRender` method first:

```
onSplitbuttonBeforeRender: function(abstractcomponent, options) {
    var lang = localStorage ? (localStorage.getItem('user-lang') ||
'en') : 'en'; // #5
    abstractcomponent.iconCls = lang; // #6
```

```
        if (lang == 'en') { // #7
            abstractcomponent.text = 'English'; // #8
        } else if (lang == 'es'){
            abstractcomponent.text = 'Español';
        } else {
            abstractcomponent.text = 'Português';
        }
    }
```

First, we will verify if there is `localStorage`, and if yes, which is the language stored already. If there is not `localStorage` or the preferred language was not stored yet (first time the user is using the application or the user has not changed the language yet), the default language will be English (`#5`). Then, we will set `iconCls` of the **Split** button as the flag of the selected language (`#6`).

If the selected language is English, we will set the **Split** button text as "English" (*#7*), if the selected language is Spanish, we will set the **Split** button text as "Español" (*#8*), otherwise we will set the text as "Português" (Portuguese).

Now let's take a look at the `onMenuitemClick` method:

```
onMenuitemClick: function(item, e, options) {
    var menu = this.getTranslation(); // #9

    menu.setIconCls(item.iconCls); // #10
    menu.setText(item.text);       // #11

    localStorage.setItem("user-lang", item.iconCls); // #12

    window.location.reload(); // #13
}
```

First, we will get the reference to the translation component (`#9`). Then, we will set the **Split** button `iconCls` and text with `iconCls` and text of the menu item selected (`#10` and `#11`). Next, we will set the new language selected by the user on `localStorage` (`#12`), and finally we will ask to reload the page (`#13`).

We also must not forget to add the new controller to the `controllers` declaration in the `app.js` file:

```
controllers: [
    'Login',
    'TranslationManager'
],
```

If we execute the application, we can change the preferred language and we can see that the result is a translated application:

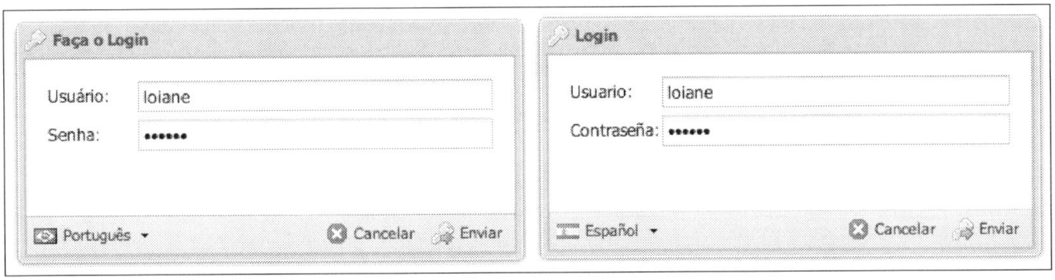

Locale – translating Ext JS

As usual, there is one thing missing. We are translating only the labels of the application. Form errors and other messages that are part of the Ext JS API are not translated. However, Ext JS provides locale support. All we need to do is to add the JavaScript `locale` file on the HTML page. To do so, we are going to add the following code inside the `translations/locale.js` file:

```
var extjsFile = 'extjs/locale/ext-lang-' + lang + '.js';
document.write('<script type="text/javascript" src="' + extjsFile +
'"></script>');
```

And now, if we try to execute the application again, we will be able to see that all the Ext JS messages will also be translated. For example, if we change the translation to Spanish, the form validation errors will also be in Spanish:

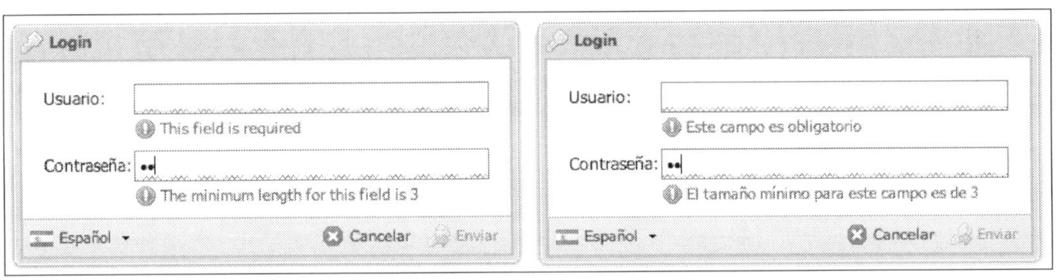

Now the translation of the application is completed! This is also one of the reasons why we are reloading the application when the user changes the language: we also need to reload the correct locale file.

Summary

We have covered how to implement the base of the application we are going to implement throughout this book and learned how to implement a **Logout** button (on Ext JS side and also on the server side). We also covered the Activity Monitor and session timeout capabilities.

And finally, we have learned how to build a translation component using HTML5 features along with Ext JS, which is able to translate all the labels of the application and also change the preferred language at runtime.

We made a great advancement in this chapter regarding the implementation of our application. We created new files and our application is growing. We will continue to create more files and components in the upcoming chapters of this book.

In the next chapter, we will learn how to build a menu dynamically using **Accordion panels** and **Trees**.

4

Advanced Dynamic Menu

We already have the login capability that we implemented throughout *Chapter 2, The Login Page*, and now it is time to start developing the screens of our project. The first thing that we are going to implement is the dynamic menu, meaning the items that will be displayed on the menu depend on the permissions that the user has. Once the user has been authenticated, we are going to display the base screen of the application, which consists of a viewport with a border layout. On the left-hand side of the viewport we are going to display a menu.

One of the options is to render all the screens of the system and then, depending on the user roles, we can hide or show them. But this is not the one we are going to use in this book. We are going to render and display only the screens the user can have access to. The approach we are going to use is to dynamically render a menu according to the capabilities the user can have access to.

So, in this chapter we will learn how to display a dynamic menu using Accordion panels and Tree panels, a more complex version of a dynamic menu. To summarize, in this chapter, we will cover:

- Creating a dynamic menu with Accordion panel and Tree panel
- Using hasMany association to load the data from server
- Handling the dynamic menu on the server
- Open a menu item dynamically

Creating the dynamic menu

So the first component that we are going to implement in this chapter is the dynamic menu. We could use only a Tree panel to display the menu, but we do like a challenge and we want to offer the best experience to the user. So, we are going to implement a dynamic menu using Accordion Layout and Tree panels, which is a more advanced dynamic menu. Our system consists of modules, and each module has subitems, which are the screens of our system. An Accordion panel will represent the modules; this way the user can expand and see the menu items of each module at a time. And for the options of each module, we will use a Tree panel; each menu item will be a node from the Tree panel.

So, at the end of this topic, we will have a dynamic menu like the following screenshot:

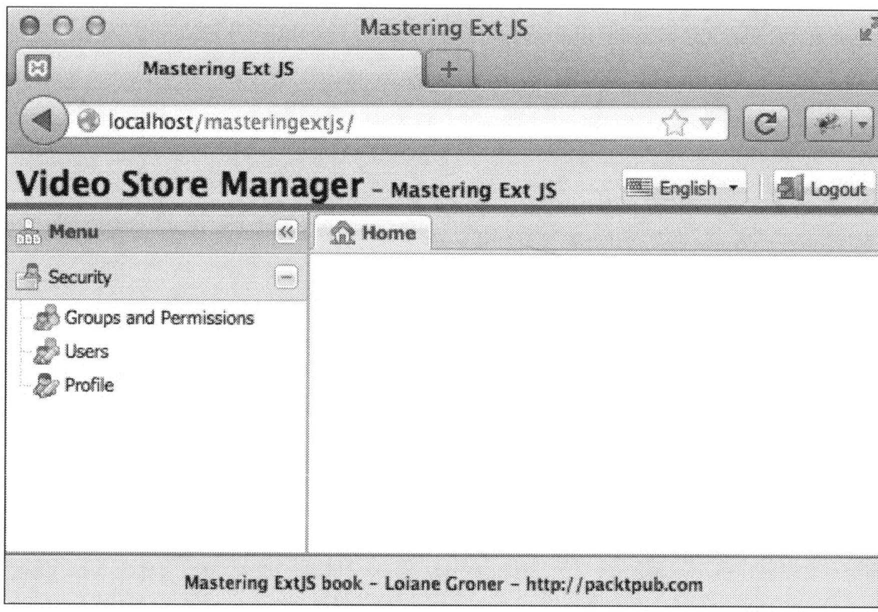

The database model – groups, menus, and permissions

We have already created the User and Groups table. To store the information of the menu and its menu items and also the permissions that each group has, we need to create two more tables, Menu and Permissions, as shown in the following screenshot:

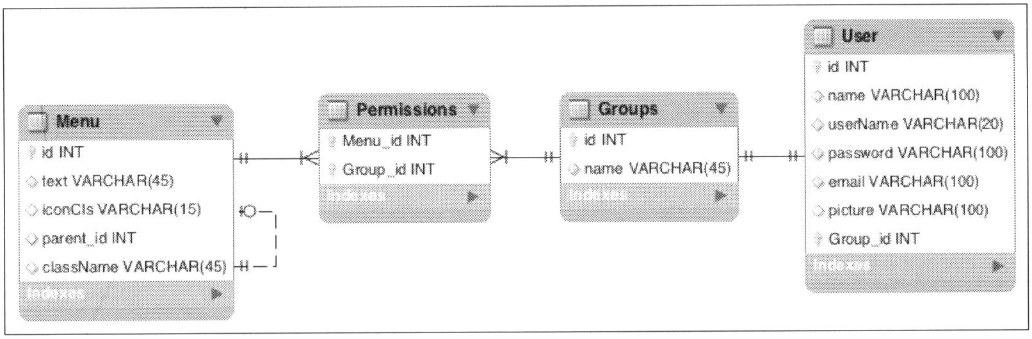

In the Menu table we will store all the menu information. As each option of the menu will be a node of a Tree panel, we will store the information in a way that represents a Tree panel. So we have an id field to identify the node, text as the text that is going to be displayed on the node (in our case, we will store the attribute of the translations file since we are using a multilingual capability), iconCls representing the css class that will be used to display the icon we are going to display for each node, className representing alias (xtype) of the class that we are going to instantiate dynamically and open at the central tab panel of the application, and finally the parent_id field representing the root node (in case, it has one: the module nodes will not have a parent_id field, but the module items will).

Then, as the Menu table has a N:N relationship with the Groups table, we have the Permissions table that will represent this relationship. We will learn more about how to assign a user to a group in the next chapter.

So to create the new table, we will use the following SQL script:

```
USE `sakila` ;
CREATE  TABLE IF NOT EXISTS `sakila`.`Menu` (
  `id` INT NOT NULL AUTO_INCREMENT ,
  `text` VARCHAR(45) NOT NULL ,
  `iconCls` VARCHAR(15) NULL ,
  `parent_id` INT NULL ,
  `className` VARCHAR(45) NULL ,
  PRIMARY KEY (`id`) ,
  INDEX `fk_Menu_Menu` (`parent_id` ASC) ,
```

```
    CONSTRAINT `fk_Menu_Menu`
      FOREIGN KEY (`parent_id` )
      REFERENCES `sakila`.`Menu` (`id` )
      ON DELETE NO ACTION
      ON UPDATE NO ACTION)
ENGINE = InnoDB;
CREATE  TABLE IF NOT EXISTS `sakila`.`Permissions` (
  `Menu_id` INT NOT NULL ,
  `Group_id` INT NOT NULL ,
  PRIMARY KEY (`Menu_id`, `Group_id`) ,
  INDEX `fk_Menu_has_Group_Group1` (`Group_id` ASC) ,
  INDEX `fk_Menu_has_Group_Menu1` (`Menu_id` ASC) ,
  CONSTRAINT `fk_Menu_has_Group_Menu1`
    FOREIGN KEY (`Menu_id` )
    REFERENCES `sakila`.`Menu` (`id` )
    ON DELETE NO ACTION
    ON UPDATE NO ACTION,
  CONSTRAINT `fk_Menu_has_Group_Group1`
    FOREIGN KEY (`Group_id` )
    REFERENCES `sakila`.`Groups` (`id` )
    ON DELETE NO ACTION
    ON UPDATE NO ACTION)
ENGINE = InnoDB;
```

And we also need to populate the `Menu` and `Permissions` table with some data. As we are going to develop the security module in this chapter as well, let's create the three menu options but for now, `className` will be `'panel'` (representing a panel) so we can test it.

```
INSERT INTO `sakila`.`menu` (`id`, `text`, `iconCls`)
VALUES (1, 'menu1', 'menu_admin');

INSERT INTO `sakila`.`menu` (`id`, `text`, `iconCls`, `parent_id`,
`className`)
VALUES
(2, 'menu11', 'menu_groups', 1, 'panel'),
(3, 'menu12', 'menu_users', 1, 'panel');

INSERT INTO `sakila`.`Permissions` (`Menu_id`, `Group_id`)
VALUES ('1', '1'), ('2', '1'), ('3', '1');
```

Creating the menu models – hasMany association

Now we can start coding. First, we will create the model classes that we are going to use to load the menu information from the server. Then, we will create a class named `Packt.model.menu.Root`. To do this, we need to create a new folder inside the `app/model` folder and also create a file named `Root.js`. The following code snippet will show the implementation of the `Packt.model.menu.Root` class:

```
Ext.define('Packt.model.menu.Root', {
    extend: 'Ext.data.Model',

    uses: [
        'Packt.model.menu.Item'
    ],

    idProperty: 'id',

    fields: [
        {
            name: 'text'
        },
        {
            name: 'iconCls'
        },
        {
            name: 'id'
        }
    ],

    hasMany: {
        model: 'Packt.model.menu.Item',
        foreignKey: 'parent_id',
        name: 'items'
    }
});
```

The information that we need for this class is the title of panel (`text`), `iconCls`, and also `id`. The `Root` class also has a `hasMany` association with the class `Packt.model.menu.Item`, which is going to represent each node from the Tree panel. Set the `name` attribute of `hasMany` association as `items`, Ext JS will create a method named `items`, so we can retrieve the collection of the class `menu.Item`. Let's implement the `Packt.model.menu.Item` class now:

```
Ext.define('Packt.model.menu.Item', {
    extend: 'Ext.data.Model',

    uses: [
        'Packt.model.menu.Root'
    ],

    idProperty: 'id',

    fields: [
        {
            name: 'text'
        },
        {
            name: 'iconCls'
        },
        {
            name: 'className'
        },
        {
            name: 'id'
        },
        {
            name: 'parent_id'
        }
    ],

    belongsTo: {
        model: 'Packt.model.menu.Root',
        foreignKey: 'parent_id'
    }
});
```

As this class is going to represent a node of a Tree panel, we need to declare `fields` according to the fields in our `Menu` table. So we have the following fields: `text`, `iconCls`, `className`, `id`, and `parent_id`. The `parent_id` field is `foreignkey` to the `menu.Root` class. And as we have a `hasMany` association on the `menu.Root` class, we will also have the inverse way using the `belongsTo` association: from `menu.Item` we can retrieve its `menu.Root` class.

With these two models and associations, we will be able to retrieve nested data from the server, as the following JSON, representing the data from the `menu.Root` class and also from the `menu.Item` class:

```
"items": [{
    "id": "1",
    "text": "menu1",
    "iconCls": "menu_admin",
    "parent_id": null,
    "className": null,
    "leaf": false,
    "items": [{
        "id": "2",
        "text": "menu11",
        "iconCls": "menu_groups",
        "parent_id": "1",
        "className": "panel",
        "leaf": true
    }, {
        "id": "3",
        "text": "menu12",
        "iconCls": "menu_users",
        "parent_id": "1",
        "className": "panel",
        "leaf": true
    }, {
        "id": "4",
        "text": "menu13",
        "iconCls": "menu_profile",
        "parent_id": "1",
        "className": "panel",
        "leaf": true
    }]
}]
```

Creating the store – loading the menu from the server

Now that we have the models, we can move on and create the store. We will create a new class named `Packt.store.Menu`, so we need to create a new file named `Menu.js` under the `app/store` folder:

```
Ext.define('Packt.store.Menu', {
    extend: 'Ext.data.Store',

    requires: [
        'Packt.model.menu.Root'
    ],

    model: 'Packt.model.menu.Root',

    proxy: {
        type: 'ajax',
        url: 'php/menu.php',

        reader: {
            type: 'json',
            root: 'items'
        }
    }
});
```

The store is going to use the model `Packt.model.menu.Root` and it will use an Ajax proxy, meaning that we will make an Ajax request to the server with the provided `url`. And this store is expecting information with the JSON format with the `root` class named as `items`, as we listed previously when we were talking about the models. Now that we know the data format that we need to retrieve from the server, let's implement it.

Handling the dynamic menu on the server

As we declared in the `Packt.store.Menu` store, we need to create a new file named `menu.php` under the `php` folder. Following is the programming logic that we need to follow:

1. Open connection with the database.
2. Get the user that is logged-in from the `session` field.

3. Select the menu IDs from the `Permission` table so we can know what are the permissions that this user has.
4. Select the modules that the user has permission to access: `parent_id` is `Null`.
5. For each module, select the nodes (menu items) that the user has access to.
6. Encode the Ext JS return from server in the JSON format.
7. Close the connection with the database.

So let's get our hands on the code:

```
require("db/db.php"); // #1

session_start(); // #2

$username = $_SESSION[username]; // #3

$queryString = "SELECT p.menu_id menuId FROM User u "; // #4
$queryString .= "INNER JOIN permissions p ON u.group_id = p.group_id
";
$queryString .= "INNER JOIN menu m ON p.menu_id = m.id ";
$queryString .= "WHERE u.username = '$username' ";

$folder = array(); // #5
```

First, we will open the connection with the database (`#1`) and then we will resume `session` (`#2`) so we can get the authenticated `username` from it (`#3`). Then, we will prepare the SQL query to get the IDs from the `Menu` table that the user has access to (`#4`). And lastly, we will declare and initiate the variable (`#5`) that we are going to return to Ext JS.

Now let's move to the next part of the code:

```
if ($resultdb = $mysqli->query($queryString)) { // #6

    $in = '('; // #7
    while($user = $resultdb->fetch_assoc()) {
        $in .=  $user['menuId'] . ","; // #8
    }
    $in = substr($in, 0, -1) . ")"; // #9

    $resultdb->free();  // #10

    $sql = "SELECT * FROM MENU WHERE parent_id IS NULL ";
    $sql .= "AND id in $in"; // #11
```

```
        if ($resultdb = $mysqli->query($sql)) { // #12

            while($r = $resultdb->fetch_assoc()) { // #13

                $sqlquery = "SELECT * FROM MENU WHERE parent_id = '";
                $sqlquery .= $r['id'] ."' AND id in $in"; // #14

                if ($nodes = $mysqli->query($sqlquery)) { // #15

                    $count = $nodes->num_rows; // #16

                    if ($count > 0){ // #17

                        $r['leaf'] = false; // #18
                        $r['items'] = array(); // #19

                        while ($item = $nodes->fetch_assoc()) {
                            $item['leaf'] = true; // #20
                            $r['items'][] = $item; // #21
                        }
                    }
                    $folder[] = $r; // #22
                }
            }
        }
        $resultdb->close(); // #23
    }
```

In this second part of the code, we will execute the query that we prepared in the first part of the code to select the IDs from the `Menu` table that the user has access to (`#6`). Then, we will concatenate all the IDs wrapped in parentheses so we can use them as an `in` operator in SQL (`#7`, `#8`, and `#9`). As we want to reuse the variable `resultdb`, we will free the result set (`#10`).

Next, we want to select all the records from the `Menu` table that represents a module (`#11`); in this case, a module has `parent_id null` and must be in the `in` variable, meaning we want to select only the modules that the logged-in user has access to. Then, we will execute this query (`#12`).

For each module (`#13`) we need to select the record from the menu that is going to represent the node from the Tree panel (instance of `Packt.model.menu.Item` model class). So we need to execute another query (`#15`) selecting all the menu items (`#14`) from the module (`parent_id`) to which the user has access (`id in $in`).

Also, we need to get the number of rows returned from the result set (#16). If the number of rows returned from the result set is larger than 0 (meaning that it returned records: #17), we are going to say that the module is not leaf (Ext JS node interface concept: #18) and we will initiate the items attribute (#19). And for each node, we will say that it is leaf (#20) and we will assign node to its parent module (#21).

And finally, we will add the module to the collection that we are going to return to Ext JS (#22) and also close the result set (#23).

Now, let's move to the last part of this server-side code:

```
$mysqli->close(); // #24

echo json_encode(array( // #25
    "items" => $folder
));
```

We are going to close the MySQL connection (#24) and encode the information into the JSON format and also wrap it into the items attribute as specified by the proxy reader.

Note that this server-side code will not work if the height of the Tree panel is greater than 2. In our case, the Tree panel will have its root and only one level of items. If you want to build a menu with more levels, you will need to use a recursive algorithm to retrieve the information from the database, and this can have a high cost.

If we execute this server-side code, it will return exactly the JSON object we listed in the models topic.

The database for the menu fits perfectly to what Ext JS needs. We designed the Menu table according to Ext JS expectations and in a way that would be easier for us to retrieve the information. The preceding server-side code also fits perfectly to Ext JS needs. Unless we have the chance to design the database ourselves in a project that we are starting from scratch, we will probably have a different design; therefore, the server-side code to retrieve the information will be a little different too. There is no problem at all. It does not matter how the database looks like or the server-side code you need to write to retrieve the information. However, Ext JS is expecting a specific format to be sent back to the frontend code and unfortunately, we need to send the information in this specific format. If the information we retrieved from the database is not in the format that Ext JS expects (the same format as our preceding code), all we need to do is to parse it, meaning there will be an extra step in our server-side code before we send it back to Ext JS.

Creating the menu with Accordion panel and Tree panel

We can go back to the Ext JS code and start implementing the dynamic menu component. First, we need to create a new folder under `app/view` and create a new file named `Accordion.js`:

```
Ext.define('Packt.view.menu.Accordion', {
    extend: 'Ext.panel.Panel',
    alias: 'widget.mainmenu',

    width: 300,
    layout: {
        type: 'accordion'
    },
    collapsible: false,
    hideCollapseTool: false,
    iconCls: 'sitemap',
    title: 'Menu'
});
```

This class is going to be a panel and it is going to wrap the menu items. It is going to use the Accordion Layout; this way the user can expand the desired module. We are going to assign `Menu` to `title` (we can add a new attribute in the `en.js`, `es.js`, and `pt_BR.js` files and use the translation) and will also have an `iconCls` to look prettier.

Next, we need to create a Tree panel to represent each module. We will create a new class named `Packt.view.menu.Item`, therefore, we need to create a new file named `Item.js` under `app/view/menu`:

```
Ext.define('Packt.view.menu.Item', {
    extend: 'Ext.tree.Panel',
    alias: 'widget.mainmenuitem',

    border: 0,
    autoScroll: true,
    rootVisible: false
});
```

The `Packt.view.menu.Item` class is a Tree panel. We do not want a border for our menu and we will also let the root to be invisible. As we can see, we are not setting many attributes. We will set the missing information dynamically on the controller.

Replacing the central container on the viewport

Before we start implementing the controller, we need to create one more component: the tab panel that will contain all the screens that we open from the menu. To do so, we will create a new class named `Packt.view.MainPanel`. Therefore, we need to create a new file named `MainPanel.js` under `app/view`:

```
Ext.define('Packt.view.MainPanel', {
    extend: 'Ext.tab.Panel',
    alias: 'widget.mainpanel',

    activeTab: 0,

    items: [
        {
            xtype: 'panel',
            closable: false,
            iconCls: 'home',
            title: 'Home'
        }
    ]
});
```

This class will have the default `activeTab` as `0`, which is the first and the only item declared on the `items` configuration. The default active item will be an empty panel that cannot be closed and that has a Home icon and also the title as **Home** (again, you need to create a new attribute in the translations file and use the translation here if you want to).

Then, on the `app/view/Viewport.js` file we will replace the `center` container with the tab panel we just created:

```
{
    xtype: 'mainpanel',
    region: 'center'
}
```

And the tab panel is now ready to receive the components we will open from the menu.

We also need to replace the `west` container with the dynamic menu we created:

```
{
    xtype: 'mainmenu',
    width: 185,
    collapsible: true,
    region: 'west'//,
    //style: 'background-color: #8FB488;'
}
```

We can comment on the `style` line or even remove it. We only need to replace `xtype` with the `xtype` of the Accordion panel. Now we can move to the controller.

Creating the menu controller-side

We already have all `views`, `models`, `stores`, and also the server side covered. Now the only thing left is to implement the controller, which is where all the magic will happen. So let's go ahead and create a new file named `Menu.js` under the `app/controller` folder:

```
Ext.define('Packt.controller.Menu', {
    extend: 'Ext.app.Controller',

    models: [
        'menu.Root',
        'menu.Item'
    ],
    stores: [
        'Menu'
    ],
    views: [
        'menu.Accordion',
        'menu.Item'
    ],

    refs: [
        {
            ref: 'mainPanel',
            selector: 'mainpanel'
        }
    ],

    init: function(application) {
        this.control({
            "mainmenu": {
```

```
                render: this.onPanelRender
            },
            "mainmenuitem": {
                select: this.onTreepanelSelect,
                itemclick: this.onTreepanelItemClick
            }
        });
    }
});
```

We added `models`, `stores`, and `views` related to `Menu`. Also, we added a reference for the `mainpanel` component, which is the tab panel located at the center of the viewport.

We will listen to three events: the first one is to render the dynamic menu. Once the user is authenticated, the viewport will be displayed. The Accordion panel that will wrap our dynamic menu (`xtype: 'mainmenu'`) is one of the items of `MyViewport` class; therefore, it will also be rendered. The other events that we need to listen are related to the nodes of the Tree panel, which will be our menu options. We will listen to the `select` and `itemclick` events. Once the user selects an option from **Menu**, we will open the desired screen on the tab panel (as a new tab). And we will listen to `itemclick` because the user can accidentally close the selected menu option and wants to open it again. As the option is already selected, the screen will not open again, so we also need to listen to the `select` event.

Rendering the menu from nested JSON (hasMany association)

So let's create the method that will be responsible for creating the dynamic menu with the information that will be received from the server:

```
onPanelRender: function(abstractcomponent, options) {
    this.getMenuStore().load(function(records, op, success){ // #1

        // #2
        var menuPanel = Ext.ComponentQuery.query('mainmenu')[0];

        Ext.each(records, function(root){ // #3

            var menu = Ext.create('Packt.view.menu.Item',{ // #4
                title: translations[root.get('text')], // #5
                iconCls: root.get('iconCls') // #6
            });
```

```
                Ext.each(root.items(), function(itens){ // #7

                    Ext.each(itens.data.items, function(item){

                        menu.getRootNode().appendChild({ // #8
                            text: translations[item.get('text')],
                            leaf: true,
                            iconCls: item.get('iconCls'),
                            id: item.get('id'),
                            className: item.get('className')
                        });
                    });
                });

                menuPanel.add(menu); // #9
            });
        });
    }
```

The first thing that we need to do is to load `MenuStore`, which is responsible for loading the nested JSON from the server (`#1`). Once `Store` is loaded (that is why we are going to handle the creation of the dynamic menu inside the `load` callback) we need to get the reference for the `Packt.view.menu.Accordion` class. As we do not have access to the controller's references (we are inside the `load` callback function), we will need to use `Ext.componentQuery.query` (`#2`) to select its reference (`xtype: 'mainmenu'`); and as the query method returns an array of references, we will need only the first one (as we only have one reference of this component on the application). Another option would be to set a reference to this (`var me = this;`) at the top of the method (in the beginning) and then, inside the callback, use the `me` variable to reference the controller.

For each record returned from `Store` (`#3`) we will create a Tree panel (`'Packt.view.menu.Item'`: `#4`) to represent each module. We will set the `title` (getting `title` from the translation file: `#5`) and `iconCls` (`#6`) to make the module look prettier.

> **Ext.create and Ext.widget**
>
> In *Chapter 2, The Login Page*, when we instantiated a class for the first time in this book we discussed the options we can use when we need to instantiate a class. Just to recapitulate, we can use `Ext.create` passing the complete name of the class as an argument or we can use `Ext.widget` passing the class alias as an argument (there are other ways as well, but these two are more commonly used). It is a matter of preference, but you can use any of the ways we mentioned in *Chapter 2, The Login Page*.

Then, for each `Packt.model.menu.Item` model instance (`#7`), we will get the root of the Tree panel and append a new node (`#8`). When appending the new node, we are setting `text`, `leaf`, and `iconCls` that are configurations from the `NodeInterface` class. The `id` and `className` fields are configurations that we are adding. So later, when we need to access these configurations we need to get them from the `raw` property.

And at last, we will add the Tree panel to the accordion menu. And after this method is executed, the dynamic menu will be rendered.

Opening a menu item dynamically

After the menu is rendered, the user will be able to select an option from it. The logic behind the method is: when the user selects an option from the menu we need to verify if the screen has already been created on the tab panel. If yes, we do not need to create it again, we only need to select the **Tab** on the tab panel and make it active. If not, then we need to create the screen selected by the user. To do so, the controller will execute the following method:

```
onTreepanelSelect: function(selModel, record, index, options) {
    var mainPanel = this.getMainPanel(); // #1

    var newTab = mainPanel.items.findBy( // #2
    function (tab){
        return tab.title === record.get('text'); // #3
    });

    if (!newTab){ // #4
        newTab = mainPanel.add({              // #5
            xtype: record.raw.className,      // #6
            closable: true,                   // #7
            iconCls: record.get('iconCls'),  // #8
            title: record.get('text')         // #9
        });
    }
    mainPanel.setActiveTab(newTab); // #10
}
```

First, we need to get the reference of the tab panel (`#1`). Then, we need to verify if the selected menu option is already created (`#2`) and we will do it by comparing the tab `title` with `text` configuration of the selected node (`#3`).

If it is not a new tab, we will add it to the tab panel, passing it as an instance to the `add` method (`#5`). So we will get `xtype` of the component that we are going to add from the node `className` (`#6`), the tab can be closed (`#7`); it will have the same `iconCls` as its node (`#8`) and will also have the same `title` as the node (`#9`: menu option).

Then, we will set it as the active tab. In case, the screen is already rendered, we will only change the active tab to the screen that the user selected from **Menu** (`#10`).

In case, the user closes the currently selected **Menu** option and clicks again on the **Node** from the Tree panel, nothing will happen. The user needs to select another **Menu** option and then select the previous one again. And this is not nice. So to avoid this behavior, we also need to listen to the `itemclick` event:

```
onTreepanelItemClick: function(view, record, item, index, event,
options){
    this.onTreepanelSelect(view, record, index, options);
},
```

This method will call the `onTreepanelSelect` method again. This way we do not need to repeat code.

Changing app.js

One last change: we also need to add the new controller to `app.js`:

```
controllers: [
    'Login',
    'TranslationManager',
    'Menu'
]
```

For every controller that we create in this book, we will always need to add it inside the `controllers` configuration inside `app.js`. Do not forget this next time we declare a new controller.

If we execute the code and open the **Menu** options, the system will open an empty panel because the screens are not ready yet (subject for the next chapter), but we will be able to see the dynamic menu working as shown in the following screenshot:

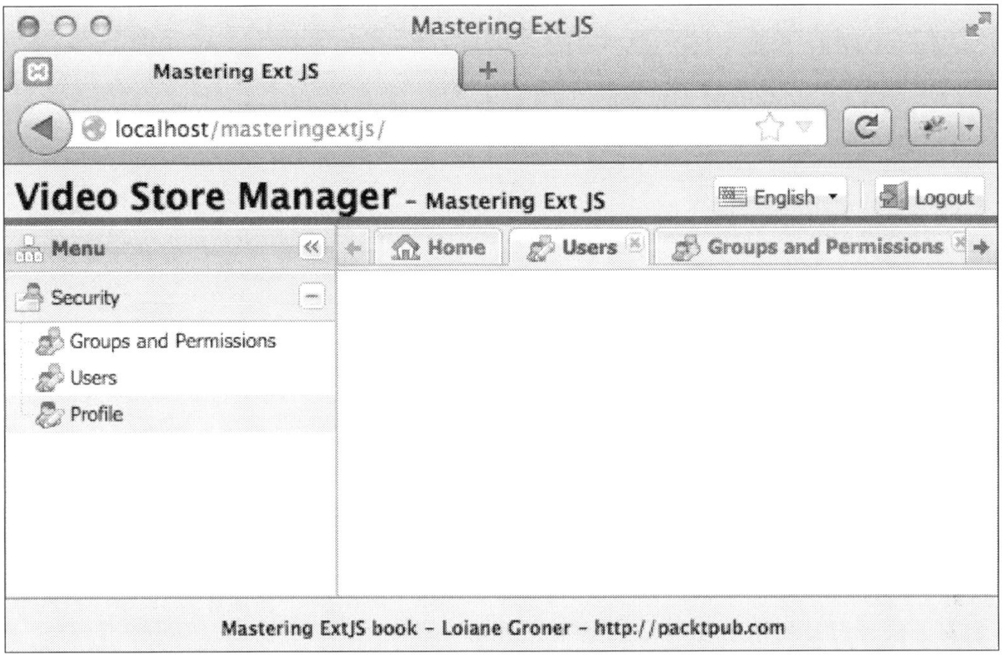

Our dynamic menu is now completed and working.

Summary

In this chapter we learned how to implement an advanced dynamic menu using an Accordion panel and also Tree panels for each module of the system. We learned how to handle the dynamic logic on the server side and also how to handle its return on the Ext JS side to build the menu dynamically. And finally, we have also learned how to open an item from the menu programmatically and display it on the center component of the application.

In the next chapter we will learn how to implement screens to list, create and update users, and also how to assign a group to the user.

5
User Identification and Security

In the previous chapters, we developed mechanisms to provide login and logout capabilities, session monitoring, and we also implemented a dynamic menu based on the user permissions. However, all the users, groups, and permissions were added to the database directly so far. We cannot do this every time that we need to grant access to the application to a new user or change the user permissions. For this reason, we will implement a screen where we can create new users and grant or change the permissions. So in this chapter, we will cover:

- Listing all the users from the system
- Creating, editing, and deleting users
- Picture preview of a file upload (user's picture)

Managing users

So the first module we are going to develop is user management. In this module, we will be able to see all the users that are registered on the system, add new users, edit, and delete current users.

When the user clicks on the **Users Menu** option, a new tab is going to be opened with the list of all users from the system as shown in the following screenshot:

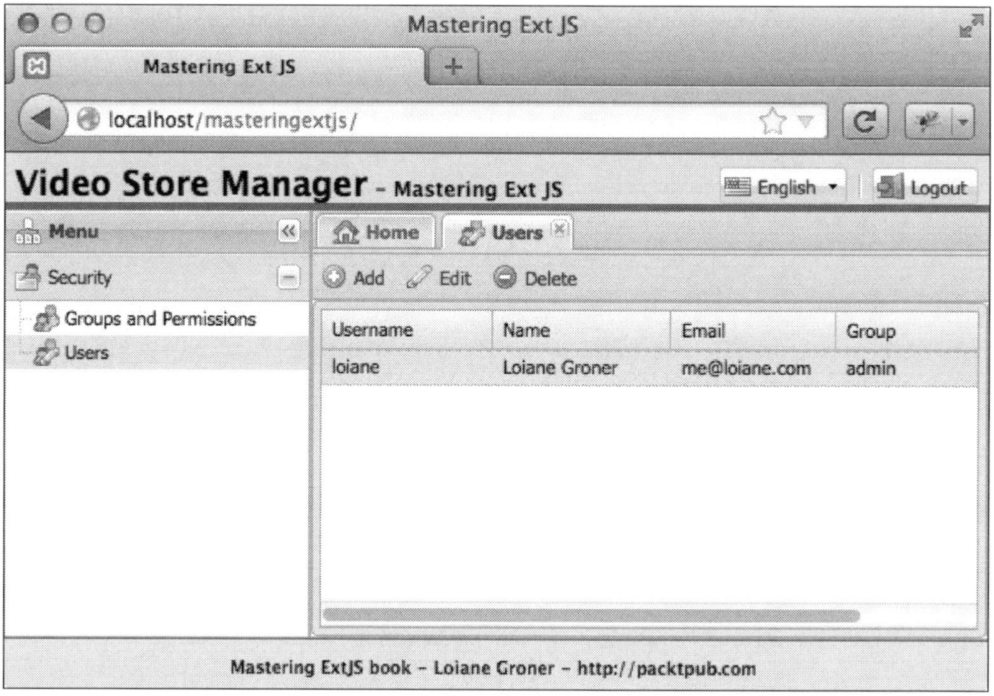

When the user clicks on the **Add** or **Edit** button, the system will display a window so the user can create a new user or edit a current user (based on the record selected on the Grid panel). The edit window will look like the following screenshot:

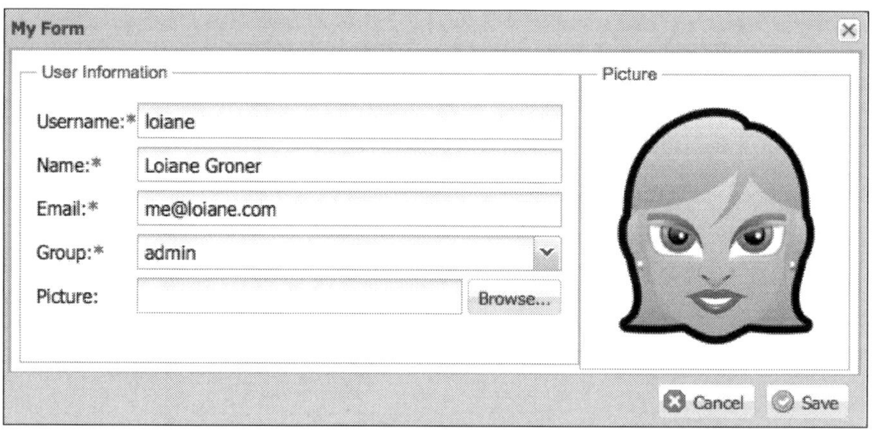

Some capabilities of creating or editing a user: we can edit the **User Information** such as **Name**, **Username** and so on. We can also upload a **Picture** representing the user. But there is an extra feature: using the HTML 5 API, we are going to display a preview of the **Picture** right after the user selects the **Picture** from the computer and before the user uploads it to the server.

So let's go ahead and implement it.

Listing all the users – simple Grid panel

We need to implement a screen similar to the first screenshot we showed in this chapter. It is a simple Grid panel. So to implement a simple Grid panel we need the following:

- A model to represent the information that is stored in the user table
- A store with a proxy to read the information from the server
- A Grid panel component representing the view
- And as we want to load the user information only after the Grid panel is rendered we will also need a controller to listen to this event

User model

So the first step is to create a model to represent the `User` table. We are going to create a new file named `User.js` under the `app/model/security` directory. This model is going to represent all the fields from the `User` table, except the `password` field, because as the password is something very personal of the user, we cannot display the user's password to any other user, including the administrator. So the user model is going to look like the following:

```
Ext.define('Packt.model.security.User', {
    extend: 'Ext.data.Model',

    idProperty: 'id',

    fields: [
        { name: 'id' },
        { name: 'name' },
        { name: 'userName' },
        { name: 'email' },
        { name: 'picture' },
        { name: 'Group_id' }
    ]
});
```

And as we mentioned previously, all the fields from the `User` table are mapped into this model, except the `password` field.

Users store

Now that we already have a model to represent the `User` table records, we need to create a store and set a proxy so we can load the collection of users from the database. So we are going to create a new file named `Users.js` (plural of "User", since we are dealing with a collection of them) under the `app/store/security` folder. Notice that we create a new folder named `security` under the `model` and `store` folders. We will do the same for the `views` and `controller`, this way maintenance in the future will be easier—we are following a pattern to create the files in each package.

Inside the users store, we will have the following code:

```
Ext.define('Packt.store.security.Users', {
    extend: 'Ext.data.Store',

    requires: [
        'Packt.model.security.User' // #1
    ],

    model: 'Packt.model.security.User', // #2

    proxy: {
        type: 'ajax',
        url: 'php/security/users.php',

        reader: {
            type: 'json',
            root: 'data'
        }
    }
});
```

This store will represent a collection of the user model (`#2`), and it is very important to declare explicitly that we need the `Packt.model.security.User` class loaded prior to loading the store (`#1`). The proxy we are going to use is the Ajax Proxy and we will receive from the server the users collection in JSON format wrapped inside the `data` attribute as the following example:

```
{
    "success": true,
    "data": [{
        "id": "1",
        "name": "Loiane Groner",
```

```
        "userName": "loiane",
        "email": "me@loiane.com",
        "picture": "FE03.png",
        "Group_id": "1"
    }]
}
```

In this chapter we will not list the server-side code. But you can get the complete code from the book support page or at: `https://github.com/loiane/masteringextjs`.

Users Grid panel

The next step is to create the views we are going to use, to manage the users of our application. But before we get our hands on the code, we need to keep one thing in mind: when we implement the edit group screen, we want to display all the users that belong to that group. And for that we will need to use a user grid as well. So that being said, we need to create a component that will list the users (in this case all the users from the application) that we can reuse later. For this reason, the component that we are going to create will only contain the list of users, and will not contain the `Add`, `Edit`, or `Delete` button. We will add a toolbar with these buttons and also wrap the users grid in another component.

So we are going to create a Grid panel. To do so, let's create a new class named `Packt.view.security.UsersList`. To create this class, we will create a new file named `UsersList.js` under the `app/view/security` directory:

```
Ext.define('Packt.view.security.UsersList', {
    extend: 'Ext.grid.Panel',
    alias: 'widget.userslist',

    frame: true,
    store: Ext.create('Packt.store.security.Users'), // #1

    columns: [
        {
            width: 150,
            dataIndex: 'userName',
            text: 'Username'
        },
        {
            width: 200,
            dataIndex: 'name',
            flex: 1,
```

```
                    text: 'Name'
                },
                {
                    width: 250,
                    dataIndex: 'email',
                    text: 'Email'
                },
                {
                    width: 150,
                    dataIndex: 'Group_id',
                    text: 'Group',
                    renderer: function(value, metaData, record ){ // #2
                        var groupsStore = Ext.getStore('groups');
                        var group = groupsStore.findRecord('id', value);
                        return group != null ? group.get('name') : value;
                    }
                }
            ]
        });
```

The preceding code was a simple Grid panel and we are going to display the information that is going to be received from the server. There are three important points that we need to discuss a little bit further on this Grid panel. The first one is `dataIndex` of each column. Notice that `dataIndex` must match the name of the field from the model. Also, we need to be very careful and remember that Ext JS is case sensitive—a field named `group_id` is not the same as `Group_id`.

The second point is the declaration of the `store` (`#1`). Notice that we are not simply declaring the store as `security.Users` as we usually do on an Ext JS **Model-View-Controller** (**MVC**) application. We are instantiating a new store explicitly. And why is that? What difference does it make? There is a very important difference. The MVC architecture uses the store manager to retrieve the reference of the store instance, and according to the store manager, there can be only one reference—because we retrieve its reference using the store ID. Having only one store reference throughout the application (and the store being shared between different components and screens) means that when we make any change on the store, all the other instances of the store will also contain the change (a new record will be added, updated, or deleted). Sometimes we do not want this to happen, we want to have different store instances for different purposes. So in this case, we want to have an independent reference of the store (we will understand this reason later when we implement the group management module—we will reuse the users grid to load users from a specific group). This is something that we really need to pay attention to.

The third point is the `renderer` function that we applied for the `Group_id` column (`#2`). When we load the store from the server, each model instance from the users store contains only the `Group_id` column and not the group name. And we do not want to display the group as a number for the user because it will not make any sense to the user. So we need to display the group name. We do not have this information, so we need to get it from somewhere. We can get the name of the group from a groups store that contains all the group information—just remember that we will create this store in a few pages ahead. So first we retrieve the store using the store manager passing the `storeId` as parameter; then we retrieve the group model instance that matches the `Group_id` that we are looking for; and then, we verify if there is a group model instance in the store with the matched `id`: if so, we display the group name, otherwise, we display the `Group_id` just to display something. We can use this approach to any **hasOne**, **hasMany**, or **Many-to-Many** relationship.

> When using approaches such as this one—retrieving a value from another store, we must be sure that the value that we are looking for exists within the store; this means that the store must contain all the values and it cannot have paging or filters applied to it. If you do have paging, we need to page the information until we find the ID we are looking for. Another strategy would be to have a model with non-persistent fields, which will be used only for display purposes, and in this case we would not need to search for the value in another store. But of course, this means bringing more information from the server. We just need to evaluate what is best for each scenario.

Now that we have the user Grid panel ready, we still need to create another component that is going to wrap the user Grid panel and will also contain the toolbar with the `Add`, `Edit`, and `Delete` buttons. The simplest component that supports docked items is the panel. So we are going to create a new class named `Packt.view.security.Users` that is going to extend from the `Ext.panel.Panel` class. To do so, we need to create a new file named `Users.js` under the `app/view/security` directory:

```
Ext.define('Packt.view.security.Users', {
    extend: 'Ext.panel.Panel',
    alias: 'widget.users',

    requires: [
        'Packt.view.security.UsersList' // #1
    ],

    layout: {
        type: 'fit' // #2
```

```
    },

    items: [
        {
            xtype: 'userslist' // #3
        }
    ]
});
```

In this class, we will have only one component being rendered in the panel's body. It is the user Grid panel (`#3`). And as we are using its `xtype` to instantiate it, we need to make sure the user Grid panel class is already loaded, and that is why we need to add the class in the `requires` declaration (`#1`). As we have only one component and we want it to occupy all the available space of the panel's body, we will use the `fit` layout (`#2`).

The next step is to add the toolbar with the `Add`, `Edit`, and `Delete` buttons, so we are going to `dock` this toolbar on the `top` and we are going to declare it inside the `dockedItems` declaration of the `Packt.view.security.Users` class:

```
dockedItems: [
    {
        xtype: 'toolbar',
        flex: 1,
        dock: 'top',
        items: [
            {
                xtype: 'button',
                text: 'Add',
                itemId: 'add',
                iconCls: 'add'
            },
            {
                xtype: 'button',
                text: 'Edit',
                itemId: 'edit',
                iconCls: 'edit'
            },
            {
                xtype: 'button',
                text: 'Delete',
                itemId: 'delete',
                iconCls: 'delete'
            }
        ]
    }
]
```

And to help us to identify each button's click event later on the controller, we will assign `itemId` to each button. And our component is ready.

Users controller

There is one last step that we need to implement to have a screen where we can load all the users from the application, which is to load the store when the user Grid panel is ready and rendered. And this is what we need to implement inside the controller. Let's create the controller then: we need to create a class named `Packt.controller.security.Users`; so we need to create a new file named `Users.js` under the `app/controller/security` directory, as shown in the following code:

```
Ext.define('Packt.controller.security.Users', {
    extend: 'Ext.app.Controller',

    views: [
        'security.Users' // #1
    ],

    init: function(application) {

        this.control({
            "userslist": { // #2
                render: this.onRender
            }
        });
    },

    onRender: function(component, options) { // #3
        component.getStore().load();         // #4
    }


});
```

First, we will declare the user Grid panel view in the `views` declaration inside the controller (`#1`). Then, we will start listening to the `render` event from the user Grid panel (`#2`). When the `render` event is fired, we will execute the `onRender` method (`#3`). What we need to do inside this method is to load the users store. Again, here comes an important detail: as we instantiated the store inside the users grid, we cannot declare the users store inside the `stores` declaration, therefore there is no method to get the store directly from the controller. We need to access the user Grid panel, and from its reference, obtain the users store reference and then load it; and that is exactly what we did inside the `onRender` method.

Now we add the controller to the `app.js` file and also change the `className` column value to `users` inside the `Menu` table (change the users record) as the following screenshot:

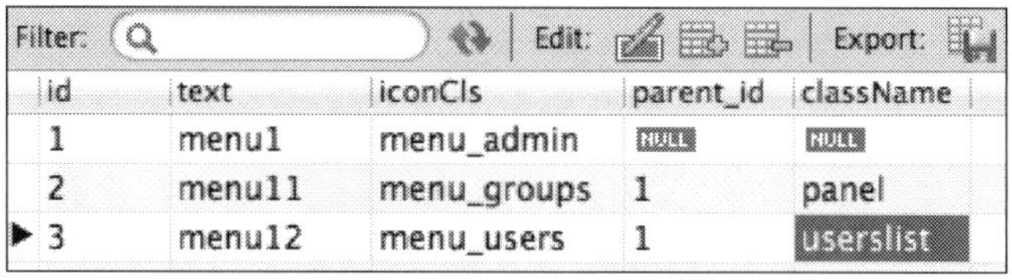

Reloading the project, we will be able to see the list of all users from the application:

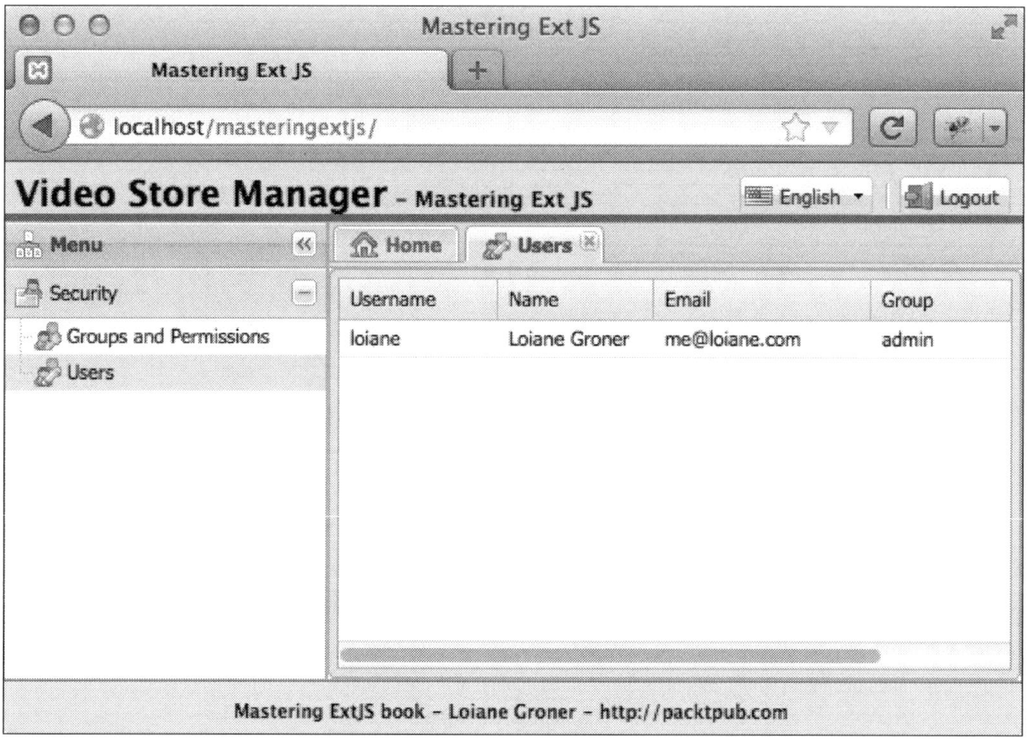

Adding and editing a new user

Now that we are capable of listing all the users from the application, we can implement add and edit capability. But before we start adding new event listeners to the controller, we need to create the new view that we are going to display to the user to edit or add a new user.

Creating the edit view – a form within a window

This new view is going to be a window, since we want to display it as a popup, and inside this window we will have a form with the user's information, and then we will have a toolbar at the bottom with two buttons: **Cancel** and **Save**. It is very similar to the login window that we developed on *Chapter 2*, *The Login Page*, but we will add new capabilities to this new form, such as form upload and also a file preview using the new HTML 5 features.

So let's get started and create a new class named `Packt.view.security.Profile` that is going to `extend` from the `Window` class:

```
Ext.define('Packt.view.security.Profile', {
    extend: 'Ext.window.Window',
    alias: 'widget.profile',

    height: 260,
    width: 550,

    requires: ['Packt.util.Util'],

    layout: {
        type: 'fit'
    },
    title: 'User',

    items: [
        {
            xtype: 'form',
            bodyPadding: 5,
            layout: {
                type: 'hbox', // #1
                align: 'stretch'
            },
            items: [

            ]
        }
    ]
});
```

There are two very important things that we need to notice in this class: the first one is that we are not using the `autoShow` attribute. And the purpose is that we can create a window, set a few settings on it, and then display it by calling the method `show`.

The second thing is the `layout` that we are using on the form. It is not the default `layout` used by the form component (which is the `anchor` layout). We are going to use the `hbox` layout (`#1`) because we want to organize the form's `items` horizontally. And we want the `items` to occupy all the available vertical space, so we will use the `align stretch`—we do not want to set a `height` for each form item.

So let's add the first item to our form. If we take a look at the window screenshot at the beginning of this chapter, we will notice that we are going to use two `fieldset` types to organize the form `items`. So the first one will be a `fieldset` to organize all the `User Information`:

```
{
    xtype: 'fieldset',
    flex: 2,
    title: 'User Information',
    defaults: {
        afterLabelTextTpl: Packt.util.Util.required, // #1
        anchor: '100%',
        xtype: 'textfield',
        allowBlank: false,
        labelWidth: 60
    },
    items: [
    ]
},
```

For all required items, we will add a red asterisk (`#1`). The `afterLabelTextTpl` is an optional string or XTemplate configuration to insert in the field markup after the label text. As most of the fields will be mandatory, we will also declare the `allowBlank false` configuration and we will also declare that the default `xtype` will be `textfield`. If any of the declared fields does not need these default configurations, we will override them with other values. So let's declare the fields that will be part of the `items` configuration of the `User Information` field set:

```
{
    xtype: 'hiddenfield',
    fieldLabel: 'Label',
    name: 'id'
},
{
    fieldLabel: 'Username',
    name: 'userName'
},
{
    fieldLabel: 'Name',
```

```
        maxLength: 100,
        name: 'name'
    },
    {
        fieldLabel: 'Email',
        maxLength: 100,
        name: 'email'
    },
    {
        xtype: 'combobox',
        fieldLabel: 'Group',
        name: 'Group_id', // #1
        displayField: 'name',  //#2
        valueField: 'id', // #3
        queryMode: 'local', // #4
        store: 'security.Groups' // #5
    },
    {
        xtype: 'filefield',
        fieldLabel: 'Picture',
        name: 'picture',
        allowBlank: true, // #6
        afterLabelTextTpl: '' // #7
    }
```

The `id` will be hidden because we do not want the user to see it (we will use it internally only), and the `username`, `name`, and `Email` are simple text fields.

Then, we have a combobox. We will map the `combobox` with the `Group_id` (`#1`) field from the user model; this way, when an existing user is loaded into the form for editing, we will get the `Group_id`, match with the `id` of the group, which is also the value of the `combobox` (`#3`), but the `combobox` will display the group `name` instead (`#2`). We will also use the groups `store` ((`#5`)—the same store instance we used on the renderer function of the user Grid panel), and the `combobox` will load the groups store only once (`#4`)—this way, when we open the `combobox` options, it will not load its values again from the server.

And then, we have the file upload field. As we do not want it to be mandatory (`#6`) and we also do not want it display that red asterisk (`#7`) we will override the `defaults` configuration.

And this is the first `fieldset` that will be displayed on the left side of the form. Next, we need to declare the other `fieldset` that is going to wrap the `Picture` and will be displayed on the right-hand side of the form.

```
{
    xtype: 'fieldset',
    title: 'Picture',
    width: 170, // #1
    items: [
        {
            xtype: 'image', // #2
            height: 150,
            width: 150,
            src: ''         // #3
        }
    ]
}
```

In this `fieldset`, we will declare a fixed `width` (`#1`). As the form is using the `hbox` layout, when a component has a fixed `width`, the layout will respect and apply the specified `width`. Then, the first `fieldset`, which has the `flex` configuration, will occupy all the remaining horizontal space.

Inside the `Picture` `fieldset` we will use an `Ext.Image` component. The `Ext.Image` (`#2`) class helps us to create and render images. It also creates an `<image>` tag in the **Document Object Model** (**DOM**) with the specified `src` (`#3`). For now the source of the image is blank. When we load an existing user and try to edit on the form, we will display the user's image (if any) in this component. Also, if the user uploads a new image, the preview will be rendered in this component.

And now, the last step is to declare the bottom toolbar with the `Save` and `Cancel` buttons:

```
dockedItems: [
    {
        xtype: 'toolbar',
        flex: 1,
        dock: 'bottom',
        ui: 'footer',
        layout: {
            pack: 'end', // #1
            type: 'hbox'
        },
        items: [
            {
```

```
                xtype: 'button',
                text: 'Cancel',
                itemId: 'cancel',
                iconCls: 'cancel'
            },
            {
                xtype: 'button',
                text: 'Save',
                itemId: 'save',
                iconCls: 'save'
            }
        ]
    }
]
```

As we want to align the buttons on the right-hand side of the toolbar, we will use the `hbox` layout as well and pack the button to the end of the toolbar. The Edit/Add window is now ready. However, there are a few other details that we still need to take care of before implementing `add` and `edit` listeners in the controller.

The group model

In the user Grid panel and in the group combobox we declared a groups store used to load all the groups from the database. We need now to implement this missing store and the first step to do it is creating the model that is going to represent a group record from the `Groups` table. So we are going to create a new model named `Packt.model.security.Group`:

```
Ext.define('Packt.model.security.Group', {
    extend: 'Ext.data.Model',

    idProperty: 'id',

    fields: [
        { name: 'id' },
        { name: 'name' }
    ]
});
```

The `Groups` table is very simple, it only contains two columns: `id` and `name`, so our group model is also simple with only these two fields.

The groups store

As we have already created the group model, now we need to create the groups store.

> Always remember the naming convention: the model name is the singular name of the entity you want to represent and the store is the plural of the name of the model/entity.

So we will create a new store named `Packt.store.security.Groups`:

```
Ext.define('Packt.store.security.Groups', {
    extend: 'Ext.data.Store',

    requires: [
        'Packt.model.security.Group'
    ],

    model: 'Packt.model.security.Group',

    storeId: 'groups', //#1

    proxy: {
        type: 'ajax',
        url: 'php/security/group.php',

        reader: {
            type: 'json',
            root: 'data'
        }
    }
});
```

This store is very similar to the ones we have already created in this and past chapters. The only thing to which we need to pay attention is that in this store, we have a `storeId` attribute. It is a good practice to declare a `storeId` if we will retrieve the store using the store manager, as we did in the `renderer` function of the group column of the user Grid panel (`Ext.getStore('groups')`). The `storeId` helps us to assign a unique ID to the store within the application.

Also, following the same pattern as the other stores, the groups information will be sent by the server within a `data` attribute in the JSON as follows:

```
{
    "success": true,
    "data": [{
        "id": "1",
        "name": "admin"
    }]
}
```

Now all the views, models, and stores needed for our user management module are created. We can focus on the controller to handle all the events we are interesting in listening to and implement all the magic!

The controller – listening to the add button

When the user clicks on the **Add** button we want to display the edit user window (`Packt.view.security.Profile` class).

So first, we will add the event listener to the `this.control` declaration within the users controller:

```
"users button#add": {
    click: this.onButtonClickAdd
}
```

The selector we are using is `users button#add` because the button we are looking for is inside the `users` component (`Packt.view.security.Users` class, which has the `users xtype`) and the `itemId` of the button is `add`. We will use a similar selector for the other buttons as well, only changing the `itemId` (`Edit` and `Delete` buttons).

When the user clicks on the **Add** button the controller will execute the `onButtonClickAdd` method:

```
onButtonClickAdd: function (button, e, options) {
    var win = Ext.create('Packt.view.security.Profile');
    win.setTitle('Add new User');
    win.show();
}
```

Inside this method we will create an instance of the edit window, set the title to `Add new User` (we can use the translation component we created to have it multilingual) and finally, we will show the window where it is possible to enter the new user information to the application's user.

The controller – listening to the edit button

We can also edit an existing user, so we also need to listen to the `click` event of the `edit` button:

```
"users button#edit": {
    click: this.onButtonClickEdit
}
```

As we can notice, the selector is very similar to `add` button, the only thing different is the `itemId` of the button.

So when the user clicks on the **Edit** button the controller will execute the `onButtonClickEdit` method:

```
onButtonClickEdit: function (button, e, options) {
    var grid = this.getUsersList(), // #1
    record = grid.getSelectionModel().getSelection();

    if(record[0]){ // #2
      var editWindow = Ext.create('Packt.view.security.Profile');

        editWindow.down('form').loadRecord(record[0]); // #3

        if (record[0].get('picture')) { //#4
            var img = editWindow.down('image');
            img.setSrc('resources/profileImages/' + record[0].
get('picture'));
        }
       editWindow.setTitle(record[0].get('name')); // #5
        editWindow.show();
    }
}
```

Our code is not complete yet. As we are going to edit an existing user, we also need to fill the form with the selected user information. So firstly, we will get the reference of the user Grid panel and get the selected records (`#1`). Then, if there is any selected `record` (`#2`) we will create the window instance; load the `form` with the information from the selected record (`#3`), set the window `title` to the `name` of the user whose information we want to edit (`#5`) and display the window.

There is one more detail: as we want to display the user's picture as well, we will check whether there is a `picture` that was updated (`#4`) and if so, we will get the Image component reference and set the `source` as the user's picture. We will see that when we upload a new user picture, we will save it inside the `resources/profileImages` folder. We could save it directly in the database, but this can bring us performance issues, so we will save it in a directory. We will learn how to handle files saved in the database in another chapter.

The controller – saving a user

Now that the user is able to open the edit window to create or edit a user, we need to implement the `save` button logic. No matter if the user is creating a new user or editing an existing user, we will use the same logic for saving the user. We will let the server side handle if it needs to use an `UPDATE` or `INSERT` query.

So first, we need to add the listener for the `save` button:

```
"profile button#save": {
    click: this.onButtonClickSave
}
```

Remember that the `save` button code is inside the `Packt.view.security.Profile` class so that is why we are limiting the selector to the button that has the `itemId` `save` to the `profile` xtype.

When the user clicks on the **Save** button, the controller will execute the `onButtonClickSave` method. As the method is a little bit long (regarding the number of lines of source code), let's implement it step-by-step:

```
onButtonClickSave: function(button, e, options) {
  var win = button.up('window'), // #1
  formPanel = win.down('form'), // #2
  store = this.getUsersList().getStore();// #3

  if (formPanel.getForm().isValid()) { // #4
      formPanel.getForm().submit({// #5
          clientValidation: true,
          url: 'php/security/saveUser.php', // #6
          //success and failure
    });
}
```

First, we will get the reference of the `window` (#1), then the `formPanel` (#2) and then the `store` (#3) of the user grid panel. This is because we want to close the window and reload the user Grid panel store after the user is saved.

Then, we will verify if the form is valid ((#4)—the user filled the form with valid values following all the rules of the client validations), then we will `submit` (#5) the form to the given `url` (#6).

We could use the store features to load, create, edit, and delete the user (as we will see later in this book). However, we are using a different approach, which is the `form submit` method to directly send the values to the server because we are also uploading a document to the server.

The next steps now are to implement the `success` and `failure` functions. Let's implement the `success` function first:

```
success: function(form, action) {
    var result = action.result; // #7
    if (result.success) {
        Packt.util.Alert.msg('Success!', 'User saved.'); // #8
        store.load();
        win.close();
    } else {
        Packt.util.Util.showErrorMsg(result.msg); // #9
    }
}
```

As usual, first we will get the response from the server (#7). If the `success` message is `true`, we will display a brief notification to the user (#8); then we will `close` the window and reload the users store to get the most up-to-date values from the server (note that if we were using the Store `sync` method to synchronize the added, edited, and deleted values from the server, we would not need to reload the store). Then, if something went wrong on the server and the `success` message is `false`, we will display an `Error alert` with the message sent by the server (#9).

Next, let's implement the `failure` function. As we implemented a default handler for the `failure` function of all our Ajax calls, we will also use a default handler for all Form Submit Failure functions:

```
failure: function(form, action) {
    switch (action.failureType) {
        case Ext.form.action.Action.CLIENT_INVALID:
            Ext.Msg.alert('Failure', 'Form fields may not be submitted
with invalid values');
            break;
```

```
            case Ext.form.action.Action.CONNECT_FAILURE:
                Ext.Msg.alert('Failure', 'Ajax communication failed');
                break;
            case Ext.form.action.Action.SERVER_INVALID:
                Ext.Msg.alert('Failure', action.result.msg);
        }
    }
```

Basically we are checking if the fields were not submitted with valid values, if there was an error with the communication, or anything else that might happen.

And now, our `save` function is ready.

The controller – listening to the cancel button

There is still one button that is left for us to implement, which is the `cancel` button. So let's add its listener on the `this.control` declaration:

```
    "profile button#cancel": {
        click: this.onButtonClickCancel
    }
```

When the user clicks on the **Cancel** button, the controller will execute the `onButtonClickCancel` method:

```
    onButtonClickCancel: function(button, e, options) {
        button.up('window').close();
    }
```

What we want to do is very simple: if the user wants to cancel all the changes made to an existing user or wants to cancel the creation of a user, the system will close the edit window. As the `cancel` button code is inside the edit window, it will search for it and call the `close` method and destroy the component.

Previewing a file before uploading it

One last thing that we will implement related to the edit window: the file upload preview. This is something that is not that hard to implement and it will bring a sparkle into the application's user's eyes!

So what we want to do is, when the user selects a new file using the file upload component, we will read the file using the HTML 5 File Reader API. Unfortunately, not every browser supports the File Reader API, only the following versions: Chrome 6+, Firefox 4+, Safari 6+, Opera 12+, Explorer 10+, iOS Safari 6+, Android 3+, Opera Mobile 12+. But do not worry, we will verify if the browser supports it first, and if it does not, we will not use it, meaning that the file preview will not happen.

> To learn more about the File Reader API please read its specification at `http://www.w3.org/TR/file-upload/` and to learn more about this and other HTML 5 features go to `http://www.html5rocks.com/`.

When the user selects a new file using the Ext JS file upload component, the change event is fired, so we need to listen to it in our controller:

```
"profile filefield": {
    change: this.onFilefieldChange
}
```

Next, we need to implement the `onFilefieldChange` method:

```
onFilefieldChange: function(filefield, value, options) {
    var file = filefield.fileInputEl.dom.files[0]; // #1

    var picture = this.getUserPicture(); // #2

    if (typeof FileReader !== "undefined" && (/image/i).test(file.
type)) {                  // #3
        var reader = new FileReader();        // #4
        reader.onload = function(e){          // #5
            picture.setSrc(e.target.result); // #6
        };
        reader.readAsDataURL(file);           // #7
    } else if (!(/image/i).test(file.type)){ // #8
        Ext.Msg.alert('Warning', 'You can only upload image files!');
        filefield.reset();                    // #9
    }
}
```

So first, we need to get the `file` (`#1`) object that is stored inside the file input element of the Ext JS file field component (also passed as a parameter to our method). Then, we will get a reference of the `Ext.Image` component that is inside our form so we can update its `source` to the file preview.

We will also test if the File Reader API is available on the browser and also if the file that the user chose is an `image` (`#3`). If both are true, we will instantiate `FileReader` (`#4`), and we will add a listener to it (`#5`), so when the File Reader is done reading the file we can set its contents to the `Ext.Image` source (`#6`). And of course, to fire the `onload` event, the `FileReader` instance needs to read the contents of the file (`#7`). One very important note: we are displaying the contents of the file before we upload to the server. If the user saves the changes made to the form, the new user information will be sent to the server (including the file upload) and next time we open the edit window, the picture will be displayed.

> How can we get the full path of the file that is being uploaded? For example, the Ext JS File Upload component displays `C:\fakepath\nameOfTheFile.jpg` and we want to get its real path such as `C:\Program Files\nameOfTheFile.jpg`. The answer is: it is not possible do to with JavaScript (and Ext JS is a JavaScript framework).
>
> This is not a restriction from Ext JS; if we try it with any other JavaScript framework or library such as jQuery it is not going to be possible, because this is a browser security restriction. Imagine if this was possible? Someone could develop a malicious JavaScript file and run it while you are navigating on the web and get all the information that you have on your computer.

Another really nice thing: if the file that the user chose is not an `image` (`#8`) we will display a message saying that only images can be uploaded and we will reset the File Upload component. Unfortunately, it is not possible to filter the file types on the browse window (that one that opens so we can choose a file from the computer) and this is a workaround so we can do this validation on the Ext JS side and not leave it to the server.

And if the File Reader is not available, nothing is going to happen. The file preview is simply not going to work. The user will select the file and that's it.

> The size limit for the file that you can upload depends on the upload limit that is set on the webserver on which you are going to deploy the Ext JS application. For example, Apache supports a limit of 2 GB. **Internet Information Services** (**IIS**) has a default value of 4 MB, but you can increase it up to 2 GB as well. Likewise for Apache Tomcat, and other webservers. So the size limit is not on Ext JS, it is on the web server; you just need to configure it.

Deleting a user

The last **Create Read Update Destroy** (**CRUD**) operation that we need to implement is the delete user operation. So let's add the `delete` listener to the controller:

```
"users button#delete": {
    click: this.onButtonClickDelete
}
```

When the user clicks on the **Delete** button, the controller will execute the `onButtonClickDelete` method.

```
onButtonClickDelete: function (button, e, options) {
    var grid = this.getUsersList(),
    record = grid.getSelectionModel().getSelection(),
    store = grid.getStore();

    if (store.getCount() >= 2 && record[0]){

        // delete logic here

    } else if (store.getCount() == 1) {
        Ext.Msg.show({
            title:'Warning',
            msg: 'You cannot delete all the users from the
application.',
            buttons: Ext.Msg.OK,
            icon: Ext.Msg.WARNING
        });
    }
}
```

The idea of this method is to verify if the user selected any row from the grid to be deleted (`record[0]` exists); and also, we will only delete a user if there are more than two users on the application. If positive, we will delete the user. If not, meaning there is only one user in the application, we cannot delete the only user that exists.

If it is possible to delete the user, the system will display a question asking if we really want to delete the selected user:

```
Ext.Msg.show({
     title:'Delete?',
     msg: 'Are you sure you want to delete?',
     buttons: Ext.Msg.YESNO,
     icon: Ext.Msg.QUESTION,
     fn: function (buttonId){
```

```
            if (buttonId == 'yes'){
                Ext.Ajax.request({
                    url: 'php/security/deleteUser.php',
                    params: {
                        id: record[0].get('id')
                    },
                    // success and failure
                });
            }
        }
    });
```

If affirmative, we will send the ID of the selected user to the server and wait for the `success` or `failure` function to be executed. As we always expect the operation to be successful, let's implement the `success` function first:

```
success: function(conn, response, options, eOpts) {
    var result = Packt.util.Util.decodeJSON(conn.responseText);
    if (result.success) {
        Packt.util.Alert.msg('Success!', 'User deleted.');
        store.load();
    } else {
        Packt.util.Util.showErrorMsg(conn.responseText);
    }
}
```

Just remember that on the server you can execute a `DELETE` query on the database, but in most cases we do a logical deletion, meaning we will perform an `UPDATE` on a column `Active` (in this case updating the user to `Inactive`).

We will get the response for the server, and if `success`, we will display the notification and `reload` the store. If not, we will display an Error message as we already did for other Ajax requests back in previous chapters.

And in case of failure:

```
failure: function(conn, response, options, eOpts) {
    Packt.util.Util.showErrorMsg(conn.responseText);
}
```

We will simply display the error message sent by the server.

Finally we need to make a last change on the `Menu` table to display all the components and screens we created in this chapter. Update the `className` to `users`, which is the `xtype` of the panel that contains the users Grid panel and also the `Add`, `Edit`, or `Delete` button:

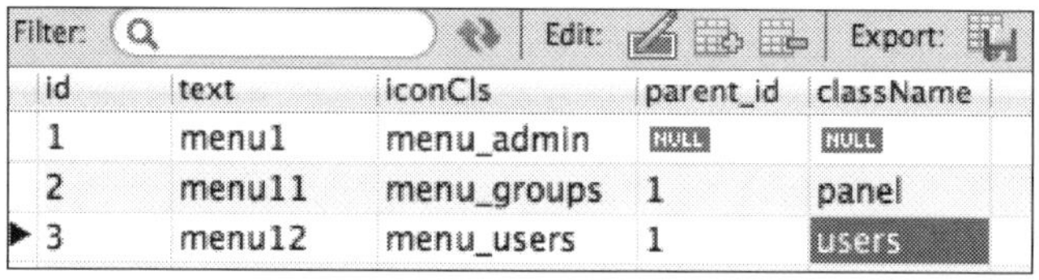

Filter: Edit: Export:

id	text	iconCls	parent_id	className
1	menu1	menu_admin	NULL	NULL
2	menu11	menu_groups	1	panel
3	menu12	menu_users	1	users

We can now reload the application and test all the functionalities.

Summary

In this chapter we covered how to create, update, delete, and list all the users from our application.

We have also learned some valuable concepts such as reusing a store throughout an Ext JS MVC application and how to retrieve its reference on the controller. We also explored a new HTML 5 feature for file upload preview capability, which is another example of how we can use other technologies along with Ext JS.

In the next chapter we will implement the MySQL table management module, meaning we will implement a screen very similar to the Edit table data screen that we find in the MySQL workbench application.

6
MySQL Table Management

So far, we have implemented capabilities related to basic features of the application. From now on, we will start implementing the application's core features, starting with the **MySQL table management**. What exactly is this? Every application has information that is not directly related with the core business, but this information is used by the core business somehow. For example, types of categories, languages, cities, and countries can exist independently of the core business and can be used by the core business information as well. We can treat this information as they are independent **MySQL** tables (because we are using MySQL as database server), and we can perform all the actions we can do on a MySQL table.

So in this chapter, we will cover:

- Creating a new system module called Static Data
- Listing all information in a MySQL table
- Creating new records on the tables
- Live search on the tables
- Filter information
- Editing and deleting records
- Creating an abstract component for reuse in all tables

Presenting the tables

If we open and analyze the **ER** (**Entity Relationship**) diagram that comes with the Sakila installation, we will notice the following tables:

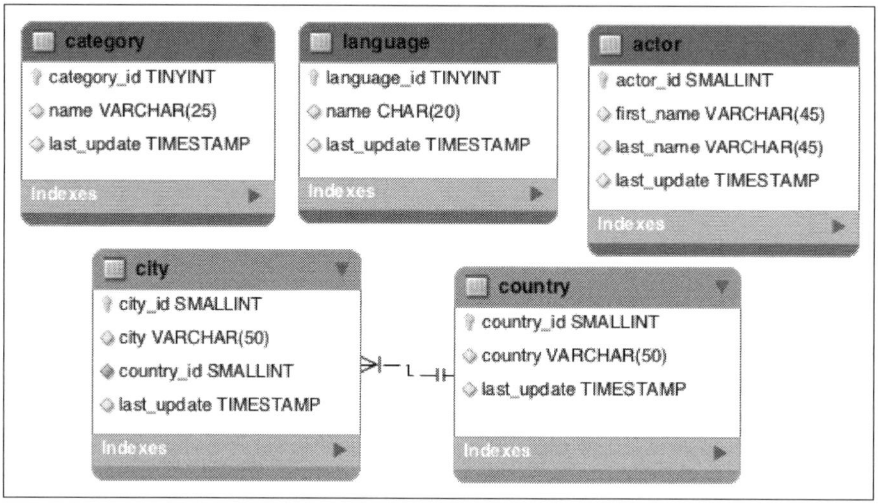

These tables can exist independently of the other tables, and we are going to work with them in this chapter.

When we open the SQL Editor in MySQL Workbench, we can select a table; right-click on it and select **Edit Table Data**. When we choose this option, a new tab will be opened and it looks like the following:

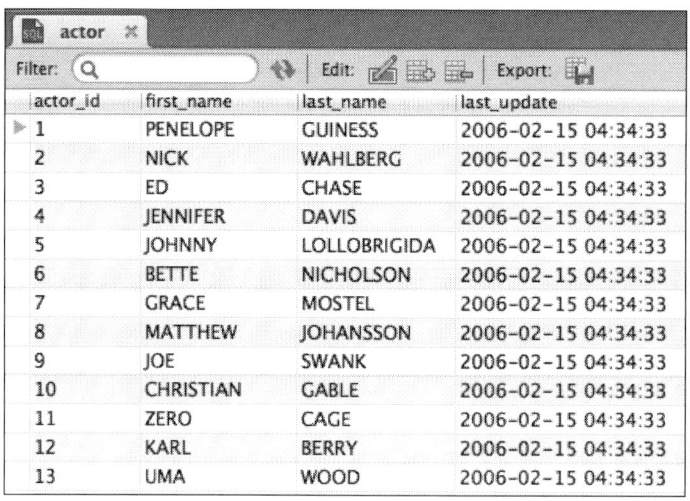

actor_id	first_name	last_name	last_update
1	PENELOPE	GUINESS	2006-02-15 04:34:33
2	NICK	WAHLBERG	2006-02-15 04:34:33
3	ED	CHASE	2006-02-15 04:34:33
4	JENNIFER	DAVIS	2006-02-15 04:34:33
5	JOHNNY	LOLLOBRIGIDA	2006-02-15 04:34:33
6	BETTE	NICHOLSON	2006-02-15 04:34:33
7	GRACE	MOSTEL	2006-02-15 04:34:33
8	MATTHEW	JOHANSSON	2006-02-15 04:34:33
9	JOE	SWANK	2006-02-15 04:34:33
10	CHRISTIAN	GABLE	2006-02-15 04:34:33
11	ZERO	CAGE	2006-02-15 04:34:33
12	KARL	BERRY	2006-02-15 04:34:33
13	UMA	WOOD	2006-02-15 04:34:33

The preceding table is the `actor` table. The idea is to implement screens that look like the preceding screenshot for each of the tables that we selected: `Actors`, `Categories`, `Languages`, `Cities`, and `Countries` as displayed in the following screenshot (which is the final result of the code that we will be implementing in this chapter):

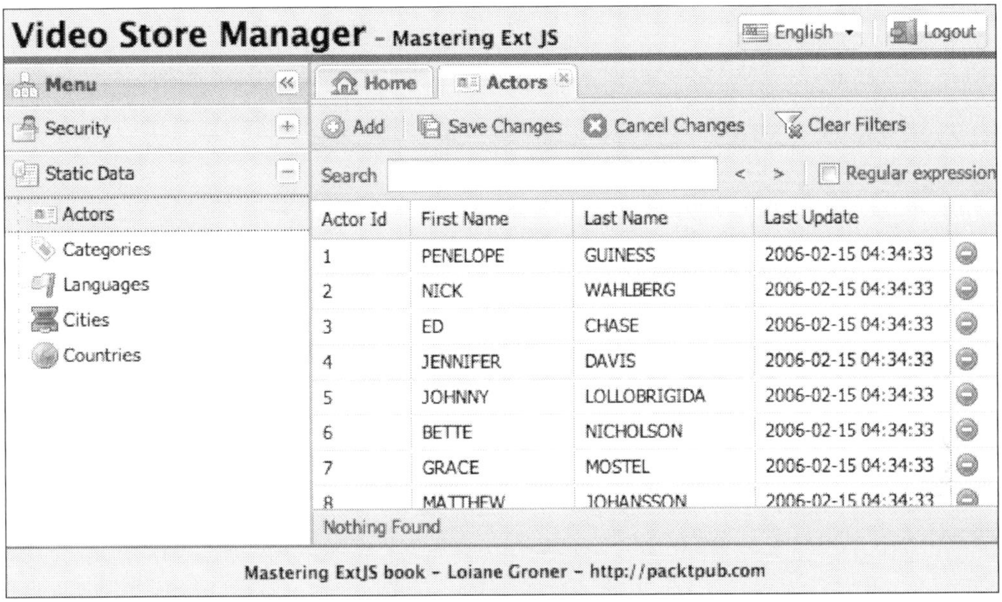

Our goal in this chapter is to minimize the amount of code to implement these five screens. This means that we want to create the most generic code possible, which will facilitate future code fixes, enhancements, and will also make it easier to create a new screen with these same features if needed.

So, let's go ahead and start the development.

Creating the models

As usual, we are going to start by creating the **models**. First, let's list the tables we will be working with and their columns:

- `Actor`: `actor_id`, `first_name`, `last_name`, `last_update`
- `Category`: `category_id`, `name`, `last_update`
- `Language`: `language_id`, `name`, `last_update`
- `City`: `city_id`, `city`, `country_id`, `last_update`
- `Country`: `country_id`, `country`, `last_update`

We could create one model for each of these entities with no problem at all, however, we want to reuse as much code as possible. Take another look at the list of tables and their columns. Notice that all tables have one column in common, the `last_update` column.

As all the tables have the `last_update` column in common we can create a super model, and then in models (which will extend the super model we do not need to declare the column) don't you think?

Abstract model

In **OOP** (**Object Oriented Programming**) there is a concept called **inheritance**, which is a way to reuse the code of existing objects. Ext JS uses an OOP approach, so we can apply the same concept in Ext JS applications. If you take a look back at the code we have already implemented, you will notice that we are already applying inheritance in most of our classes (with the exception of the `util` package), but we are creating classes that inherit from Ext JS classes. Now we will start creating our own super classes.

As all the models that we will be working with have the `last_update` column in common (if you take a look, all the `sakila` tables have this column), we can create a super model with this field. So, we will create a new file under `app/model/sakila` named `Sakila.js`:

```
Ext.define('Packt.model.sakila.Sakila', {
    extend: 'Ext.data.Model',

    fields: [
        {
          name: 'last_update',
          type: 'date',
          dateFormat: 'Y-m-j H:i:s'
        }
    ]
});
```

We will learn how to do the production build later on this book with Sencha Command, and it uses **YUI Compressor** to minify the code. For this reason, we cannot use the word "abstract" as a package name. It would be much nicer if we could have a class named `Packt.model.abstract.Sakila`, but we cannot use it.

This model has only one column, that is, `last_update`. On the tables, the `last_update` column has the `type` timestamp, so the type of the field needs to be `date` and we will also apply a date format `Y-m-j H:i:s` which is *year-month-day hour:minutes:seconds* following the same format as we have in the database (`2006-02-15 04:34:33`).

And now we can create each model representing the tables, and we will not need to declare the `last_update` field again.

Specific models

Now we create all the models representing each table. Let's start with the **Actor model**. We will create a new class named `Packt.model.staticData.Actor`, therefore we need to create a new file name `Actor.js` under `app/model/staticData`:

```
Ext.define('Packt.model.staticData.Actor', {
    extend: 'Packt.model.sakila.Sakila', // #1

    idProperty: 'actor_id', // #2

    fields: [
        { name: 'actor_id' },
        { name: 'first_name'},
        { name: 'last_name'}
    ]
});
```

Two things are different from the other models we created before. The `extend` class (`#1`) is not `Ext.data.Model` but `Packt.model.sakila.Sakila`. The Sakila model is already extending from the `Ext.data.Model` class, and the class `Packt.model.staticData.Actor` is extending from Sakila model. This means our Actor model inherits from the Sakila model that inherits from `Ext.data.Model` class. This way our Actor model class has all the `Ext.data.Model` features along with the `last_update` field inherited from the Sakila model.

And the other different thing is the `idProperty` (`#2`). By default, the `idProperty` has the value `id`. This means that when we declare a model with a field named `id`, Ext JS already knows that this is the unique field of this model. When it is different from `id`, we need to specify it using the `idProperty` configuration. As all Sakila tables do not have a unique field called `id`, it is always of the form name of the entity + `_id`. We will need to declare this configuration in all the models.

Now we can do the same for the other models. We need to create four more classes:

- `Packt.model.staticData.Category`
- `Packt.model.staticData.Language`
- `Packt.model.staticData.City`
- `Packt.model.staticData.Country`

At the end, we will have five model classes created inside the `app/model/staticData` package. If we create a UML class diagram for the model classes, we will have the following diagram:

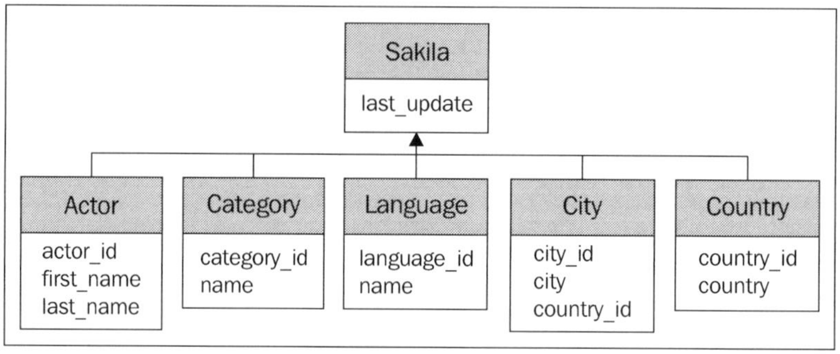

The Actor, Category, Language, City, and Country Models extend the Sakila Model, which extends from the `Ext.data.Model` class.

Creating the stores

The next step is to create the stores for each model. As we did with the models, we will try to create a generic store as well. Although the common configurations are not in the store, but in the proxy, having a super store class can help us to listen to events that are common for all the Static Data stores.

We will create a super store named `Packt.store.staticData.Abstract`.

As we need a store for each model, we will create the following stores:

- `Packt.store.staticData.Actors`
- `Packt.store.staticData.Categories`
- `Packt.store.staticData.Languages`
- `Packt.store.staticData.Cities`
- `Packt.store.staticData.Countries`

The most important configurations will be declared inside the proxy as `url`, `reader`, `writer`, and so on. Some of these configurations will be the same for all stores of the `staticData` package. For this reason, we can also create a super proxy to reuse most of the code. We will create a proxy named `Packt.proxy.StaticData`.

At the end of this topic, we will have created all the preceding classes. If we create a UML diagram for them, we will have something like the following diagram:

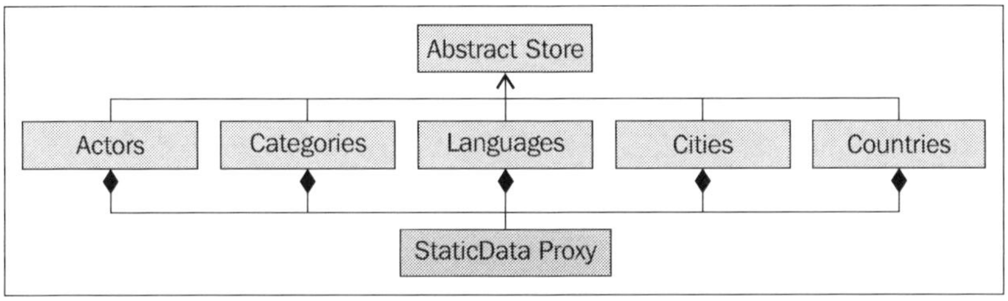

All the store classes extend from the Abstract Store and all the store classes have the StaticData proxy in their configurations.

Now that we know what we need to create, let's get our hands dirty!

The Abstract Store

The first class we need to create is the `Packt.store.staticData.Abstract` class. Inside this class, we will not declare any configuration, as the only objective of this class is to have the same store `id` property for all stores inside the `store.staticData` package:

```
Ext.define('Packt.store.staticData.Abstract', {
    extend: 'Ext.data.Store',

    storeId: 'staticDataAbstract'
});
```

All the specific stores that we will create will extend this store. Creating a super store like this can feel pointless; however, we do not know if during future maintenance we will need to add some common store configuration. Another reason is that inside the controller we can also listen to store events (available since Ext JS 4.2). If we want to listen to the same event belonging to a set of Stores and if we execute exactly the same method, having a super store, it will save us some lines of code.

The Abstract Proxy

The next step is to create a super proxy. Inside this Proxy we will code all the common configurations of the `staticData` stores.

Let's do it step by step. First, we need to create a new folder inside the `app` folder called `proxy`. Then, inside this folder we will create a new file named `StaticData.js` as shown in the following screenshot:

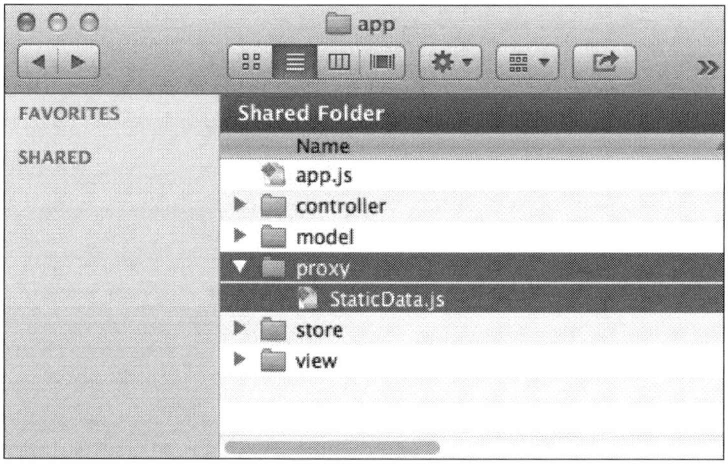

That being said, our class name will be `Packt.proxy.StaticData`. Let's declare the base of the class first:

```
Ext.define('Packt.proxy.StaticData', {
    extend: 'Ext.data.proxy.Ajax',
    alias: 'proxy.staticdataproxy', // #1

    type: 'ajax' // #2
});
```

We can also assign `alias` to this proxy (`#1`). For all classes that extend from a component class of Ext JS (the Grid panel, the Tree Panel, the Form Panel, and so on), when we assign `alias`, we use `widget.` as the prefix and then the name of the `xtype` of the class that we want to assign to it (all in lowercase). For proxies, we can do the same thing, but the prefix we will use is `proxy.` + the name of the proxy.

Next, we will configure the type of the proxy (#2). All staticData stores will communicate with the server using Ajax calls.

Next, we will configure reader, which describes the way we will read data from the server:

```
reader: {
    type: 'json',
    messageProperty: 'msg',
    root: 'data'
}
```

As always, we will use JSON as the exchange format between the server and Ext JS. The attribute inside the JSON object that will wrap the collection of models will be data, and in case we want to send an additional message to Ext JS we can use the attribute msg.

We described how we will be reading the data from the server using reader; we will also describe how we will send data back to server using writer:

```
writer: {
    type: 'json',           // #3
    writeAllFields: true, // #4
    encode: true,           // #5
    allowSingle: false,    // #6
    root: 'data'            // #7
}
```

We will also use JSON to send data back to server (#3). Here is an example of the data we will send back to the server (Actor model):

```
{
    "data": [{
        "last_update": "2013-01-28 13:42:00",
        "actor_id": "1",
        "first_name": "PENELOPE",
        "last_name": "GUINESS"
    }]
}
```

The writeAllFields configuration (with the value true) indicates Ext JS will always send all the model fields back to the server, irrespective of whether the field has updates or not (#4). For example, let's use the Actor model. Consider that we edited the last_name column of the actor class, and now we need to send the actor class's information back to the server to execute an UPDATE query in the database. With writeAllFields set to true, we will send back the id, first_name (which did not have any update on it), and last_name (with the new value) fields. With all the fields, we can execute the following update query (even if all the columns have not been updated):

```
UPDATE Actor
SET
  first_name = {first_name: },
  last_name = {last_name: },
  last_update = {last_update: CURRENT_TIMESTAMP}
WHERE actor_id = {actor_id};
```

If writeAllFields were set to false, we would have to verify what fields have been sent to the server and create the SET statement dynamically. So to save some work, we will set writeAllFields to true in our application.

Then we have the encode configuration set to true (#5). This means that we will send the information encoded in the JSON format and not form data format.

Next, we have the allowSingle configuration set to false (#6). This means that we will always wrap the information we will send to the server in square brackets ([]), even if we need to send only information about one model instance. This can give us a big headache if we do not treat one scenario on the server.

When you send a model instance to the server (to create, update, or delete), it does not mean that the action will be completed with no errors (we always hope for this, but unfortunately, errors and exceptions can happen). When you edit or create a record from the store, this model instance is marked as dirty. This way the store knows what information needs to be sent to the server when we use the sync method. When the action is completed, we send it back to Ext JS as an **ACK** (**acknowledgment**) stating that the action is OK and the store can remove the dirty mark from the model instance. When it is not OK and the server gives an exception or the success value takes the value false, the store will not remove the dirty mark from the model instance we are trying to save.

However, consider that we are editing another model and then we try to save it. If the previous model was not saved, when we call the `sync` method from the store again, the store will send two model instances to the server and the information will be wrapped inside brackets. If we do not have the code on the server side to handle this situation, we will have an error or an exception thrown by the server. So to avoid this verification, we will also wrap the information inside brackets; this way we will have only one piece of code.

And at last, we will wrap the information inside a `data` attribute; likewise we do for reading data from the server.

Next, we will add a security configuration to the proxy. We will change the action method for the reading action:

```
actionMethods: {
    create: "POST",
    read: "POST", //changed to POST
    update: "POST",
    destroy: "POST"
}
```

When using Ajax to exchange data with the server, the `create`, `update`, and `destroy` (delete) actions will use the `POST HTTP` method to send information to the server. The read action uses the `GET HTTP` method by default. However, we will also change the read action to the `POST` method. This way, all the parameters will be retrieved from the `POST` method and will not be sent as query string parameters (added in the URL, for example: `http://localhost/masteringextjs/php/staticData/actor/create.php?entity=Actor`).

Before we go to the next step, let's focus on the idea of why we can create a super proxy. We have five models: Actor, Category, Language, City, and Country. On the server side, we want to execute a `SELECT` query like the following:

```
SELECT * FROM Actor
```

`Actor` is the name of the table that we want to retrieve all the records from. In this case for the Static Data module, we will not apply remote sorting, filtering, or paging, so a simple `SELECT` statement will do the work. We can replace `Actor` with the name of the other tables: `Category`, `Language`, `City`, and `Country`. And if we could send the name of the table to the server that we want to retrieve the records, it would be great; this way we could use the same URL to retrieve the records from the database, and this is exactly what we will do.

For deleting, updating, and creating a record, when using simple PHP code instead of Object Oriented PHP, using the same code to execute a `DELETE`, `UPDATE`, and `INSERT` statement is not possible. However, we will use the same URL, get the name of the table, and redirect to the specific code.

That being said, this means we can use the same URL for all four **CRUD** operations: `create`, `read`, `update`, and `destroy`:

```
api: {
    read    : 'php/staticData/list.php',
    create  : 'php/staticData/create.php',
    update  : 'php/staticData/update.php',
    destroy : 'php/staticData/delete.php'
}
```

And at last, we will add an `exception` listener to display a message to the user in case of any exception:

```
listeners: {
    exception: function(proxy, response, operation){
        Ext.MessageBox.show({
            title: 'REMOTE EXCEPTION',
            msg: operation.getError(),
            icon: Ext.MessageBox.ERROR,
            buttons: Ext.Msg.OK
        });
    }
}
```

Now we have all the configurations done! And the best of it is that we have all of them in only one piece of code, and we will not need to repeat it in every single specific store.

Specific stores

Our next step is to implement the **Actors**, **Categories**, **Languages**, **Cities**, and **Countries** stores.

So let's start with the **Actors** store:

```
Ext.define('Packt.store.staticData.Actors', {
    extend: 'Packt.store.staticData.Abstract', // #1

    requires: [
        'Packt.model.staticData.Actor',    // #2
        'Packt.proxy.StaticData'           // #3
    ],
```

```
    model: 'Packt.model.staticData.Actor', // #4

    proxy: {
        type: 'staticdataproxy',          // #5
        extraParams: {
            entity: 'Actor'               // #6
        }
    }
});
```

After the definition of the store, we need to extend from the Ext JS store class. As we are using a super store, we can extend directly from the super store (#1) that is extending from the `Ext.data.Store` class.

Next, we have the `requires` declaration. We usually always require the `model` class (#2 and #4). However, as we are using `xtype` of the Static Data proxy (#5), we need to have this class already loaded in the memory (#3) so that Ext JS can instantiate the proxy by its `xtype` with no problems (if Ext JS tries to instantiate the proxy—which is not a native proxy—and it is not loaded in the memory yet, Ext JS will throw an exception because it does not know this class).

And lastly, we have the proxy declaration. The proxy type is Static Data proxy that we created. The only configuration specific for each store now is `entity` (#6), which is the name of the table that we will retrieve the records from. This parameter will be sent in every request from the store to the server.

One thing that is very important to notice is the URLs for creating, deleting, reading, and updating the `reader`, `writer`, and other information that we usually configure in a proxy are not listed here. This is because we do not have to do it, as all of this information is in the super proxy.

Creating the menu items

Before we create the screens, we need to add the menu items in our dynamic menu. To do so, we will execute the following scripts in the `Menu` table:

```
INSERT INTO `sakila`.`Menu` (`id`, `text`, `iconCls`)
VALUES ('4', 'staticData', 'menu_staticdata');
```

First, we add the new Menu Module that we will call Static Data.

```
INSERT INTO `sakila`.`Menu` (`text`, `iconCls`, `parent_id`,
`className`)
VALUES
('actor', 'menu_actor', '4', 'actorsgrid'),
```

```
('category', 'menu_category', '4', 'categoriesgrid'),
('language', 'menu_language', '4', 'languagesgrid'),
('city', 'menu_city', '4', 'citiesgrid'),
('country', 'menu_country', '4', 'countriesgrid');
```

Next, we add each menu item that has the Static Data menu as its parent.

Our `Menu` table looks like the following as of now:

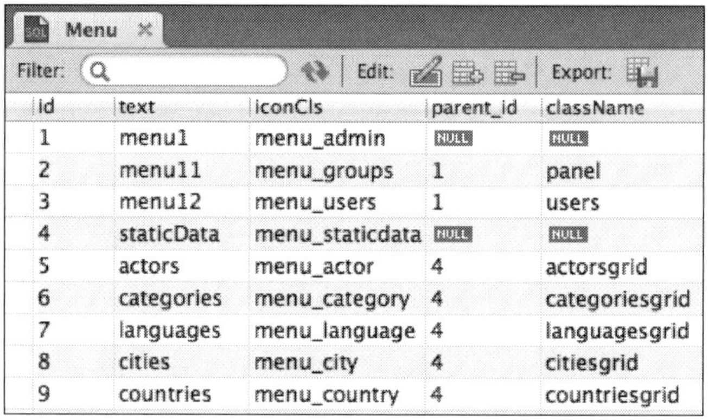

id	text	iconCls	parent_id	className
1	menu1	menu_admin	NULL	NULL
2	menu11	menu_groups	1	panel
3	menu12	menu_users	1	users
4	staticData	menu_staticdata	NULL	NULL
5	actors	menu_actor	4	actorsgrid
6	categories	menu_category	4	categoriesgrid
7	languages	menu_language	4	languagesgrid
8	cities	menu_city	4	citiesgrid
9	countries	menu_country	4	countriesgrid

And as the username we are using to log in to the application is a part of the `admin` group, we will also manually add to the database all the permissions to this group:

```
INSERT INTO `sakila`.`Permissions` (`Menu_id`, `Group_id`)
VALUES
('4', '1'),
('5', '1'),
('6', '1'),
('7', '1'),
('8', '1'),
('9', '1');
```

In the translations files (`en.js`, `es.js`, and `pt.js`), we will also add the attributes and their translations:

```
staticData: 'Static Data',
actors: 'Actors',
categories: 'Categories',
languages: 'Languages',
cities: 'Cities',
countries: 'Countries'
```

The following screenshot shows the output we will get:

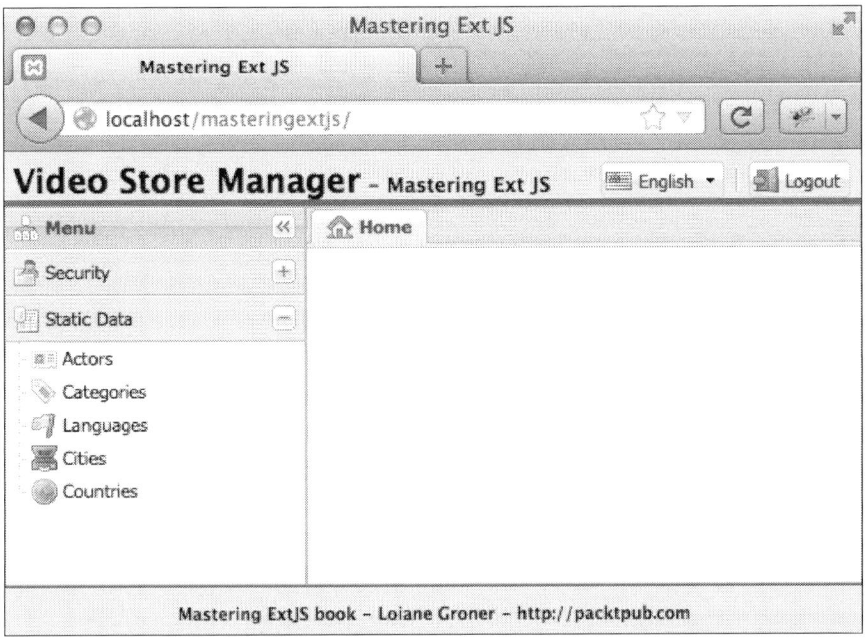

Creating an abstract Grid panel for reuse

Now is the time to implement **views**. We have to implement five views: one to perform the CRUD operations for Actors, one for Categories, one for Languages, one for Cities, and one for Countries.

The following screenshot represents the final result we want to achieve after implementing the **Actors** screen:

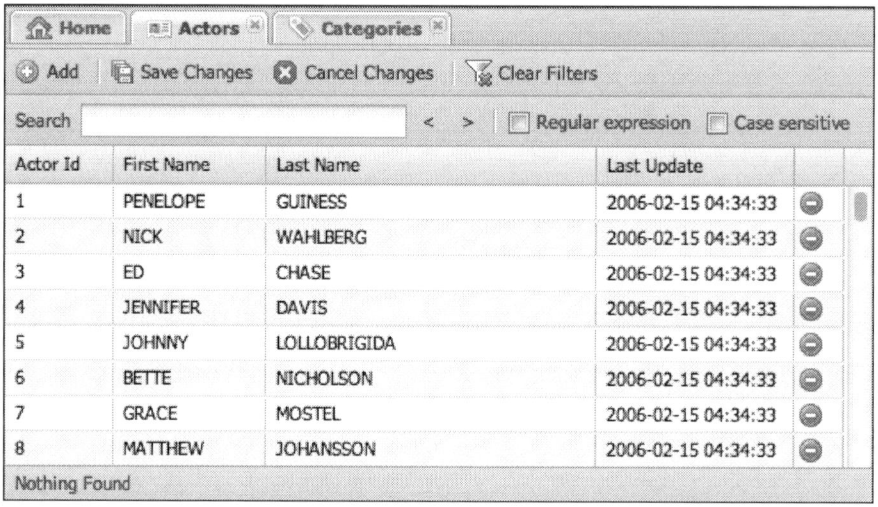

And the following screenshot represents the final result we want to achieve after implementing the **Categories** screen:

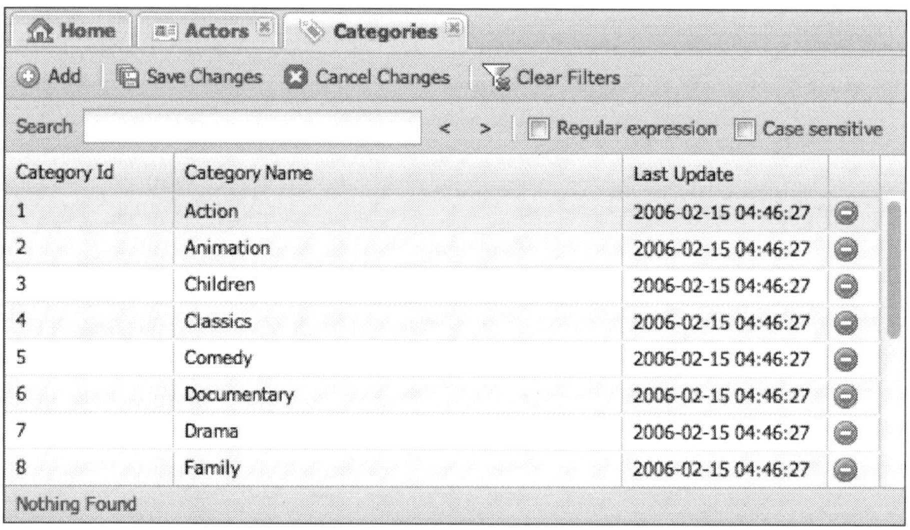

Noticed anything similar between these two screens? Let's take a look again:

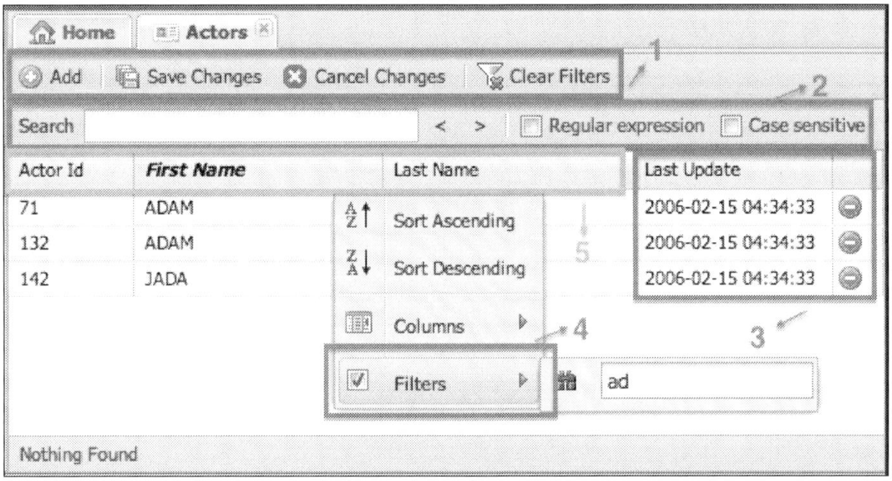

The top-most toolbar is the same (**1**); there is a live **Search** capability (**2**), a **Filters** plugin (**4**), and the **Last Update** and **action** columns (**3**). Going a little bit further, both the Grid panels can be edited using a cell editor plugin. The things that are different between these two screens are the columns that are specific to each screen (**5**). Does this mean we can reuse a good part of the code if we use inheritance by creating a super Grid panel with all these common capabilities? Yes!

So this is what we are going to do. Now, let's create a new class named `Packt.view.staticData.AbstractGrid`:

```
Ext.define('Packt.view.staticData.AbstractGrid', {
    extend: 'Ext.ux.LiveSearchGridPanel', // #1
    alias: 'widget.staticdatagrid',

    columnLines: true, // #2
    viewConfig: {
        stripeRows: true // #3
    },
});
```

We will extend the `Ext.ux.LiveSearchGridPanel` class instead of `Ext.grid.Panel`. The `Ext.ux.LiveSearchGridPanel` class already extends the `Ext.grid.Panel` class and also adds the Live Search toolbar (**2**). The `LiveSearchGridPanel` class is a plugin that is distributed with Ext JS SDK. You can find it inside the `sdk/examples/ux` directory. We will place the `ux` directory inside the `extjs` directory (`extjs/ux`).

The configurations #2 and #3 are for showing the border of each cell of the grid and to alternate between a white background and a light gray background.

As this is the first time we are going to use an `Ext.ux` namespace, we need to tell the `Loader` class where to find these files. Opening the `app.js` file, we will add this mapping inside the `Loader` class:

```
Ext.Loader.setConfig({
    enabled: true,
    paths: {
        Ext: '.',
        'Ext.ux': 'extjs/ux',
        'Packt.util': 'app/util'
    }
});
```

The next step is to create an `initComponent` method. As we are creating a superclass, some of the configurations will be overridden, and some will not. Usually, the ones that we expect to override we declare in the class as configurations. The ones we do not want to override, we declare them inside the `initComponent` method. As there are a few configurations we do not want to override, we will declare them inside the `initComponent` class:

```
initComponent: function() {
    var me = this;

    me.selModel = {
        selType: 'cellmodel' // #4
    };

    me.plugins = [
        Ext.create('Ext.grid.plugin.CellEditing', { // #5
            clicksToEdit: 1,
            pluginId: 'cellplugin'
        })
    ];

    me.features = [
        Ext.create('Ext.ux.grid.FiltersFeature', { // #6
            local: true
        })
    ];

    //docked items

    //columns

    me.callParent(arguments);
}
```

> **me versus this**
>
> If we take a look around some Ext JS code over the Internet, we will notice that a lot of developers use `me` instead of `this`. Why is that? If `this` is going to be used a lot of times, you should consider using `me` because it saves you 16 bits and also compresses better (after we make a production build and the code is compressed). Also, `me` is also used in cases where we need to maintain the scope of the current context within another function.

We can also define how the user can select information from the Grid panel: the default configuration is the row selection model. As we want the user to be able to edit cell by cell, we will use the cell selection model (`#4`) and also the cell editor plugin (`#5`), which is a part of the Ext JS SDK.

To be able to filter the information (the Live Search will only highlight the matching records), we will use the filter feature (`#6`). The filter feature is not a part of the Ext JS SDK, and you can find it inside the ux folder as well.

Next, we have the declaration of the docked items. As all the Grid panels will have the same toolbar, we can declare it on the superclass we are creating:

```
me.dockedItems = [
    {
        xtype: 'toolbar',
        dock: 'top',
        itemId: 'topToolbar',
        items: [
            {
                xtype: 'button',
                itemId: 'add',
                text: 'Add',
                iconCls: 'add'
            },
            {
                xtype: 'tbseparator'
            },
            {
                xtype: 'button',
                itemId: 'save',
                text: 'Save Changes',
                iconCls: 'save_all'
            },
            {
                xtype: 'button',
```

```
                    itemId: 'cancel',
                    text: 'Cancel Changes',
                    iconCls: 'cancel'
                },
                {
                    xtype: 'tbseparator'
                },
                {
                    xtype: 'button',
                    itemId: 'clearFilter',
                    text: 'Clear Filters',
                    iconCls: 'clear_filter'
                }
            ]
        }
    ];
```

We will have **Add**, **Save Changes**, **Cancel Changes**, and **Clear Filter** buttons.

And finally, we will add those two columns that are common for all the screens (`Last Update` and the action column—`Delete`) along with the columns already declared in each specific Grid panel:

```
me.columns = Ext.Array.merge(me.columns,
    [{
        xtype    : 'datecolumn',
        text     : 'Last Update',
        width    : 120,
        dataIndex: 'last_update',
        format: 'Y-m-j H:i:s',
        filter: true
    },
    {
        xtype: 'actioncolumn',
        width: 30,
        sortable: false,
        menuDisabled: true,
        items: [
            {
                handler: function(view, rowIndex, colIndex, item, e) {
                    this.fireEvent('itemclick', this, 'delete', view,
rowIndex, colIndex, item, e);
                },
                iconCls: 'delete',
```

```
                    tooltip: 'Delete'
                }
            ]
        }]
    );
```

Handling the action column in the MVC architecture

Let's take a look again at the action column declared in the super Grid panel, especially in the handler configuration:

```
handler: function(view, rowIndex, colIndex, item, e) {
    this.fireEvent('itemclick', this, 'delete', view, rowIndex,
colIndex, item, e);
}
```

The buttons we add to an action column are not components (because they are not buttons, they are only an image/icon); therefore we cannot listen to their events on the controller. However, using the handler configuration to handle their events means breaking the MVC architecture. That is why firing a custom event on the action column (which is a component) and passing an extra parameter, which is the name of the action we clicked (delete). This way, we will be able to listen to this event on the controller.

Setting iconCls instead of icon on the action column

Usually, when we declare an action column's item, we set the icon configuration with the path of the image we will use as the icon in the action column. However, this is not very practical. Imagine that the same icon is used in another place of the application and we want to change to something else. We will have to search for all places where this icon is used and make the change manually.

When we want to assign an icon to a button, we can create a style on a CSS file and use the `iconCls` configuration. This way it is easier to make a change if we need to; we just need to change the style and the change will be applied to all the places in the application where that icon was being used.

Can we do the same for the Action Columns? Use the `iconCls` configuration instead of the `icon` (and the complete path)? Of course we can! Let's see how to do it.

First, we need to create the style to represent the icon. We will use the delete `iconCls` we already used in other buttons of the application:

```
.delete {
  background-image:url('../icons/delete.png') !important;
}
```

Next, we need to add a new style in our CSS file:

```
.x-action-col-cell img {
    height: 16px;
    width: 16px;
    cursor: pointer;
}
```

This is the style that will do all the magic for us! Then, we can apply `iconCls` to the item of the action column:

```
{
    xtype: 'actioncolumn',
    width: 30,
    sortable: false,
    menuDisabled: true,
    items: [
        {
            iconCls: 'delete',
            tooltip: 'Delete'
        }
    ]
}
```

The Live Search plugin versus the Filter plugin

Both the Live Search and Filter plugins have the objective of helping the user to search for information quickly. In our project, we are using both.

The Live Search plugin will search for any matching result in all the columns of the Grid panel. The search is also performed locally, meaning if we use the paging toolbar, this plugin will not work as expected. In our case, we are displaying all the records from the database at once, so the plugin works as expected. For example, if we search for `ada`, we will get the following output:

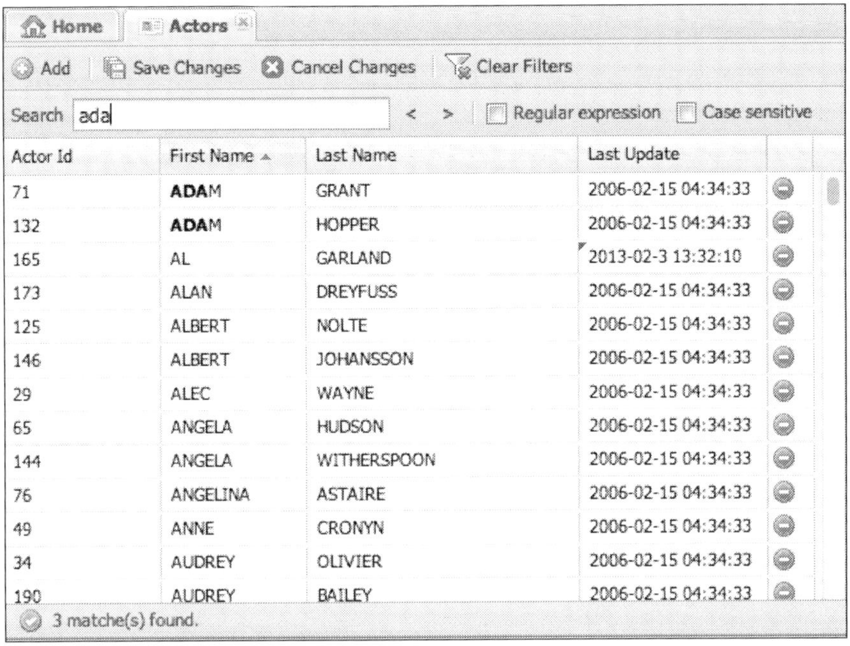

The Filter plugin will apply the filters on the store as well, so it will only display the matching results to the user:

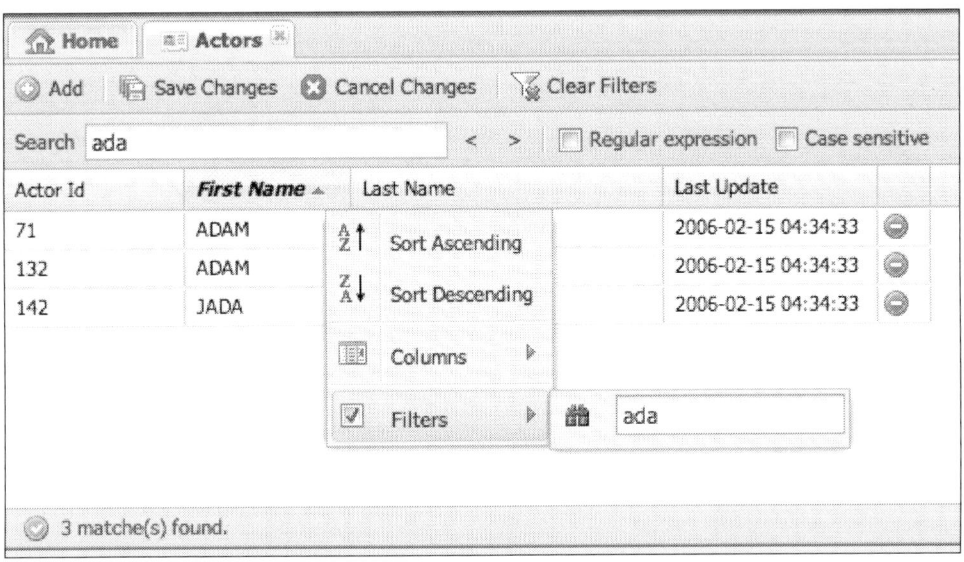

Specific Grid panels for each table

Our last step before we implement the controller are the specific Grid panels. We have already created the super Grid panel that contains most of the capabilities that we need. Now we just need to declare the specific configurations for each Grid panel.

We will create five Grid panels that will extend from the `Packt.view.staticData.AbstractGrid` class:

- `Packt.view.staticData.Actors`
- `Packt.view.staticData.Categories`
- `Packt.view.staticData.Languages`
- `Packt.view.staticData.Cities`
- `Packt.view.staticData.Countries`

Let's start with the **Actors** Grid panel:

```
Ext.define('Packt.view.staticData.Actors', {
    extend: 'Packt.view.staticData.AbstractGrid',
    alias: 'widget.actorsgrid',

    store: 'staticData.Actors', // #1

    columns: [
        {
            text: 'Actor Id',
            width: 100,
            dataIndex: 'actor_id',
            filter: {
                type: 'numeric' // #2
            }
        },
        {
            text: 'First Name',
            flex: 1,
            dataIndex: 'first_name',
            editor: {
                allowBlank: false, // #3
                maxLength: 45      // #4
            },
            filter: {
                type: 'string'    // #5
            }
        },
```

```
            {
                text: 'Last Name',
                width: 200,
                dataIndex: 'last_name',
                editor: {
                    allowBlank: false, // #6
                    maxLength: 45      // #7
                },
                filter: {
                    type: 'string'     // #8
                }
            }
        ]
    });
```

The first declaration that is specific to the **Actors** Grid panel is the store (#1). We are going to use the Actors store. Because the Actors store is inside the staticData folder (store/staticData), we also need to pass the name of the subfolder, otherwise, Ext JS will think that this store file is inside the app/store folder, which is not true.

Then, we need to declare the columns specific for the **Actors** Grid panel (we do not need to declare the Last Update and the Delete action columns because they are already in the super Grid panel).

What we need to pay attention to now are the editor and filter configurations for each column. editor is for editing. We will only apply this configuration to the columns we want the user to be able to edit, and filter is the configuration that we will apply to columns we want the user to be able to filter information.

For example, for the id column we do not want the user to be able to edit it, as it is a sequence provided by the MySQL database auto-increment, so we will not apply the editor configuration to it. However, the user can filter the information based on the ID, so we will apply the filter configuration (#2).

For the other two columns, first_name and last_name, we want the user to be able to edit them, so we will add the editor configuration. We can apply client validations as we can do on a field of a form too. For example, we want both fields to be mandatory (#3 and #6) and the maximum number of characters the user can enter is 45 (#4 and #7).

And at last, as both columns are rendering text values (string), we will also apply a filter configuration (#5 and #8). All the other capabilities will be provided by the super Grid panel.

A generic controller for all tables

Now it is time to implement the last piece of the Static Data module. The goal is to implement a controller that has the most generic code that will provide the functionalities for all the screens without us creating any specific methods for any screens.

So let's start with the base of the controller. We are going to create a new class named `Packt.controller.staticData.AbstractController`:

```
Ext.define('Packt.controller.staticData.AbstractController', {
    extend: 'Ext.app.Controller',

    requires: [  // #1
        'Packt.util.Util'
    ],

    stores: [    // #2
        'staticData.Actors',
        'staticData.Categories',
        'staticData.Cities',
        'staticData.Countries',
        'staticData.Languages'
    ],

    views: [    // #3
        'staticData.AbstractGrid',
        'staticData.Actors',
        'staticData.Categories',
        'staticData.Cities',
        'staticData.Countries',
        'staticData.Languages'
    ],

  init: function(application) {
      this.control({
      });
  }
});
```

For now, we are going to declare `requires` (`#1`—where we are going to use the `Util` class in some methods), `stores` (`#2`—where we can list all the stores of this module), and also `views` (`#3`—where we can list all views of this module including the abstract Grid panel).

And as usual, we have the `init` function and `this.control` where we are going to listen to all component events.

Loading the Grid panel store when the grid is rendered

We want to load the stores on demand. When the user clicks on the dynamic menu, and the application opens the screen, the Grid panel will be rendered. When the Grid panel is rendered, we want to load the store. So to do this, we need to listen to the event `render` from the Grid panel.

Now comes the best part; when declaring the selector of the component that the controller will be listening to, we cannot use `grid` or `gridpanel` as the `xtype` because we are only interested in the Grid panels of the Static Data module. Using each Static Data Grid panel `xtype` (`actorsgrid`, `categoriesgrid`, `languagesgrid`, `citiesgrid`, and `countriesgrid`) is also not what we want, as we are looking for generic code that can provide the same functionality to all these components. The good news is that we used inheritance and we have a super Grid panel (`Packt.view.staticData.AbstractGrid`) of which `xtype` is `staticdatagrid`.

For example, to listen to an event from the Actors Grid panel, we can use `xtype` `actorsgrid`, its superclass `xtype` (`staticdatagrid`) or `xtype` `grid` or `gridpanel`. Inheritance is such a beautiful thing!

So going back to the selector, we are going to use `staticdatagrid` and listen to the event `render`:

```
"staticdatagrid": {
    render: this.render
}
```

Now we need to declare the `render` method:

```
render: function(component, options) {
    component.getStore().load();
}
```

There are a few ways we can do this. We could get each store and load it depending on the component that is being rendered. But, as the Grid panel is being passed as a parameter to the `render` event (`component`), we can use the method `getStore` to get the store that is being used by the Grid panel and call the method `load`.

This way, when we load the **Actors** Grid panel, its store (**Actors** store) is going to be loaded, when we load the **Categories** Grid panel, its store (**Categories** store) is going to be loaded, and so on.

With only one line of code, we can make the call and the code generic and provide the same capability to all Static Data Grid panels.

Adding a new record on the Grid panel

On the toolbar from each Static Data Grid panel, we have a button with the text **Add**. When we click on this button, we want to add a new model in the store (and consequently, add a new record on the Grid panel) and enable the editing so that the user can fill the values to save it for later (when we click on the **Save Changes** button).

So first, we need to listen to the `click` event of the **Add** button:

```
"staticdatagrid button#add": {
    click: this.onButtonClickAdd
}
```

Then, we need to implement the method `onButtonClickAdd`:

```
onButtonClickAdd: function (button, e, options) {
    var grid = button.up('staticdatagrid'), // #1
    store = grid.getStore(),                // #2
    modelName = store.getProxy().getModel().modelName, // #3
    cellEditing = grid.getPlugin('cellplugin'); // #4

    store.insert(0, Ext.create(modelName, {  // #5
        last_update: new Date()              // #6
    }));

    cellEditing.startEditByPosition({row: 0, column: 1}); // #7
}
```

From the parameters, we only have the button reference. We need to get the Grid panel reference. So we are going to use the method `up` to get it (`#1`). Again, we are going to use the super Grid panel `xtype` as the selector (`staticdatagrid`) because this way we have the most generic code possible.

When we have the Grid panel reference, we can get the store reference using the `getStore` method (`#2`).

We need to have the model name to instantiate it (`#5`) so that we can insert in the first position of the store (this way it will be the first line of the Grid panel). So still targeting generic code, we can get the model name of the proxy from the store (`#3`). We can pass some configurations to the model when we instantiate it. We want the `Last Update` column to be updated as well, so we will only pass it as configuration with the most current date and time.

And at last, we also want to focus on a cell of the row so that the user can be aware that the cell can be edited; so we will focus on the second column of the grid (the first one is the `id` column, which is not editable) of the first row (`#7`). But to do so, we need a reference to the cell editor plugin; we can get it by using the method `getPlugin`, passing `pluginId` as the parameter (`#4`).

Just to remember, we declare `pluginId` for the `CellEditing` plugin of the `Packt.view.staticData.AbstractGrid` class:

```
Ext.create('Ext.grid.plugin.CellEditing', {
    clicksToEdit: 1,
    pluginId: 'cellplugin'
})
```

Editing an existing record

The editing of a cell will be done automatically by the `CellEditing` plugin. However, when the user clicks on a cell to edit and finishes the editing, we need to update the `Last Update` value to the current date and time.

The `CellEditing` plugin has an event named `edit` that allows us to listen to the event we want. Unfortunately, the controller is not able to listen to plugin events. Fortunately, the Grid panel class also fires this event (the `CellEditing` plugin forwards the event to the Grid panel), so we can listen to it. As we declared an event for the super Grid panel, already, we will add the `edit` event to it as highlighted in the following code snippet:

```
"staticdatagrid": {
    render: this.render,
    edit: this.onEdit
}
```

Next, we need to implement the `onEdit` method:

```
onEdit: function(editor, context, options) {
    context.record.set('last_update', new Date());
}
```

The second parameter is the event (`context`). From this parameter, we can get the model instance (`record`) that the user edited, and then set the `last_update` field to the current date and time.

Deleting – handling the action column on the controller

Well, the read, create, and update actions are already implemented. Now we need to implement the delete action. We do not have a button for the delete action, but we do have `item` of an action column. In the previous sections, we learned how to fire the event from `item` of the action column so that we can handle it on the Controller. We cannot listen to the event fired by the action column's `item`; however, we can listen to the event fired by the action column:

```
"staticdatagrid actioncolumn": {
    itemclick: this.handleActionColumn
}
```

Now, let's see how to implement the `handleActionColumn` method:

```
handleActionColumn: function(column, action, view, rowIndex, colIndex, 
item, e) {
        var store = view.up('staticdatagrid').getStore(),
        rec = store.getAt(rowIndex);

        if (action == 'delete'){
            store.remove(rec);
            Ext.Msg.alert('Delete', 'Save the changes to persist the 
removed record.');
        }
    }
```

As this is a custom event, we need to get the parameters that were passed by the item of the action column.

So first, we need to get the store and also record that the user clicked to delete. Then, using the second parameter, which is the name of the action of the action column's `item`, we have a way to know which item fired the event. So if the action is `delete`, we are going to remove the record from the store and ask the user to commit the changes by pressing the button **Save Changes**, which is going to synchronize the models from the store with the information we have on the server.

Saving the changes

After the user performs an update, delete, or create action, the cells that were updated will have a mark (the "dirty" mark so that the store knows what models were modified) as shown in the following screenshot:

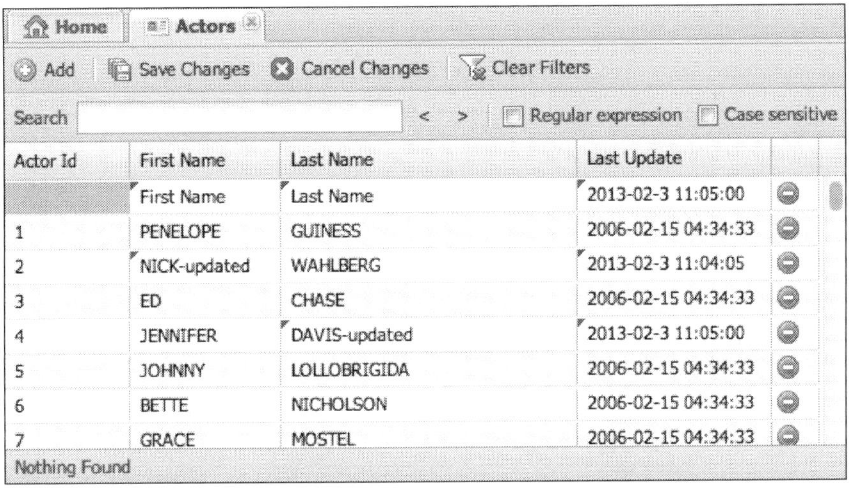

In the same way we can perform changes on the MySQL table by saving the changes (commit). That is why we created the **Save Changes** button; this way we will synchronize all the changes at once to the server.

So first, we need to add a listener to `this.control`:

```
"staticdatagrid button#save": {
    click: this.onButtonClickSave
}
```

Then, we need to implement the `onButtonClickSave` method:

```
onButtonClickSave: function (button, e, options) {
  button.up('staticdatagrid').getStore().sync();
}
```

The implementation of the method is pretty straightforward. We simply need to get the store from the Grid panel and call the method `sync`.

autoSync configuration

The store has a configuration named `autoSync`. The default value is `false`, but if we set it to `true`, the store will automatically synchronize with the server whenever a change is detected. This can be good or bad, it depends on how we are going to use it.

It is going to depend on how often the user is going to make a change. For example, for the **Categories** screen, it is not that often that the user is going to add, update, or delete a category. The changes are going to be rare. In this case, there is no issue in using the `autoSync` configuration as `true`.

Now, imagine a situation where the user is going to delete, create, or update records very often. Having the `autoSync` configuration as `true` can be very dangerous. Depending on the periodicity, Ext JS will be sending a lot of requests to the server and the server can interpret it as a **DoS attack** (**denial-of-service attack**—true story!). This is because for every delete, update, or create action, Ext JS will send a request to the server, different from when `autoSync` is `false`. This is going to send only one request for create, one for update, and one for delete (when there is any record to create, update, or delete). So think very carefully when using `autoSync` as `true`.

> To learn more about the DoS attack, please read `http://en.wikipedia.org/wiki/Denial-of-service_attack`.

Canceling the changes

As the user can save the changes (commit), the user can also cancel them (roll back). All we have to do is to reload the store so that we get the most updated information from the server, and the changes made by the user will be lost.

So we need to listen to the event:

```
"staticdatagrid button#cancel": {
    click: this.onButtonClickCancel
}
```

And implement the method:

```
onButtonClickCancel: function (button, e, options) {
  button.up('staticdatagrid').getStore().reload();
}
```

If you would like to, you can add a message asking if the user really wants to roll back the changes. Calling the `reload` method from the store is what we need to do to make it work.

Clearing the filter

When using the **Filters** plugin on the Grid panel, it will do everything that we need (when used locally). But there is one thing that it doesn't provide to the user, the option to clear all the filters at once. So that is why we implemented a **Clear Filter** button.

So first let's listen to the event:

```
"staticdatagrid button#clearFilter": {
    click: this.onButtonClickClearFilter
}
```

And implement the method:

```
onButtonClickClearFilter: function (button, e, options) {
  button.up('staticdatagrid').filters.clearFilters();
}
```

When using the Filters plugin, we are able to get a property named `filters` from the Grid panel. Then, all we need to do it is to call the `clearFilters` method. It will clear the filter values from each column that was filtered, and will also clear the filters from the store.

Listening to store events on the controller

And the last event we will be listening to is the `write` event from the store. We have already added an `exception` listener to the proxy. Now we need to add a listener in case of success.

The first step is to listen to the event from the store in the controller. But attention! If you are using Ext JS 4.0.x or 4.1.x, it will not work. This feature is only present in Ext JS 4.2.x+.

Inside the `init` function of the controller, we will add the following code:

```
this.listen({
    store: {
        '#staticDataAbstract': {
            write: this.onStoreSync
        }
    }
});
```

We can listen to the `store` events inside the store option. As we have a super `store` class, when we say we want to listen to its events, all the child classes will also be in the scope. That is why we created a super `store` class, this way we do not need to listen to every Static Data store event.

The `write` event is fired whenever the store receives the response from the server. So let's implement the method:

```
onStoreSync: function(store, operation, options){
  Packt.util.Alert.msg('Success!', 'Your changes have been saved.');
}
```

We will simply display a message saying the changes have been saved. Notice that the message is also generic, this way we can use it for all the Static Data module.

Summary

In this chapter, we covered how to implement screens that look very similar to the MySQL table editor. The most important concept we covered in this chapter is how to implement abstract classes, using the inheritance concept from OOP. Usually, we are used to using these concepts on server-side languages, such as PHP, Java, .NET, and so on. And this chapter demonstrated that it is important to use these concepts on the Ext JS side. This way we can reuse a lot of code and also implement generic code that provides the same capability for more than one component.

We created abstract models, stores, views, and controller. We also learned how to create a custom proxy. We also used the plugins: the cell editor for the Grid panel, Live Search grid, and Filters plugin for the Grid panel as well. We learned how to perform CRUD operations using the store capabilities and that the `autoSync` configuration can be dangerous if not used carefully. We also learned how to create custom events and handle the action column's item events on the controller.

In the next chapter, we will learn how to implement the Content Management module, which goes further than just managing one single table as we did in this chapter. We will manage information from the table (related to the business of the application) and all its relations within the database.

7
Content Management

In the previous chapter we developed the static data module that consisted of emulating the editing of a table from a database. Basically, it was a CRUD of a single table with some extra capabilities. In this chapter, we will learn more about the complexity of managing information from a table. Usually, in real-world applications, the table information that we want to manage has relationships with other tables, and we have to manage these relationships as well. This is what this chapter is all about; how to build screens and manage complex information in Ext JS.

In this chapter we will cover:

- Managing complex information with Ext JS
- How to handle many-to-many associations
- Forms with associations
- Reusing components

Managing information – films, clients, and rentals

The Sakila database has four major modules within it: `Inventory`, which consists of the information about films along with inventory information (the number of movies available for rental in each store); `Customer Data`, which consists of customer information; `Business`, which consists of the stores, staff, rental, and payment information (it depends on `Inventory` and `Customer Data` to feed some information); and `Views`, which consists of data we can use for reports and charts.

For now we are only interested in `Inventory`, `Customer Data`, and `Business`, which contains the core business information of the application. Let's take a look at `Inventory`, which has more tables than the other two:

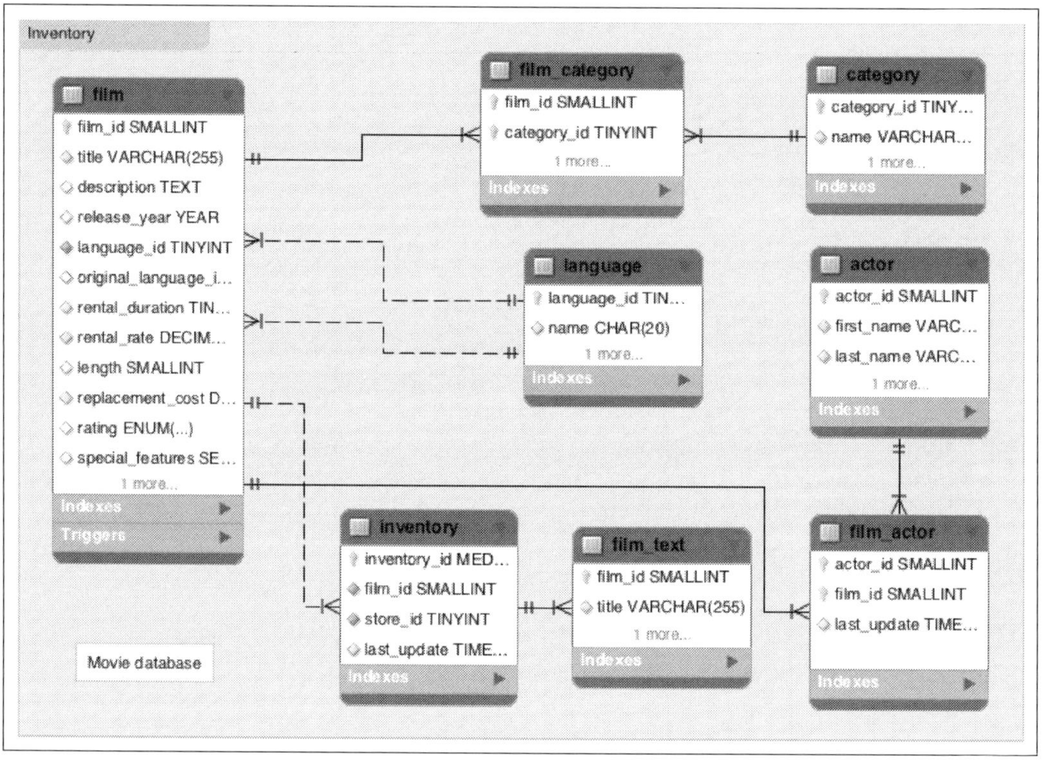

According to the Sakila documentation:

> *The film table is a list of all films potentially in stock in the stores. The actual in-stock copies of each film are represented in the inventory table.*
>
> *The film table refers to the language table and is referred to by the film_category, film_actor, and inventory tables.*

The `Film` table has a many-to-many relationship with the `Category` and `Actor` tables. It has two many-to-one relationships with the `Language` table. In the previous chapter, we have already developed code to manage the `Category`, `Actor`, and `Language` tables. Now we need to manage the relationships between the `Film` table and these other tables.

So, let's take a brief look at the screens that we are going to develop in this chapter. Even though we have the `Customer` and `Business` Sakila modules, in this chapter we will work only with `Films`. But do not worry or panic, the `Customer` and `Business` modules follow the same approach and you can find all the `Customer` and `Business` module-associated code within the source code distributed with this book.

First, we need a screen to list the films we have:

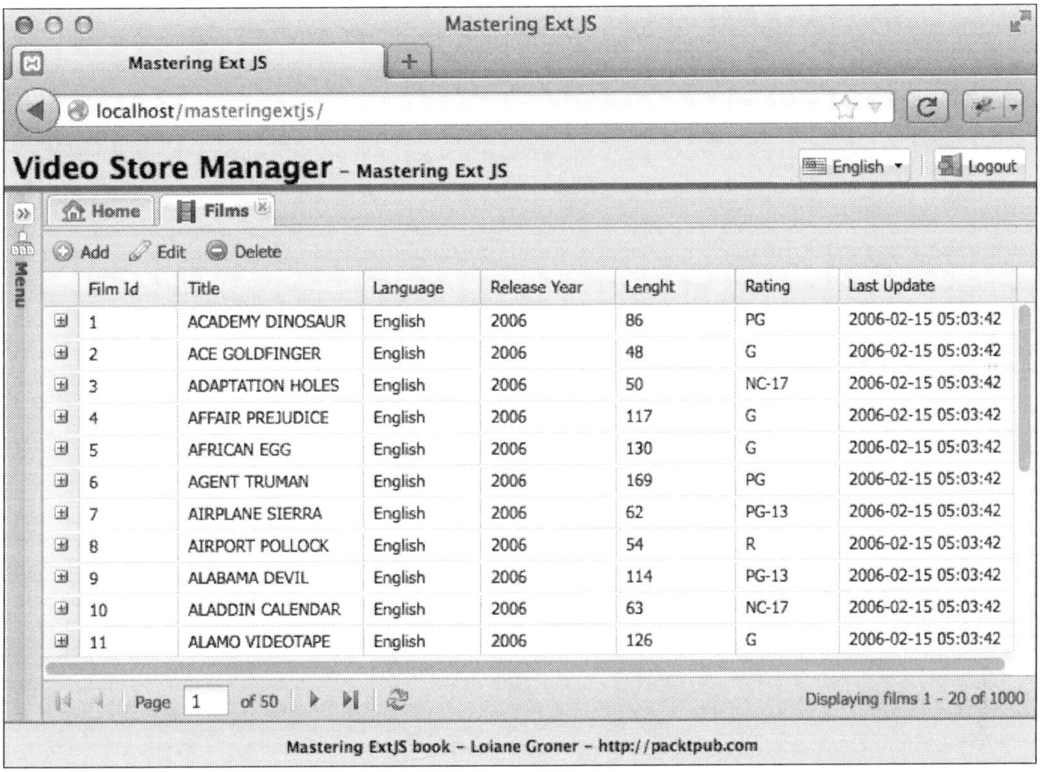

Then, in case we want to create or edit a film, we will create a Form panel within a window so that we can edit its information:

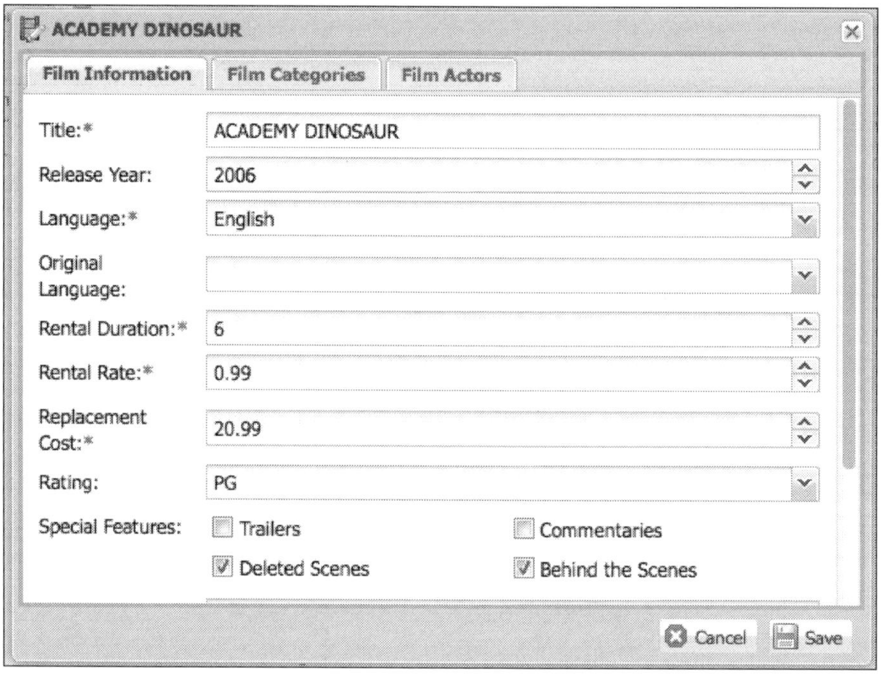

As the film has a many-to-many association with the `Categories` table, we also need to handle it within the Form panel using a different tab:

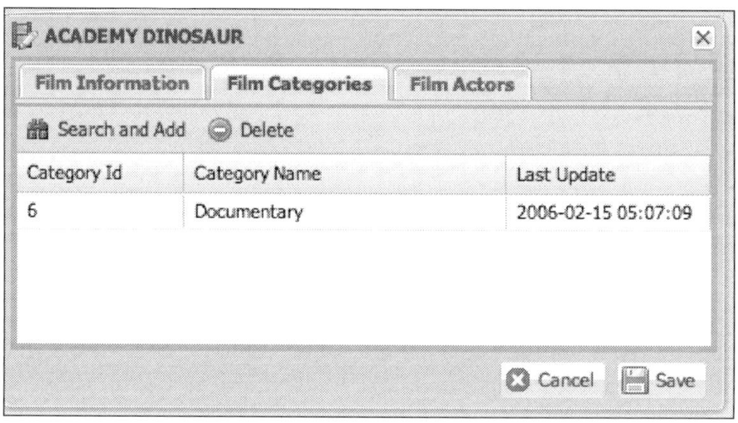

In case we want to add more categories to the film, we can **Search and Add**:

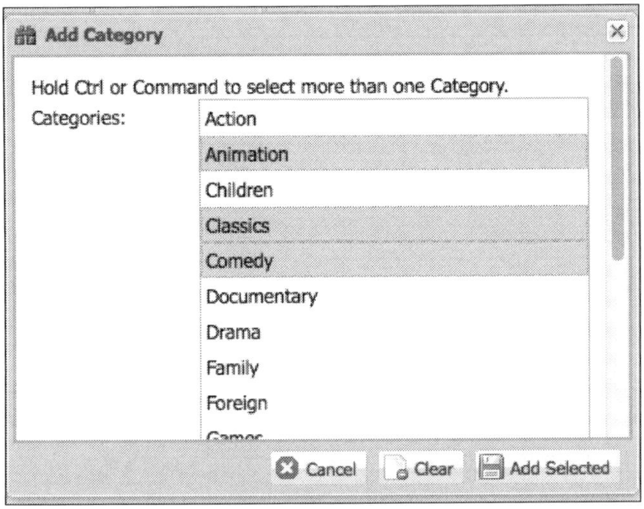

Likewise, the film also has a many-to-many association with the `Actors` table, so we also need to handle it within the Form panel:

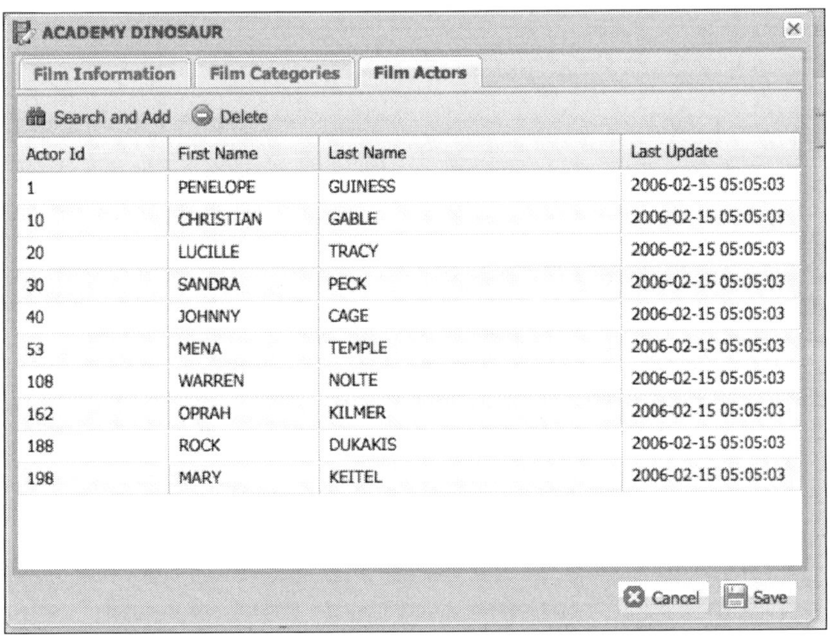

In case we want to add more actors to the film, we can use Search and Add Actor:

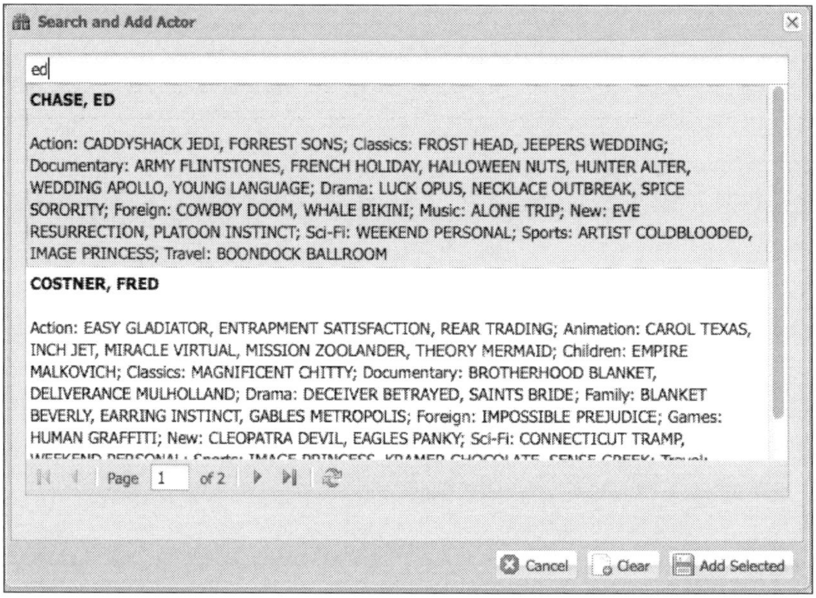

Notice that we are taking a different approach for each screen. This way we can learn more ways of handling these scenarios in Ext JS.

So now that we have an idea of what we will implement throughout this chapter, let's have some fun and get our hands dirty!

Displaying the Film data grid

First, let's start with the basics. Whenever we need to implement a complex screen, we need to start with the simplest component we can develop. After we have it working 100 percent, we can increment it and add more complex capabilities. So first, we need to create a model and a store to represent the `Film` table. And after we have this part of the code working, we can work with the Category, Language, and Actor relationships.

The Film model

First, we are going to create the model to represent the `Film` table. Let's not worry about the relationships this table has for now.

We need to create a new class named `Packt.model.film.Film`:

```
Ext.define('Packt.model.film.Film', {
    extend: 'Packt.model.sakila.Sakila',

    idProperty: 'film_id',

    fields: [
        { name: 'film_id' },
        { name: 'title', type: 'string' },
        { name: 'description', type: 'string'},
        { name: 'release_year', type: 'int'},
        { name: 'language_id'},
        { name: 'original_language_id'},
        { name: 'rental_duration', type: 'int'},
        { name: 'rental_rate', type: 'float'},
        { name: 'length', type: 'int'},
        { name: 'replacement_cost', type: 'float'},
        { name: 'rating'},
        { name: 'special_features'}
    ]
});
```

As all Sakila tables have the `last_update` column, we will extend `Packt.model.sakila.Sakila` to avoid declaring this field in every single model we create that represents a Sakila table.

For the fields, we will have the same ones we have on the `Film` table.

Films store

Our next step is to create a store to load the collection of films. Let's create a store named `Packt.store.film.Films` (remember that the store name is always the plural of the name of the model—if you want to follow the Sencha convention):

```
Ext.define('Packt.store.film.Films', {
    extend: 'Ext.data.Store',

    requires: [
        'Packt.model.film.Film',
        'Packt.proxy.Sakila'
    ],

    model: 'Packt.model.film.Film',
```

```
        pageSize: 20, // #1

        storeId: 'films',

        proxy: {
            type: 'sakila', // #2
            url: 'php/inventory/list.php'
        }
    });
```

In this store, we are declaring the model as usual, and we are also declaring the `pageSize` as `20` (`#1`), meaning we will use the Paging toolbar in the Films data grid and we will retrieve sets of 20 films at a time to display in the Grid panel.

Notice that the proxy `type` we declared is `sakila`, and this means it is not a native proxy. Why is there a need to create a custom proxy? Most of the times we declared a proxy in this book, the proxy `type` was `Ajax` and the configurations used for the `reader` and `writer` were always the same. So to avoid declaring the same configuration every time we declare a proxy, we can create our own custom proxy.

Remember to create this proxy inside the `app/proxy` folder:

```
    Ext.define('Packt.proxy.Sakila', {
        extend: 'Ext.data.proxy.Ajax',
        alias: 'proxy.sakila',

        type: 'ajax',

        reader: {
            type: 'json',
            messageProperty: 'msg',
            root: 'data'
        },

        writer: {
            type: 'json',
            writeAllFields: true,
            encode: true,
            allowSingle: false,
            root: 'data'
        },

        listeners: {
            exception: function(proxy, response, operation){
                Ext.MessageBox.show({
```

```
                title: 'REMOTE EXCEPTION',
                msg: operation.getError(),
                icon: Ext.MessageBox.ERROR,
                buttons: Ext.Msg.OK
            });
        }
    }
});
```

To use this proxy inside a store, we only need to add the proxy class name inside the `requires` declaration and use the proxy type. If you would like to, go ahead and refactor the stores that we have already created in the previous chapters.

Film data grid (with paging)

Now that we have the model and store, we need to create the Films data grid:

```
Ext.define('Packt.view.film.Films', {
    extend: 'Packt.view.sakila.SakilaGrid', // #1
    alias: 'widget.filmsgrid',

    requires: [
        'Ext.ux.RowExpander' // #2
    ],

    store: 'film.Films',

    columns: [
        {
            text: 'Film Id',
            width: 100,
            dataIndex: 'film_id'
        },
        {
            text: 'Title',
            flex: 1,
            dataIndex: 'title'
        },
        {
            text: 'Language',
            width: 100,
            dataIndex: 'language_id', // #3
            renderer: function(value, metaData, record ){
                var languagesStore = Ext.getStore('languages');
```

```
var lang = languagesStore.findRecord('language_id', value);
                return lang != null ? lang.get('name') : value;
            }
        },
        {
            text: 'Release Year',
            width: 90,
            dataIndex: 'release_year'
        },
        {
            text: 'Lenght',
            width: 80,
            dataIndex: 'length'
        },
        {
            text: 'Rating',
            width: 70,
            dataIndex: 'rating'
        }
    ],

    dockedItems: [
        {
            dock: 'bottom',
            xtype: 'pagingtoolbar', // #4
            store: 'film.Films',
            displayInfo: true,
            displayMsg: 'Displaying films {0} - {1} of {2}',
            emptyMsg: "No films to display"
        }
    ],

    plugins: [{ // #5
        ptype: 'rowexpander',
        rowBodyTpl : [
            '<p><b>Description:</b> {description}</p><br>',
            '<p><b>Special Features:</b> {special_features}</p><br>',
            '<p><b>Rental Duration:</b> {rental_duration}</p><br>',
            '<p><b>Rental Rate:</b> {rental_rate}</p><br>',
            '<p><b>Replacement Cost:</b> {replacement_cost}</p><br>'
        ]
    }]
});
```

As our application starts to grow, we notice that we use some of the configurations a lot in the same components. For example, for most of the Grid panels, we use a toolbar with the **Add**, **Edit**, and **Delete** buttons. As all Sakila tables have the Last Update column, this column is also common to all the Grid panels we use to list information from Sakila tables. For this reason, we can create a super-Grid panel (as we did specifically for the static data module). So for the Films grid panel, we will extend from the `SakilaGrid` (`#1`) that we will create next.

Next, we have the `requires RowExpander` (`#2`) because we will use it to display some extra information about the Film that would be too big to display on the columns.

The next important code is the `renderer` of the `language_id` column (`#3`). Again, we are using the `renderer` function to display a value from a store that is already loaded. We could use a HasOne association for this column; however, there are a few things we need to ask ourselves before we start coding: even though Ext JS has the association, is it worth using it in this scenario, since we already have a store with the values we need loaded? If we do use association, the JSON that will be loaded from the server will be bigger, and some of them can be duplicated for different models. In this case, all Films have the `language_id` as `1` which is English. So the same language model would be loaded 20 times (pageSize).

> If we consider we have a HasOne association between the Film and Language models of the `language_id` field. In this case, we could have a getter method named `getLanguage` generated because of the association. In this case, we still would need to use the `renderer` function as follows:
>
> ```
> dataIndex: 'language_id',
> renderer: function(value, metaData, record ){
>     return record.getLanguage().get('name');
> }
> ```

Next we have the Paging toolbar (`#4`). We need to specify the store, which is the same used by the Grid panel. `pageSize` is already declared inside the store, so we do not need to configure it again on the Paging toolbar.

Finally, we have the configuration for the `RowExpander` plugin (`#5`). We need to configure a template to display the extra information we want. In this case, we are displaying the `description` of the film and some other information that could not fit in the columns such as the `rental` information. Unfortunately, it is not possible to use the `RowExpander` plugin with associated models.

The Films grid panel is already created. Now we need to implement `SakilaGrid` that we mentioned earlier. Notice that the Films data grid does not have the toolbar with the **Add**, **Edit**, and **Delete** buttons nor the `Last Update` column. So the super-grid we are going to create will have these configurations.

As we are creating all the super-views inside the `app/view/sakila` folder, let's create another file named `SakilaGrid.js` with the following content:

```
Ext.define('Packt.view.sakila.SakilaGrid', {
    extend: 'Ext.grid.Panel',
    alias: 'widget.sakilagrid',

    requires: [
        'Packt.view.toolbar.AddEditDelete' // #1
    ],

    columnLines: true,
    viewConfig: {
        stripeRows: true
    },

    dockedItems: [
        {
            xtype: 'addeditdelete' // #2
        }
    ],

    initComponent: function() {
        var me = this;

        me.columns = Ext.Array.merge(me.columns, // #3
            [{
                xtype    : 'datecolumn',
                text     : 'Last Update',
                width    : 120,
                dataIndex: 'last_update',
                format: 'Y-m-j H:i:s',
                filter: true
            }]
        );

        me.callParent(arguments);
    }
});
```

There are two important points to note in the preceding code: the first one is the `AddEditDelete` toolbar (#1 and #2). If we want to, we can create a class only to declare the toolbar. This way, if this same toolbar needs to be used in another component, we can reuse it. Also, having the same toolbar, we are creating a pattern and it is easier to create the controller code later (to listen to the events fired by `Views`). Next, we have the declaration of the `Last Update` column (`#3`). We used the same approach on the last chapter when we implemented the static data module.

So far, we have not created the `AddEditDelete` toolbar. So let's create it. To do so, we are going to create a new folder inside `app/view` named `toolbar`. Inside this `toolbar` folder, we will create all the toolbars for the application:

```
Ext.define('Packt.view.toolbar.AddEditDelete', {
    extend: 'Ext.toolbar.Toolbar',
    alias: 'widget.addeditdelete',

    flex: 1,
    dock: 'top',
    items: [
        {
            xtype: 'button',
            text: 'Add',
            itemId: 'add',
            iconCls: 'add'
        },
        {
            xtype: 'button',
            text: 'Edit',
            itemId: 'edit',
            iconCls: 'edit'
        },
        {
            xtype: 'button',
            text: 'Delete',
            itemId: 'delete',
            iconCls: 'delete'
        }
    ]
});
```

This toolbar will be located at the top of the component `dockedItem` configuration. But if we need to change it, we simply need to declare the `dock` configuration along with the `xtype: 'addeditdelete'` configuration.

Notice that it is the same code we have used in previous classes. What we are doing is removing it from the class declaration and creating a new custom component to reuse within the application. If you want to, go ahead and refactor the previous classes that we have created. Do not forget to add the `required` declaration with the name of this class, otherwise the Ext JS dynamic loading engine will not know which class we want to instantiate (if it is not loaded in the memory already).

Handling paging on the server side

Since we are using the Paging toolbar, it is important to remember some concepts. Ext JS provides tools to help us to page the content, but let's emphasize on the word provide. Ext JS will not do the paging for us if we retrieve all the records from the database at once. If we take a look at the request Ext JS sends to the server, it sends 3 extra parameters when we use the Paging toolbar:

These parameters are `start`, `limit`, and `page`. For example, as we can see, when we load the Grid panel information for the first time, `start` is **0**, `limit` is the `pageSize` configuration we set on the store (in this case **20**), and `page` is **1**:

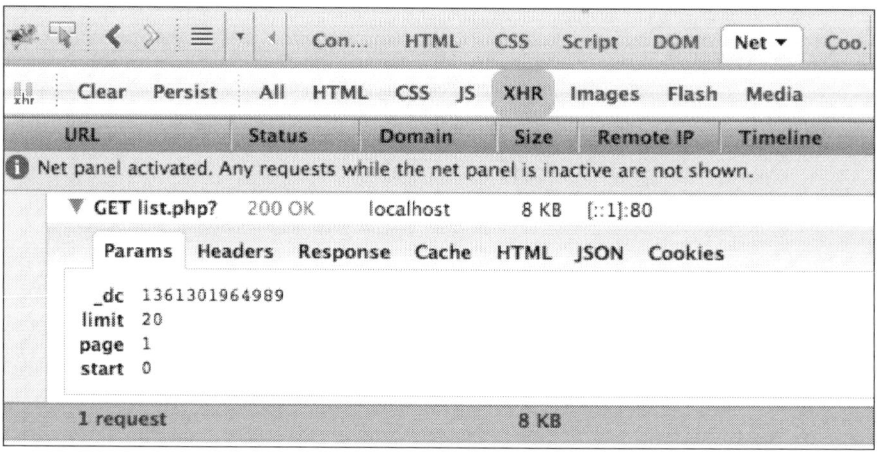

When we click on the next page of the Grid panel, `start` will be **20**, `limit` will have the same value (always, unless we change the `pageSize` dynamically), and `page` will be **2**:

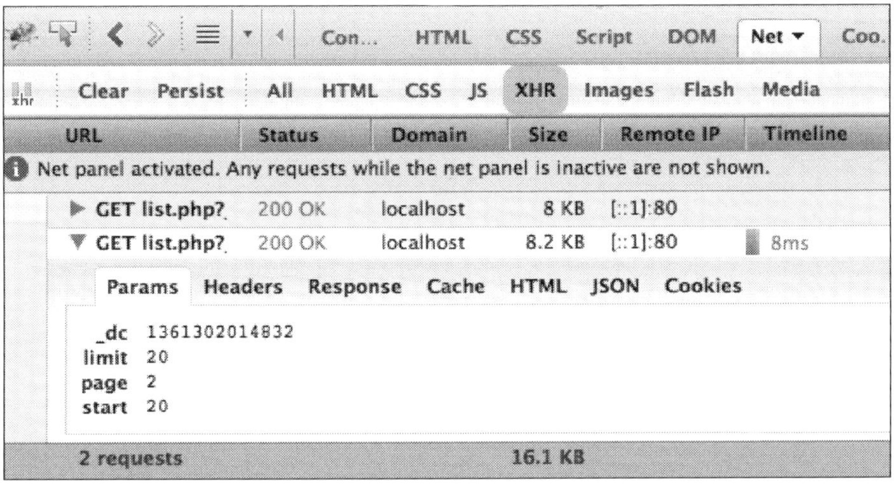

> There is a third-party plugin that can change the `pageSize` dynamically, according to the user's selection: `https://github.com/loiane/extjs4-ux-paging-toolbar-resizer`.

These parameters help us to page the information on the database as well. For example, for MySQL, we only need `start` and `limit`, so we need to get them from the request:

```
$start = $_REQUEST['start'];
$limit = $_REQUEST['limit'];
```

Then, after we execute the `SELECT` query, we need to add `LIMIT $start, $limit` at the end (after the `WHERE`, `ORDER BY`, and `GROUP BY` clauses—if any).

```
$sql = "SELECT * FROM Film LIMIT $start,  $limit";
```

This will provide the information we need from the database. Another very important detail is that the Paging toolbar displays the total number of records we have in the database:

```
$sql = "SELECT count(*) as num FROM Film";
```

So we also need to return a `total` property in the JSON with the count of the table:

```
echo json_encode(array(
  "success" => $mysqli->connect_errno == 0,
  "data" => $result,
  "total" => $total
));
```

Then Ext JS will receive all the information required to make the paging work as expected.

Paging queries on MySQL, Oracle, and Microsoft SQL Server

We need to be careful because if we use a different database, the query to page the information directly from the database is different.

If we were using an Oracle database, the `SELECT` query with paging would be:

```
SELECT * FROM
  (select rownum as rn, f.* from
    (select * from Film order by film_id) as f
  ) WHERE rn > $start  and rn <= ($start + $limit)
```

This is much more complicated than MySQL. Now let's see the query for Microsoft SQL Server (prior to SQL Server 2012):

```
SELECT  *
FROM ( SELECT ROW_NUMBER() OVER ( ORDER BY film_id ) AS RowNum, *
          FROM Films
        ) AS RowConstrainedResult
WHERE   RowNum > $start
    AND RowNum <= ($start + $limit)
ORDER BY RowNum
```

It is simpler in SQL Server 2012:

```
SELECT * FROM Film
ORDER BY film_id
OFFSET $start ROWS
FETCH NEXT $limit ROWS ONLY
```

In Firebird, it is even simpler than MySQL:

```
SELECT FIRST $limit SKIP $start * FROM Film
```

So be careful with the SQL syntax if you are using a different database from MySQL.

Creating the controller

So far we have the Film grid panel. Following our pattern, we need a controller. So we will create a controller named `Packt.controller.film.Films`:

```
Ext.define('Packt.controller.cms.Films', {
    extend: 'Ext.app.Controller',

    requires: [  // #1
        'Packt.util.MD5',
        'Packt.util.Alert',
        'Packt.view.MyViewport',
        'Packt.util.Util'
    ],

    views: [
        'film.Films'
    ],

    stores: [
        'film.Films'
    ],

    init: function(application) {
        this.control({
            "filmsgrid": {
                render: this.render // #2
            }
        });
    },

    render: function(component, options) {
        component.getStore().load();     // #3
    }
});
```

So this is our basic controller that already listens to the `render` event (`#2`) from the Film grid panel. And when the Film grid panel renders, we ask Ext JS to `load` its store (`#3`). As usual, we require Ext JS to load the `Util` classes we created for this application (`#1`).

Editing in the Film grid panel

Now that the Film grid panel is already being rendered and loaded, we can implement the create and edit functionalities.

As we could see in the screenshots at the beginning of this chapter, the Edit window has three tabs: one for editing the Film details, one to edit the categories related to the Film, and another one to edit the actors related to the Film. For now, we are going to work with the Film details only.

So inside the `app/view/film` folder we are going to create a new view named `Packt.view.film.FilmWindow`. This class will be a window that has a form with a Tab panel as an item. Inside one of the tabs, we will place the fields to edit the Film details:

```
Ext.define('Packt.view.film.FilmWindow', {
    extend: 'Packt.view.sakila.WindowForm', // #1
    alias: 'widget.filmwindow',

    requires: [
        'Packt.util.Util' // #2
    ],

    width: 537,
    title: 'Edit Film',
    iconCls: 'film_add',

    items: [
        {
            xtype: 'form',
            autoScroll: true,
            layout: {
                type: 'fit'
            },
            items: [
                {
                    xtype: 'tabpanel',
                    activeTab: 0,
                    items: [
                        {
                            xtype: 'panel',
                            autoScroll: true,
                            bodyPadding: 10,
                            layout: {
                                type: 'anchor'
```

```
                        },
                        title: 'Film Information',
                        defaults: {
                            anchor: '100%',
                            msgTarget: 'side'
                        },
                        items: [ // #3
                            //Film detail fields
                        ]
                    },
                    //Tab Film Categories
                    //Tab Film Actors
                ]
            }
        ]
    }
  ]
});
```

So we have the basic configurations already. One important detail: we are extending (`#1`) from `Packt.view.sakila.WindowForm`, which is a class that extends from window and has the **Save** and Cancel **buttons**. Again, let's try to create superclasses, so that we can reuse as many configurations as possible. We will implement this class in the next topic.

The `requires` for the `Util` class is to use the red asterisk (*) in all required fields (`#3`). Now, on the first item of the Tab panel (`#3`), we need to place the fields that represent each field of the Film table.

Let's go back to the Sakila documentation and take a look at the fields of the `Film` table (`http://dev.mysql.com/doc/sakila/en/sakila-structure-tables-film.html`):

- `film_id`: The primary key of the table that has a unique value. So for this field we can use a Hidden field to control this.
- `title`: The title of the film. So we can use a text field for it. As the maximum length of values on the database is 255, we also need to add validation.
- `description`: A short description or plot summary of the film. As the description can have a length of 5000 characters, we can use a Text area to represent it.
- `release_year`: The year in which the movie was released. This can be a numeric field, with minimum value of 1950 until the current year + 1 (let's say we want to add a film that is going to be released next year).

- `language_id`: A foreign key pointing at the language table; identifies the language of the film. This can be a combobox with the Language store (already populated when we load the application).
- `original_language_id`: A foreign key pointing at the language table that identifies the original language of the film. Used when a film has been dubbed into a new language. This can also be a combobox with the Language store (already populated when we load the application).
- `rental_duration`: The length of the rental period, in days. This can be a number field, with minimum value `1` and maximum value `10` (let's give a limit to the maximum value).
- `rental_rate`: The cost to rent the film for the period specified in the `rental_duration` column. This can also be a number field with minimum value as `0` and maximum value as `5`, and we need to allow decimal values we well.
- `length`: The duration of the film, in minutes. The `length` can also be a number field between `1` and `999`.
- `replacement_cost`: The amount charged to the customer if the film is not returned or is returned in a damaged state. Also a numeric field. Let's give a minimum value of 0 and maximum value of 100.
- `rating`: The rating assigned to the film. It can be one of the following: G, PG, PG-13, R, or NC-17. As this has fixed values, we can represent them on a radio button group or a combobox. We are going to use a combobox.
- `special_features`: Lists which common special features are included on the DVD. It can be zero or more, for example trailers, commentaries, deleted scenes, or behind the scenes. As this can be one or more, we can use either a checkbox or a combobox allowing multiselection. Let's go with checkboxes.

So let's declare the first three fields as `film_id`, `title`, and `release_year`:

```
{
    xtype: 'hiddenfield',
    name: 'film_id'
},
{
    xtype: 'textfield',
    name: 'title',
    fieldLabel: 'Title',
    afterLabelTextTpl: Packt.util.Util.required,
    allowBlank: false,
    maxLength: 255
},
```

```
{
    xtype: 'numberfield',
    name: 'release_year',
    fieldLabel: 'Release Year',
    maxValue: (new Date().getFullYear()) + 1,
    minValue: 1950,
    allowDecimals: false
}
```

So far nothing new. Then the language fields:

```
{
    xtype: 'combobox',
    name: 'language_id',
    fieldLabel: 'Language',
    displayField: 'name',
    valueField: 'language_id',
    queryMode: 'local',
    store: 'staticData.Languages',
    afterLabelTextTpl: Packt.util.Util.required,
    allowBlank: false
},
{
    xtype: 'combobox',
    name: 'original_language_id',
    fieldLabel: 'Original Language',
    displayField: 'name',
    valueField: 'language_id',
    queryMode: 'local',
    store: 'staticData.Languages'
}
```

Notice that we are using the same store for both fields; we want them to have the same values, meaning that if the user goes to the Language grid panel on static data and adds or changes a language, we want these changes to be applied to these stores at the same time, and that is why we are using the same store used by the static data module.

The numeric fields are `rental_duration`, `rental_rate`, `length`, and `replacement_cost`:

```
{
    xtype: 'numberfield',
    name: 'rental_duration',
    fieldLabel: 'Rental Duration',
    maxValue: 10,
```

```
        minValue: 1,
        allowDecimals: false,
        afterLabelTextTpl: Packt.util.Util.required,
        allowBlank: false
    },
    {
        xtype: 'numberfield',
        name: 'rental_rate',
        fieldLabel: 'Rental Rate',
        maxValue: 5,
        minValue: 0,
        step: 0.1,
        afterLabelTextTpl: Packt.util.Util.required,
        allowBlank: false
    },
    {
        xtype: 'numberfield',
        name: 'length',
        fieldLabel: 'Lenght (min)',
        maxValue: 999,
        minValue: 1
    },
    {
        xtype: 'numberfield',
        name: 'replacement_cost',
        fieldLabel: 'Replacement Cost',
        maxValue: 100,
        minValue: 0,
        step: 0.1,
        afterLabelTextTpl: Packt.util.Util.required
    }
```

It is very important to note that, whenever we have numeric fields and we want to load them from a model, we need the field from the model to be numeric as well (`int` or `float`), otherwise, the form will not load the values.

Then the `rating` combobox with its store will be as follows:

```
    {
        xtype: 'combobox',
        name: 'rating',
        fieldLabel: 'Rating',
        displayField: 'text',
        valueField: 'text',
        queryMode: 'local',
        store: 'film.Ratings'
    }
```

The values for the rating are fixed; this means we can create an `ArrayStore` with the values we have:

```
Ext.define('Packt.store.film.Ratings', {
    extend: 'Ext.data.ArrayStore',

    fields: [
        {name: 'text'},
    ],

    data : [ // ENUM('G','PG','PG-13','R','NC-17')
        ['G'],
        ['PG'],
        ['PG-13'],
        ['R'],
        ['NC-17']
    ],

    autoLoad: true
});
```

This is the simplest store we can create to populate a combobox.
The `special_features` CheckBox group is shown as follows:

```
{
    xtype: 'checkboxgroup',
    fieldLabel: 'Special Features',
    columns: 2,
    name: 'special_features',
    items: [
        {
            xtype: 'checkboxfield',
            boxLabel: 'Trailers',
            inputValue: 'Trailers',
            name: 'trailers'
        },
        {
            xtype: 'checkboxfield',
            boxLabel: 'Commentaries',
            inputValue: 'Commentaries',
            name: 'commentaries'
        },
        {
            xtype: 'checkboxfield',
            boxLabel: 'Deleted Scenes',
```

```
                inputValue: 'Deleted Scenes',
                name: 'deleted'
            },
            {
                xtype: 'checkboxfield',
                boxLabel: 'Behind the Scenes',
                inputValue: 'Behind the Scenes',
                name: 'behind'
            }
        ]
    }
```

The CheckBox group is the most complicated field to populate in a form. Each checkbox field behaves like an independent field; so it needs to have its name and its input value. We will learn how to populate it once we start working on the controller.

And finally, the description as a text area:

```
    {
        xtype: 'textareafield',
        name: 'description',
        fieldLabel: 'Description',
        maxLength: 5000
    }
```

Packt.view.sakila.WindowForm

The last piece of code we need to complete the **Edit Film** window is the `WindowForm` superclass. So far, all the window components that we have implemented use the Fit Layout and usually have a Form panel inside it. The window also has a **Cancel** and a **Save** button. As all these configurations are default for our components, we can create a super-window for them:

```
Ext.define('Packt.view.sakila.WindowForm', {
    extend: 'Ext.window.Window',
    alias: 'widget.windowform',

    requires: [
        'Packt.view.toolbar.CancelSave'
    ],

    height: 400,
    width: 550,
    autoScroll: true,
```

```
    layout: {
        type: 'fit'
    },
    modal: true,

    //items must be overridden in subclass

    dockedItems: [
        {
            xtype: 'cancelsave'
        }
    ]
});
And we can do the same thing for the Cancel Save Toolbar:
Ext.define('Packt.view.toolbar.CancelSave', {
    extend: 'Ext.toolbar.Toolbar',
    alias: 'widget.cancelsave',

    flex: 1,
    dock: 'bottom',
    ui: 'footer',
    layout: {
        pack: 'end',
        type: 'hbox'
    },
    items: [
        {
            xtype: 'button',
            text: 'Cancel',
            itemId: 'cancel',
            iconCls: 'cancel'
        },
        {
            xtype: 'button',
            text: 'Save',
            itemId: 'save',
            iconCls: 'save'
        }
    ]
});
```

Again, feel free to refactor the code we have implemented so far. This is what is nice about Ext JS and the MVC Architecture: it allows you to reuse code and you can refactor it as you can do in any other object-oriented language and you do not need to have headaches to get it done.

Film categories

Now that we have the film details part covered, we can handle the most complex part, which is the association with the `Category` and `Actor` tables. The `Category` and `Actor` tables have a many-to-many association with the `Film` table. Before we start coding an association we need to ask ourselves again: is it really necessary to have an association? Is it worth it? Is it going to overload the size of the data we are exchanging between the server and Ext JS?

Taking a look at the database we can see each film has only one category, even though there is a many-to-many relationship. Even though Ext JS has the association capability, we are not going to use it right now. This is because we want to load the associated information only when the user opens the Edit window to see the film information, meaning we will load the associated data on demand.

But in case you really want to do the association, how can we handle a many-to-many association in Ext JS? There is no native support for it. You can have a Has Many association between the `Film` and `Film_Category` table called `FilmCategory` and then the `FilmCategory` has a Has One association with the Category.

Store

As we want to display only the categories associated with a particular film, we can reuse the Category model, but we need a different store:

```
Ext.define('Packt.store.film.FilmCategories', {
    extend: 'Ext.data.Store',

    requires: [
        'Packt.model.staticData.Category',
        'Packt.proxy.Sakila'
    ],

    model: 'Packt.model.staticData.Category',

    proxy: {
        type: 'sakila',

        api: {
            create: 'php/inventory/film_category_create.php',
            read: 'php/inventory/film_category.php',
            update: 'php/inventory/film_category_update.php',
            destroy: 'php/inventory/film_category_destroy.php'
        }
    }
});
```

To perform the CRUD operations on the `Film_Category` table, we will use the store features to do it. But the one we are going to focus on first is the `read` action.

The idea is to pass the `film_id` we are interested in getting to the `Categories` table and then to the server. We will retrieve the information from the `Category` table that we are looking for using the following query:

```
SELECT c.category_id, c.name, f.last_update FROM category c
INNER JOIN film_category f ON f.category_id = c.category_id
WHERE f.film_id = $film_id
```

This way we do not need to use associations and we can get the information we are looking for with a single `SELECT`.

Edit view

The next step is to implement the Grid panel to display the film categories on the **Edit Film** window:

```
Ext.define('Packt.view.film.FilmCategories', {
    extend: 'Packt.view.sakila.SakilaGrid',
    alias: 'widget.filmcategories',

    requires: [
        'Packt.view.toolbar.SearchAddDelete'
    ],

    store: 'film.FilmCategories',

    columns: [
        {
            text: 'Category Id',
            width: 100,
            dataIndex: 'category_id'
        },
        {
            text: 'Category Name',
            flex: 1,
            dataIndex: 'name'
        }
    ],

    dockedItems: [
        {
            xtype: 'searchadddelete' // #1
        }
    ]
});
```

It is a simple Grid panel very similar to the ones we already create, but this one has the Search Add Delete toolbar (`#1`) instead of the Add Edit Delete toolbar. This is also an example showing that we can override any configuration from the superclass (`SakilaGrid`, which originally has the Add Edit Delete toolbar in its configuration). If we do not override any configuration, it will use the ones we have declared on the `SakilaGrid` class. As we are overriding the `dockedItem` configuration, it will use the one we are declaring on the child class.

The Search Add Delete toolbar

This toolbar component is new to us. We have never used it before. As the **Film Actors** screen will also use a **Search**, **Add**, and **Delete** button, let's create a specific component for it:

```
Ext.define('Packt.view.toolbar.SearchAddDelete', {
    extend: 'Ext.toolbar.Toolbar',
    alias: 'widget.searchadddelete',

    flex: 1,
    dock: 'top',
    items: [
        {
            xtype: 'button',
            text: 'Search and Add',
            itemId: 'add',
            iconCls: 'find'
        },
        {
            xtype: 'button',
            text: 'Delete',
            itemId: 'delete',
            iconCls: 'delete'
        }
    ]
});
```

It is a simple toolbar with two buttons on it, very similar to the other toolbars we have declared already as showed in the following screenshot:

Search categories – MultiSelect

When the user clicks on the **Search and Add** button, a new window will be displayed and it contains a MultiSelect component where the user can select one or more categories to add to the film categories:

```
Ext.define('Packt.view.film.SearchCategory', {
    extend: 'Packt.view.sakila.SearchWindow',
    alias: 'widget.searchcategory',

    requires: [
        'Ext.ux.form.MultiSelect'
    ],

    title: 'Add Category',

    items: [
        {
            xtype: 'form',
            itemId: 'filmForm',
            autoScroll: true,
            bodyPadding: 10,
            items: [
                {
                    xtype: 'label', // #1
                    text: 'Hold Ctrl or Command to select more than
one Category.'
                },
                {
                    anchor: '100%',
                    xtype: 'multiselect', // #2
                    msgTarget: 'side',
                    fieldLabel: 'Categories',
                    name: 'multiselect',
                    allowBlank: false,
                    store: 'staticData.Categories', // #3
                    valueField: 'category_id', // #4
                    displayField: 'name',      // #5
                    ddReorder: true            // #6
                }
            ]
        }
    ]
});
```

So we have a form and the Form panel has two items inside it: the first one (`#1`) is a label informing the user to hold down the *Ctrl* or *command* key to select more than one category, and the second one is a MultiSelect field. This field is not Ext JS native, although it comes inside the `ux` folder of the examples directory, so this is why we need to add the class declaration inside the `requires`.

The MultiSelect component is very similar to the combobox component. You also need to set a Store (`#3`), the `valueField` (`#4`), and the `displayField` (`#5`). The difference is in how the information is going to be displayed for the user. Instead of a drop-down list, it is a panel with multiple values.

To make it fun, we can allow drag-and-drop reorder, where the user can reorder the values using drag-and-drop (`#6`).

Packt.view.sakila.SearchWindow

As the `SearchCategory` class extends from `SearchWindow`, we also need to create this component. This is also a new component, since it is the first time we are using it. In case we need a **Search and Add** window again, we can extend from this class:

```
Ext.define('Packt.view.sakila.SearchWindow', {
    extend: 'Ext.window.Window',
    alias: 'widget.searchWindow',

    requires: [
        'Packt.view.toolbar.CancelClearAdd'
    ],

    height: 300,
    width: 400,
    autoScroll: true,
    layout: {
        type: 'fit'
    },
    iconCls: 'find',
    modal: true,

    //items must be overridden in subclass

    dockedItems: [
        {
            xtype: 'cancelclearadd'
        }
    ]
});
```

As we can see, it is very similar to the Edit window, the difference is that we use the Cancel, Clear, and Add buttons instead of the Cancel and Save toolbar.

The Cancel, Clear, and Add toolbar is also very simple (nothing different from what we have done so far):

```
Ext.define('Packt.view.toolbar.CancelClearAdd', {
    extend: 'Ext.toolbar.Toolbar',
    alias: 'widget.cancelclearadd',

    flex: 1,
    dock: 'bottom',
    ui: 'footer',
    layout: {
        pack: 'end',
        type: 'hbox'
    },
    items: [
        {
            xtype: 'button',
            text: 'Cancel',
            itemId: 'cancel',
            iconCls: 'cancel'
        },
        {
            xtype: 'button',
            text: 'Clear',
            itemId: 'clear',
            iconCls: 'clear'
        },
        {
            xtype: 'button',
            text: 'Add Selected',
            itemId: 'save',
            iconCls: 'save'
        }
    ]
});
```

We will handle all the events fired by these buttons on the controller, later.

Film actors

The actor's relationship with the film is similar to the relationship between the `Category` and `Film` tables, meaning it is also a many-to-many relationship. We will handle the `Actor` table's many-to-many relationship with the `Film` table the same way we handled Film Categories.

Store

Again, we can reuse the `Actor` model, we simply need to create a new store to handle the information about this relationship:

```
Ext.define('Packt.store.film.FilmActors', {
    extend: 'Ext.data.Store',

    requires: [
        'Packt.model.staticData.Actor',
        'Packt.proxy.Sakila'
    ],

    model: 'Packt.model.staticData.Actor',

    proxy: {
        type: 'sakila',

        api: {
            create: 'php/inventory/film_actor_create.php',
            read: 'php/inventory/film_actor.php',
            update: 'php/inventory/film_actor_create.php',
            destroy: 'php/inventory/film_actor_delete.php'
        }
    }
});
```

On the server side, we will do the same as with the `Film_Category` table: we will send the `film_id` to the server and will retrieve only the information we are interested in getting from the `Actors` table:

```
SELECT c.actor_id, c.first_name, c.last_name, f.last_update
FROM actor c
INNER JOIN film_actor f ON f.actor_id = c.actor_id
WHERE f.film_id = $film_id
```

The `Film_Actor` table will be modified or populated with new records when we save the editing of a film.

Edit view

Similar to what we did to the `Film_Category` table, we also need a Grid panel to display the film actors. Again, we are going to extend the `SakilaGrid` class and display the columns for the actor, which are `Actor Id`, `First Name`, and `Last Name` (`Last Update` will be displayed because of the `SakilaGrid` class):

```
Ext.define('Packt.view.film.FilmActors', {
    extend: 'Packt.view.sakila.SakilaGrid',
    alias: 'widget.filmactors',

    requires: [
        'Packt.view.toolbar.SearchAddDelete'
    ],

    store: 'film.FilmActors',

    columns: [
        {
            text: 'Actor Id',
            width: 100,
            dataIndex: 'actor_id'
        },
        {
            text: 'First Name',
            flex: 1,
            dataIndex: 'first_name'
        },
        {
            text: 'Last Name',
            width: 200,
            dataIndex: 'last_name'
        }
    ],

    dockedItems: [
        {
            xtype: 'searchadddelete'
        }
    ]
});
```

This Grid panel will also have the **Search and Add** and **Delete** buttons.

Searching for actors – live search combobox

The idea of the **live search combobox** is to display the Search screen and a combobox field for the user, where the user can enter a few characters and then the system will do a live search displaying the actor that matches the search made by the user and also the films this actor has already made. All the actors that match the search will be displayed as items of the combobox and the combobox will also have paging. When the user selects the actor, we will display its last name and first name. It is a very nice component, a bit more complex than the other, and we will apply some advanced configurations to the combobox.

Model

First, we need a model to represent the information we want to retrieve from the server. We will retrieve the actor's information plus the films the actor has already made. So we can create a model extending the `Actor` model and in the `SearchActor` model we only need to declare the missing field:

```
Ext.define('Packt.model.film.SearchActor', {
    extend: 'Packt.model.staticData.Actor',

    fields: [
        { name: 'film_info' }
    ]
});
```

Store

Next we need a Store to load the `SearchActor` model collection:

```
Ext.define('Packt.store.film.SearchActors', {
    extend: 'Ext.data.Store',

    requires: [
        'Packt.model.film.SearchActor'
    ],

    model: 'Packt.model.film.SearchActor',

    pageSize: 2,

    proxy: {
        type: 'ajax',
        url: 'php/inventory/searchActors.php',
```

```
            reader: {
                type: 'json',
                root: 'data'
            }
        }
    });
```

On the server, we will use the `actor_info` view to retrieve the information. However, the combobox also passes three extra parameters—`start` and `limit` for the paging and a parameter named `query` with the text the user entered to do the live search.

So our `SELECT` query will be something like the following:

```
$start = $_REQUEST['start'];
$limit = $_REQUEST['limit'];
$query = $_REQUEST['query'];

//select the information
$sql = "SELECT * FROM actor_info ";
$sql .= "WHERE first_name LIKE '%" . $query . "%' OR ";
$sql .= "last_name LIKE '%" . $query . "%' ";
$sql .= "LIMIT $start,  $limit";
```

As we are working with paging, we must not forget to `COUNT` how many records we have that match the search and return the result inside the `total` attribute of the JSON:

```
$sql = "SELECT count(*) as num FROM actor_info ";
$sql .= "WHERE first_name LIKE '%" . $query . "%' OR ";
$sql .= "last_name LIKE '%" . $query . "%' ";
```

Now, we are able to retrieve the information according to the search text entered by the user.

Live search combobox

Our next step now is to implement the view that is going to provide the tools for searching. So we are going to create a class that extends from `SearchWindow` and inside this class we will have a combobox that will provide all the features to do the live search.

```
Ext.define('Packt.view.film.SearchActor', {
    extend: 'Packt.view.sakila.SearchWindow',
    alias: 'widget.searchactor',
```

```
        width: 600,
        bodyPadding: 10,
        layout: {
            type: 'anchor'
        },
        title: 'Search and Add Actor',

        items: [
            {
                //combobox // #1
            }, {
                xtype: 'component',
                style: 'margin-top:10px',
                html: 'Live search requires a minimum of 2 characters.'
            }
        ]
    });
```

At the bottom, there is just a comment for the user to know that it is required to enter at least two characters so the live search can work as shown in the following screenshot:

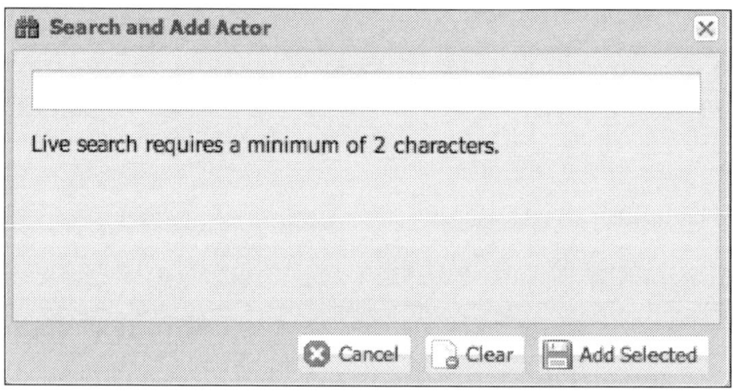

Now, let's see the code for the combobox that goes in the place of #1 in the previous code:

```
xtype: 'combo',
store: 'film.SearchActors', // #1
displayField: 'first_name', // #2
valueField: 'actor_id',     // #3
typeAhead: false,
hideLabel: true,
hideTrigger:true,   // #4
```

```
    anchor: '100%',
    minChars: 2,        // #5
    pageSize: 2,        // #6

    displayTpl: new Ext.XTemplate(        // #7
        '<tpl for=".">' +
            '{[typeof values === "string" ? values : values["last_
name"]]}, ' +
            '{[typeof values === "string" ? values : values["first_
name"]]}' +
        '</tpl>'
    ),

    listConfig: {         // #8
        loadingText: 'Searching...',
        emptyText: 'No matching posts found.',

        // Custom rendering template for each item
        getInnerTpl: function() {         // #9
            return '<h3><span>{last_name}, {first_name}</span></h3></br>'
+
                '{film_info}';
        }
    }
```

As always, we need a Store (#1) to populate the combobox and we have already declared it. Then we need a `displayField` (#2). The `displayField` will only show the `first_name` of the actor when an actor is selected from the live search. However, we want to display the `last_name` and the `first_name`. So to be able to do it, we need to overwrite the `displayTpl` template (#7) so we can have it as we want to. This is the result we will get:

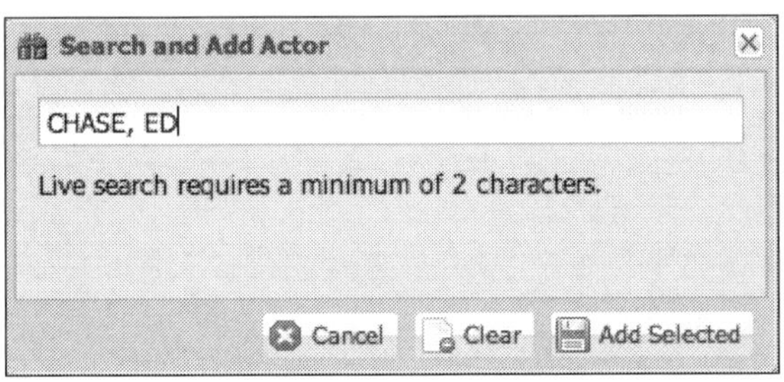

Next, we have the `valueField` (#3), which is the `id` of the selected actor; we are going to hide the down arrow, called `trigger` (#4); to make the live search work, the user needs to enter at least two characters (#5) and the combobox will display only two actors per page.

Then we have the `listConfig` (#8), where we can configure the loading text and the empty text and also, the template to display the actor's information. Basically, we are displaying `last_name, first_name` on the top and bolded, and on the next line we are displaying all the films already made by this actor.

The films controller

In the previous chapters, we have gone through some examples of how to save data. We used Form `submit`, Ajax `request`, and also the writing resource from the store. In this chapter, let's focus on the functionalities we have not implemented yet. But don't worry, the complete implementation is available in the source code distributed with this book.

Loading the existing film information within the Edit form

We have loaded a Form panel using the `loadRecord` method. Let's try a different approach now. Let's try using the `setValues` method. This is also useful because we have a `CheckBox` group, and it can be a little tricky to load their values on the Form panel. So when the user selects a record from the Film grid panel and clicks on the **Edit** button, we will open the Edit window and load its values. For this reason, we need to listen to the click event of the **Edit** button and implement a method that receives the `button` as parameter:

```
var grid = button.up('filmsgrid'),
record = grid.getSelectionModel().getSelection();

if(record[0]){ // #1

    var editWindow = Ext.create('Packt.view.film.FilmWindow');

    var form = editWindow.down('form');

    var values = { // #2
        film_id: record[0].get('film_id'),
        title: record[0].get('title'),
        description: record[0].get('description'),
        release_year: record[0].get('release_year'),
        language_id: record[0].get('language_id'),
        original_language_id: record[0].get('original_language_id'),
        rental_duration: record[0].get('rental_duration'),
        rental_rate: record[0].get('rental_rate'),
```

```
            length: record[0].get('length'),
            replacement_cost: record[0].get('replacement_cost'),
            rating: record[0].get('rating')
        };

        Ext.each(record[0].get('special_features').split(','),
    function(feat){ // #3
            if (feat === 'Trailers') {
                values.trailers = 'Trailers';
            } else if (feat === 'Commentaries') {
                values.commentaries = 'Commentaries';
            } else if (feat === 'Deleted Scenes') {
                values.deleted = 'Deleted Scenes';
            } else if (feat === 'Behind the Scenes') {
                values.behind = 'Behind the Scenes';
            }
        });

        var filmCategories = editWindow.down('form filmcategories');
        filmCategories.getStore().load({   // #4
            params: {
                filmId: record[0].get('film_id')
            }
        });

        var filmActors = editWindow.down('form filmactors');
        filmActors.getStore().load({       // #5
            params: {
                filmId: record[0].get('film_id')
            }
        });

        form.getForm().setValues(values); // #6

        editWindow.setTitle(record[0].get('title'));
        editWindow.setIconCls('film_edit'); // #7
        editWindow.show();
    }
```

First, if a `record` was selected from the grid panel (`#1`), we will create the Edit window, get the reference for the Form panel, and extract the values from the `record` (`#2`). This is where, if the field was not set with the correct type in the model, we need to do the conversion (numeric fields only accept numbers, not strings).

But there is one field missing: the Special Features are stored in the database separated by a comma (`,`) and we need to get each value (`#3`). Each checkbox is like an independent field, so we need to set the input value in each one we would like to have checked.

Next, we will get the `film_id` and ask for the `FilmCategories` (`#4`) and `FilmActors` (`#5`) stores to be loaded, but retrieve only the information associated with the desired film.

When everything is ready, we call the `setValues` method passing the JSON object we created with all the form values we want to set.

Then, we can set the `Title` and `Icon` of the window (`#7`) dynamically and finally display the window to the user.

Getting the MultiSelect values

Once the user has selected the categories desired to be associated with the selected film, the user will click on the **Save** button. When this happens, we need to handle the click event of this button. Here is what will happen:

```
var searchWindow = button.up('searchcategory');
var values = searchWindow.down('multiselect').getValue();
var store = Ext.getStore('categories');
var filmCategoriesStore = this.getFilmCategories().getStore();

Ext.each(values, function(value){

   var model = store.findRecord('category_id', value);

      if (model){
            model.set('last_update', new Date());
            filmCategoriesStore.add(model);
      }
});

searchWindow.close();
```

First, we get the reference for the `SearchWindow`, and then we can locate the `multiselect` field and get its values. We will then get the reference for the categories store, since the `multiselect` field is only going to send back the `id` of the selected values. And finally, we need the reference for the `FilmCategories` store as well, to add the selected values.

Then, for each value, we will search in the categories store and if the model is found, we will add it to the FilmCategories store and it will be displayed in the FilmCategories grid panel.

But, to make it work, we need the this.getFilmCategories method to work. Creating a reference for the filmCategories grid panel does the trick:

```
{
        ref: 'filmCategories',
        selector: 'filmcategories'
}
```

Getting the selected actor from live search

To get the details of the actor selected in live search we will use the same approach as we did for film categories. As we are using different components, the implementation is a bit different:

```
var searchWindow = button.up('searchactor');
var value = searchWindow.down('combo').getValue();
var store = Ext.getStore('actors');
var model = store.findRecord('actor_id', value);

if (model){
        model.set('last_update', new Date());
        this.getFilmActors().getStore().add(model);
}

searchWindow.close();
```

First, we get the reference for the SearchWindow, and then we can locate the combobox field and get its selected value. Then, we will get the reference for the Actors store, since the combobox field is only going to send back the id of the selected value. And finally, we need the reference for the FilmActors store as well to add the selected value.

Then, we will search in the Actors store and if the model was found, we will add it to the FilmActors store and it will be displayed in the FilmActors grid panel.

But, to make it work, we need the this.getFilmActors method to work. Creating a reference for the filmCategories grid panel does the trick:

```
{
        ref: ' filmActors',
        selector: ' filmactors'
}
```

Summary

In this chapter, we learned how to implement a more complex screen to manage the inventory information from the database. We have also learned how to handle a many-to-many association in two different ways.

We learned how to use the MultiSelect component and also how to use the Form and combobox component to do a live search.

In the next chapter, we will learn how to add some extra capabilities that are not native to the Ext JS API to the screens we have already developed so far, such as printing, exporting to Excel, and exporting to PDF the contents of a grid panel. We will also learn how to implement charts, and export them to image and PDF.

8

Adding Extra Capabilities

We are on the final stage of our application and Ext JS provides great capabilities, but there are some capabilities that we need to code ourselves with the help of other technologies. Although, having a Grid panel with paging, sorting, and filter capabilities, sometimes the user is going to expect more from the application. Adding features such as printing, export to Excel, export charts to images, and PDF can add a great value to the application and please the final user.

So in this chapter, we will cover:

- Printing records of a Grid panel
- Exporting Grid panel information to PDF and Excel
- Creating charts
- Exporting charts to PDF and images
- Using third-party plugins

Exporting the Grid panel to PDF and Excel

The first capability we are going to implement is to export the contents of a Grid panel to PDF and Excel. We will implement these features for the **Films** Grid panel we implemented in the last chapter. However, the logic is the same for any Grid panel you may have in an Ext JS application.

The first thing we are going to do is to add the export buttons to the Grid panel's toolbar. We will add three buttons: one to **Print** the contents of the Grid panel (we will develop this feature later, but let's add this button right now), one button to **Export to PDF** and one button to **Export to Excel**:

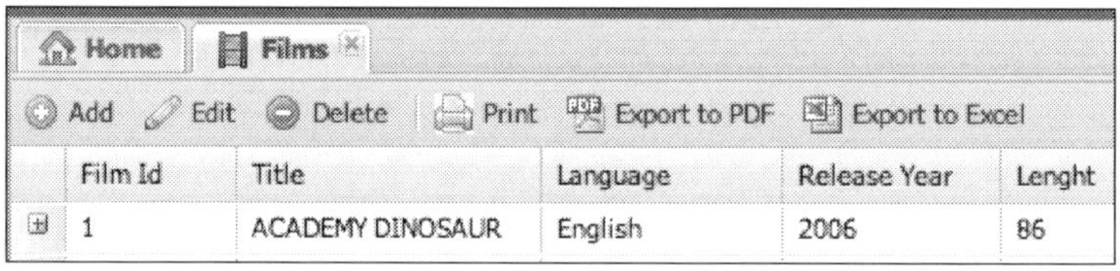

Remember that in the last chapter we created a toolbar named `AddEditDelete` that we used for the Grid panels? We are going to add these three buttons on this toolbar:

```
Ext.define('Packt.view.toolbar.AddEditDelete', {
    extend: 'Ext.toolbar.Toolbar',
    alias: 'widget.addeditdelete',

    items: [
        // Add Edit and Delete Buttons
        {
            xtype: 'tbseparator'
        },
        {
            xtype: 'button',
            text: 'Print',
            itemId: 'print',
            iconCls: 'print'
        },
        {
            xtype: 'button',
            text: 'Export to PDF',
            itemId: 'pdf',
            iconCls: 'pdf'
        },
        {
            xtype: 'button',
            text: 'Export to Excel',
            itemId: 'excel',
            iconCls: 'excel'
        }
    ]
});
```

We cannot forget to give `itemId` for each button so we can listen to the specific `button` event on the controller later. If you did refactor the code and added this toolbar to every Grid panel, you cannot forget to add these capabilities for each Grid panel.

Also, we are adding three more buttons to this toolbar. This could also be a chance for us to refactor the code and change the name of the class and the alias as well. And of course, if we do it, we cannot forget to change all the places on the code that we are using as a reference to the `AddEditDelete` class.

Exporting to PDF

Now that the button is being displayed on the **Films** Grid panel, it is time to go back to the Films Controller and add these capabilities.

The first button we are going to listen to is the **Export to PDF** click event. When the user clicks on the **Export to PDF** button, the following method is executed:

```
onButtonClickPDF: function(button, e, options) {
    var mainPanel = Ext.ComponentQuery.query('mainpanel')[0];//#1

    newTab = mainPanel.add({ // #2
        xtype: 'panel',
        closable: true,
        iconCls: 'pdf',
        title: 'Films PDF',
        layout: 'fit',
        items: [{
            xtype: 'uxiframe', // #3
            src: 'php/pdf/exportFilmsPdf.php' // #4
        }]
    });

    mainPanel.setActiveTab(newTab);
}
```

What we want to implement is that when the user clicks on the **Export to PDF** button, a new tab will be opened with the PDF file in it. This means that we need to get the main panel we declared as the center item of the viewport of the application (`#1`) and add a new tab to it (`#2`); as the PDF file will be inside it, we can implement it as an iFrame. To implement an iFrame in Ext JS, we can use the `IFrame` plugin that is distributed with the SDK and it is inside the `examples/ux` folder (`#3`). As we already have `Ext.ux` mapped in the loader configuration on `app.js`, we simply need to require the plugin in the `requires` declaration, this way, when we load the controller, the plugin will be loaded and when Ext JS tries to instantiate using its `xtype` (`#3`), the plugin will be already loaded:

```
requires: [
    //other requires here
    'Ext.ux.IFrame'
]
```

Now comes the most important part: Ext JS does not provide the Export to PDF capability natively. If we want the application to have it, we need to implement it using a different technology. In this case, the PDF will be generated on the server side (`#4`) and we will only display its output inside the iFrame.

When we execute the preceding code, we will get the following output:

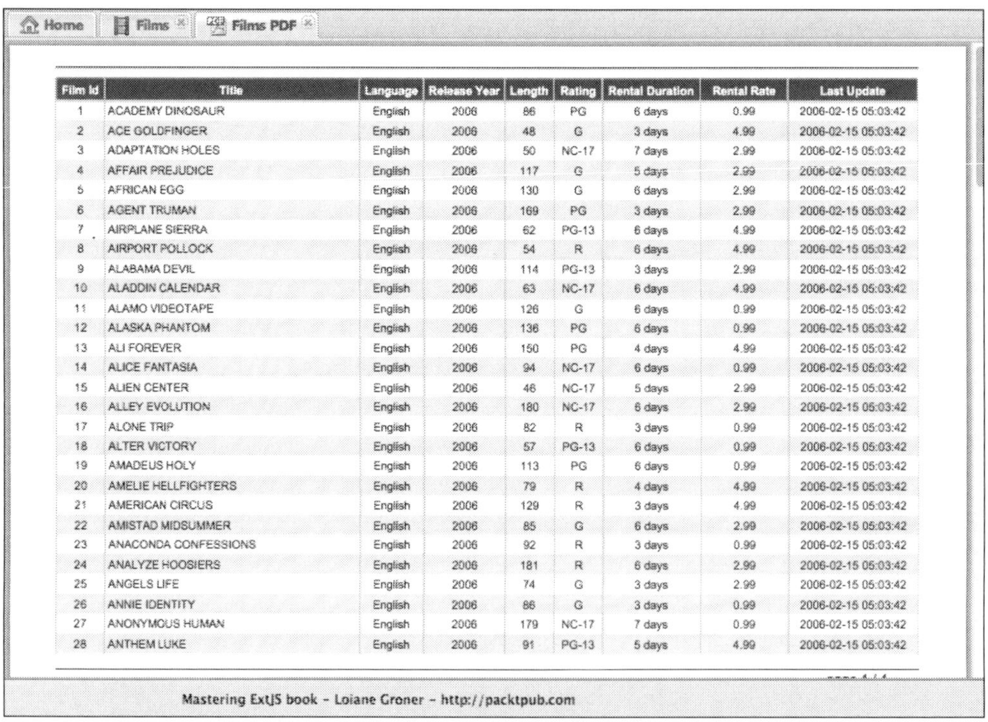

Film Id	Title	Language	Release Year	Length	Rating	Rental Duration	Rental Rate	Last Update
1	ACADEMY DINOSAUR	English	2006	86	PG	6 days	0.99	2006-02-15 05:03:42
2	ACE GOLDFINGER	English	2006	48	G	3 days	4.99	2006-02-15 05:03:42
3	ADAPTATION HOLES	English	2006	50	NC-17	7 days	2.99	2006-02-15 05:03:42
4	AFFAIR PREJUDICE	English	2006	117	G	5 days	2.99	2006-02-15 05:03:42
5	AFRICAN EGG	English	2006	130	G	6 days	2.99	2006-02-15 05:03:42
6	AGENT TRUMAN	English	2006	169	PG	3 days	2.99	2006-02-15 05:03:42
7	AIRPLANE SIERRA	English	2006	62	PG-13	6 days	4.99	2006-02-15 05:03:42
8	AIRPORT POLLOCK	English	2006	54	R	6 days	4.99	2006-02-15 05:03:42
9	ALABAMA DEVIL	English	2006	114	PG-13	3 days	2.99	2006-02-15 05:03:42
10	ALADDIN CALENDAR	English	2006	63	NC-17	6 days	4.99	2006-02-15 05:03:42
11	ALAMO VIDEOTAPE	English	2006	126	G	6 days	0.99	2006-02-15 05:03:42
12	ALASKA PHANTOM	English	2006	136	PG	6 days	0.99	2006-02-15 05:03:42
13	ALI FOREVER	English	2006	150	PG	4 days	4.99	2006-02-15 05:03:42
14	ALICE FANTASIA	English	2006	94	NC-17	6 days	0.99	2006-02-15 05:03:42
15	ALIEN CENTER	English	2006	46	NC-17	5 days	2.99	2006-02-15 05:03:42
16	ALLEY EVOLUTION	English	2006	180	NC-17	6 days	2.99	2006-02-15 05:03:42
17	ALONE TRIP	English	2006	82	R	3 days	0.99	2006-02-15 05:03:42
18	ALTER VICTORY	English	2006	57	PG-13	6 days	0.99	2006-02-15 05:03:42
19	AMADEUS HOLY	English	2006	113	PG	6 days	0.99	2006-02-15 05:03:42
20	AMELIE HELLFIGHTERS	English	2006	79	R	4 days	4.99	2006-02-15 05:03:42
21	AMERICAN CIRCUS	English	2006	129	R	3 days	4.99	2006-02-15 05:03:42
22	AMISTAD MIDSUMMER	English	2006	85	G	6 days	2.99	2006-02-15 05:03:42
23	ANACONDA CONFESSIONS	English	2006	92	R	3 days	0.99	2006-02-15 05:03:42
24	ANALYZE HOOSIERS	English	2006	181	R	6 days	2.99	2006-02-15 05:03:42
25	ANGELS LIFE	English	2006	74	G	3 days	2.99	2006-02-15 05:03:42
26	ANNIE IDENTITY	English	2006	86	G	3 days	0.99	2006-02-15 05:03:42
27	ANONYMOUS HUMAN	English	2006	179	NC-17	7 days	0.99	2006-02-15 05:03:42
28	ANTHEM LUKE	English	2006	91	PG-13	5 days	4.99	2006-02-15 05:03:42

Generating the PDF file on the server (PHP)

As we need to generate the file on the server side, we can use any framework and library that is available for the language we are using on the server. We can use TCPDF (`http://www.tcpdf.org/`) to generate PDF files in PHP. There are other libraries as well, and you can use the one you are most familiar with.

> In case, you are using Java, you can use iText (`http://itextpdf.com/`) and if you are using .NET, you can use iTextSharp (`http://itextpdf.com/`).

Exporting to Excel

To export the Grid panel to an Excel we will also use a server-side technology to help us. We will use PHPExcel (`http://phpexcel.codeplex.com/`).

On the Ext JS side, the only thing we need to do is to call the URL that will generate the Excel file as follows:

```
onButtonClickExcel: function(button, e, options) {
    window.open('php/pdf/exportFilmsExcel.php');
}
```

> If you are using Java, you can use the Apache POI library (`http://poi.apache.org/`) and if you are using .NET, you can use ExcelLibrary (`https://code.google.com/p/excellibrary/`).

In case, you want to export the Grid panel of any other content from an Ext JS component to Excel, PDF, Text, and Word document, you can use the same approach.

Printing Grid panel content with the Grid printer plugin

The next functionality we will implement is to print the contents of the Grid panel. When the user clicks on the **Print** button, the application will open a new browser window and display the contents of the Grid on this new window.

To do this, we will use a plugin named `Ext.ux.grid.Printer`, which receives the Grid panel reference to be printed, get the information that is in the store and generate HTML from this content and display on a new window.

> The Grid printer plugin is a third-party plugin available at `https://github.com/loiane/extjs4-ux-gridprinter`. This plugin will only print the information that is available on the Grid panel's store, meaning if you are using the paging toolbar, the plugin will only generate the HTML of the current page. The plugin also supports the Row Expander plugin. Please feel free to contribute to this plugin (or any other Ext JS plugin) and in this way we can help growing the Ext JS community.

After installing the plugin (get the contents of the `ux` folder and paste it inside the `masteringextjs/extjs/ux` folder) we simply need to add it in the `requires` declaration of the Films Controller:

```
requires: [
    // other requires here
    'Ext.ux.grid.Printer'
]
```

When the user clicks on the **Print** button, the controller will execute the following method:

```
onButtonClickPrint: function(button, e, options) {
    Ext.ux.grid.Printer.printAutomatically = false;
    Ext.ux.grid.Printer.print(button.up('filmsgrid'));
}
```

The `printAutomatically` property means if you want the print window to be displayed automatically. If set to `false`, the plugin will display the print window, and then, if the user wants to print it, they need to go to the browser's menu and select **Print** (*Ctrl* + *P*).

To make the plugin work, we need to pass the Grid panel reference to the `print` method. In this case, we can use the `button.up` method to get the Films Grid panel reference.

When we execute the code, we will get the following output:

Print Close

Film Id	Title	Language	Release Year	Lenght	Rating	Last Update
1	ACADEMY DINOSAUR	English	2006	86	PG	02/15/2006
Description: A Epic Drama of a Feminist And a Mad Scientist who must Battle a Teacher in The Canadian Rockies **Special Features:** Deleted Scenes,Behind the Scenes **Rental Duration:** 6 **Rental Rate:** 0.99 **Replacement Cost:** 20.99						
2	ACE GOLDFINGER	English	2006	48	G	02/15/2006
Description: A Astounding Epistle of a Database Administrator And a Explorer who must Find a Car in Ancient China **Special Features:** Trailers,Deleted Scenes **Rental Duration:** 3 **Rental Rate:** 4.99 **Replacement Cost:** 12.99						
3	ADAPTATION HOLES	English	2006	50	NC-17	02/15/2006
Description: A Astounding Reflection of a Lumberjack And a Car who must Sink a Lumberjack in A Baloon Factory **Special Features:** Trailers,Deleted Scenes **Rental Duration:** 7 **Rental Rate:** 2.99 **Replacement Cost:** 18.99						
4	AFFAIR PREJUDICE	English	2006	117	G	02/15/2006

Creating the Sales by Film Category chart

Ext JS provides a great set of visual charts we can implement, and the users love things like this. For this reason, we will implement a chart using three different series (Pie, Column, and Bar) where the user can see the **Sales by Film Category**.

Following is a screenshot of the final result we will have at the end of this topic. As we can see on the following screenshot, we have the chart. Above it we have a toolbar with two buttons: **Change Chart Type**, where the user will be able to change the chart series from Pie to Column or Bar, and **Download Chart**, where the user will be able to download the chart in the following formats: image, SVG, or PDF.

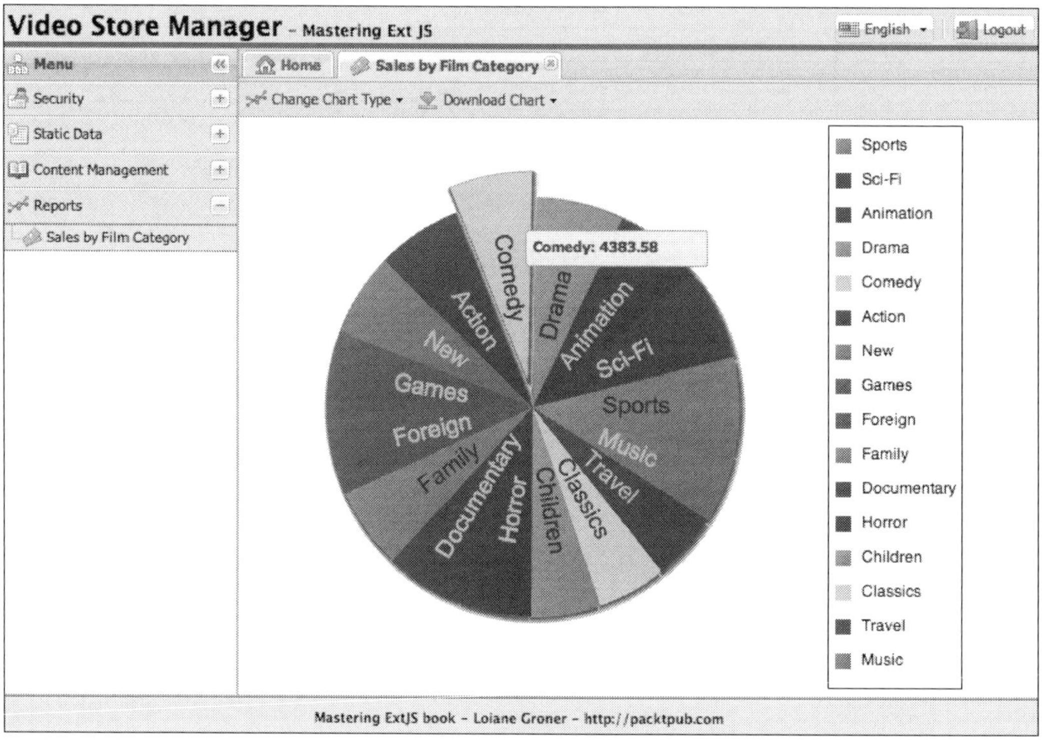

The following parts compose a chart: `store`, which is going to provide the data; the `series`, which represents the type of chart we want to create (Pie, Bar, Column, and so on) and the `axis` (if it is a cartesian chart which contains the X and Y axes).

So, no matter if we want to create a Pie or Column or Bar chart, we need a store to provide the information we want to display on the chart. So for this reason, we need to create a new store and we will call it `SalesFilmCategory` store:

```
Ext.define('Packt.store.reports.SalesFilmCategory', {
    extend: 'Ext.data.Store',

    requires: [
        'Packt.proxy.Sakila'
    ],
```

```
        fields: [ // #1
            {name: 'category'},
            {name: 'total_sales'}
        ],

        autoLoad: true,

        proxy: {
            type: 'sakila', // #2
            url: 'php/reports/salesFilmCategory.php'
        }
    });
```

For this store, we will not declare a model; we are going to declare its `fields` (#1) directly on it. As this store is going to be used exclusively by the chart, there is no need to create a specific model for it, as we do not intend to reuse it later.

We can reuse the Sakila Proxy (#2), since we still need to return the same data structure from the server (the collection of information wrapped in the `data` attribute).

On the server side, we can query the data that will feed the chart from the `sales_by_ film_category` view from the `Sakila` database as follows:

```
SELECT * FROM sales_by_film_category
```

Pie chart

Now that we are able to retrieve the information we need, let's work on the implementation of the chart. First, we will develop the Pie chart:

```
Ext.define('Packt.view.reports.SalesFilmCategoryPie', {
    extend: 'Ext.chart.Chart',
    alias: 'widget.salesfilmcategorypie',

    animate: true,
    store: 'reports.SalesFilmCategory', // #1
    shadow: true,
    legend: {
        position: 'right' // #2
    },
    insetPadding: 60,
    theme: 'Base:gradients',
    series: [{
        type: 'pie', // #3
```

```
            field: 'total_sales', // #4
            showInLegend: true, // #5
            tips: {
                  trackMouse: true, // #6
                  width: 140,
                  height: 28,
                  renderer: function(storeItem, item) {
                    this.setTitle(storeItem.get('category') + ': ' +
storeItem.get('total_sales'));
                  }
            },
            highlight: {
              segment: {
                margin: 20
              }
            },
            label: {
                field: 'category', // #7
                display: 'rotate',
                contrast: true,
                font: '18px Arial'
            }
        }]
    });
```

Let's go through the most important parts of the preceding code: first, we need to bind `store` we just declared with the chart (`#1`). Then, we can add `legend` to the chart; in this case, we want it to be displayed on the right-hand side of the chart (`#2`).

Next there is the `series` configuration, which defines what `type` of chart we are implementing (`#3`), which is the `Pie` chart in this case. The `Pie` chart needs a field that is going to be used to do the sum and then calculate the fraction of each piece. We only have two fields and the `total_sales` field (`#4`) is the numeric one, so we will use this field. The `showInLegend` configuration means if we want to add the elements on `legend` (`#5`).

On the `tips` configuration we can define whether we want to display a quick tip or not. In this case, we want Ext JS to track the movements of the mouse (`#6`) and in case, the user can mouse over any item of the chart, Ext JS will display a tip with the name of the `category` field and `total_sales` number.

And lastly, `label` that will be used to represent each piece of the Pie chart (on the chart and on the legend) is the `category` field (`#7`).

Column chart

As we can change the chart type, we will also implement a Column chart that looks like the following screenshot:

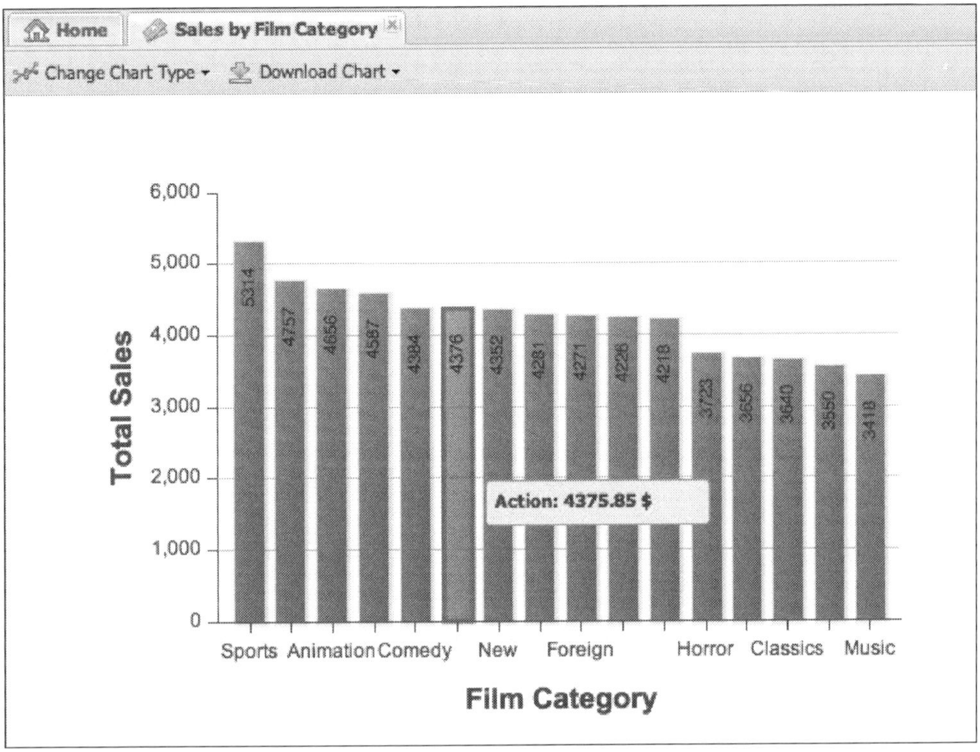

So let's get our hands dirty:

```
Ext.define('Packt.view.reports.SalesFilmCategoryColumn', {
    extend: 'Ext.chart.Chart',
    alias: 'widget.salesfilmcategorycol',

    animate: true,
    store: 'reports.SalesFilmCategory', // #1
    shadow: true,
    insetPadding: 60,
    theme: 'Base:gradients',
    axes: [{
        type: 'Numeric', // #2
        position: 'left',
        fields: ['total_sales'], // #3
        label: {
```

```
            renderer: Ext.util.Format.numberRenderer('0,0')
        },
        title: 'Total Sales',
        grid: true,
        minimum: 0
    }, {
        type: 'Category', // #4
        position: 'bottom',
        fields: ['category'], // #5
        title: 'Film Category'
    }],
    series: [{
        type: 'column', // #6
        axis: 'left',
        highlight: true,
        tips: {
          trackMouse: true,
          width: 140,
          height: 28,
          renderer: function(storeItem, item) {
            this.setTitle(storeItem.get('category') + ': ' +
                storeItem.get('total_sales') + ' $');
          }
        },
        label: {
          display: 'insideEnd',
          'text-anchor': 'middle',
            field: 'total_sales',
            renderer: Ext.util.Format.numberRenderer('0'),
            orientation: 'vertical',
            color: '#333'
        },
        xField: 'category', // #7
        yField: 'total_sales' // #8
  }]
});
```

The Column chart will use the same `store` as the Pie chart (`#1`). As the Column chart is a Cartesian chart, we need to define the X and Y axis. We will have a `Numeric` axis (#2) that will be located on the left-hand side and will be placed vertically. The numeric axis is represented by the `total_sales` field (`#3`). Next we have the `Category` axis (`#4`), which is the `label` field that represents each column of the chart. The category axis is represented by the `category` field (`#5`).

Next we have the definition of the series, which defines the type of chart we are implementing. In this case, we are implementing a `column` chart (`#6`). We also need to define which are going to be the X and Y axis fields, so the chart can read and apply the correct field in each axis. The X field (which is the horizontal one) is represented by the `category` field (`#7`). The Y field (which is the vertical one) is represented by the `total_sales` field (`#8`). A very important note is that `xField` (`#7`) matches the `Category` axis (`#4`) and `yField` (`#8`) matches the `Numeric` axis (vertical/ left position: `#2`).

The Bar chart code is exactly the Column chart with a small change. We need to invert the `axis` (category will be left and numeric will be bottom), `xField` (will be total_sales instead of category), and `yField` (will be category instead of total_sales).

The Bar chart is going to look like the following screenshot:

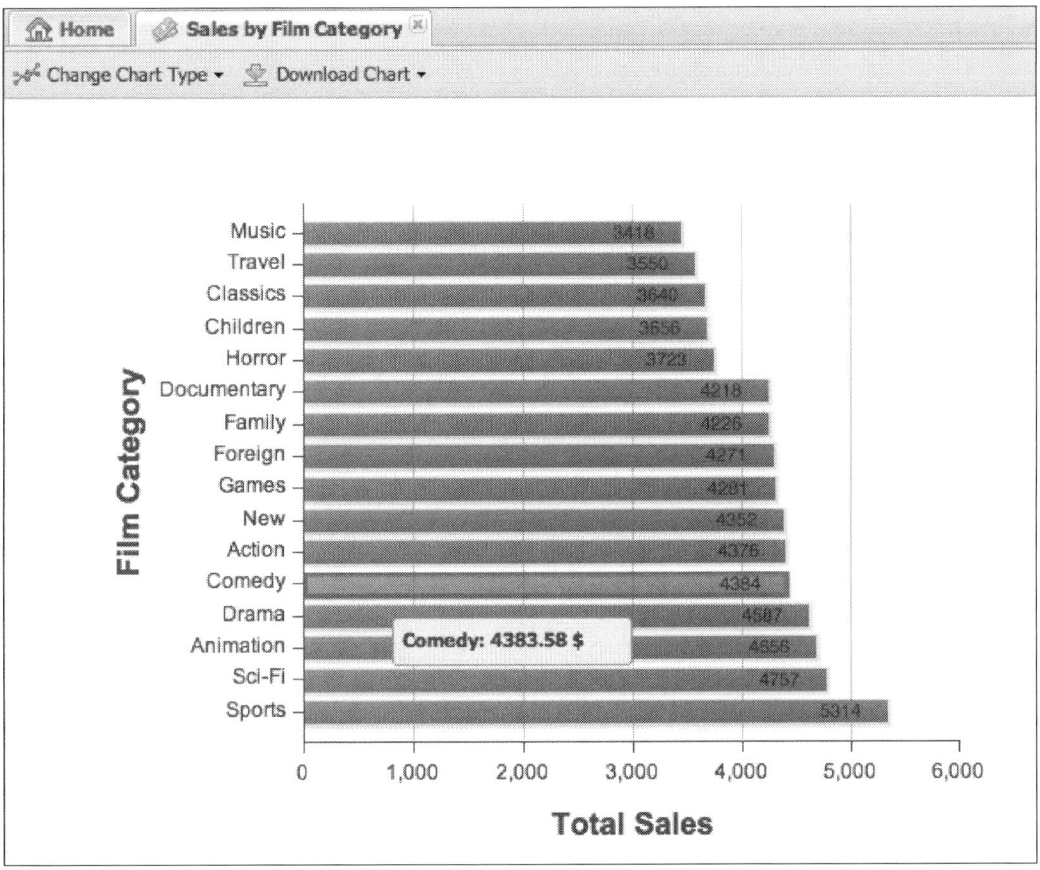

The chart panel

As we want to display a panel and offer the user the possibility to change the chart type, we will create a panel and use the card layout. To refresh our memory, the card layout is mostly used for wizards and also when we have several items, but we want to display only one at a time. And the item that is currently being displayed uses the Fit layout.

So let's create our chart panel:

```
Ext.define('Packt.view.reports.SalesFilmCategory', {
    extend: 'Ext.panel.Panel',
    alias: 'widget.salesfilmcategory',

    layout: 'card',
    activeItem: 0,

    items: [
        {
            xtype: 'salesfilmcategorypie' // #1
        },
        {
            xtype: 'salesfilmcategorycol' // #2
        },
        {
            xtype: 'salesfilmcategorybar' // #3
        }
    ],

    dockedItems: [{
        xtype: 'toolbar',
        flex: 1,
        dock: 'top',
        items: [
            // items here #4
        ]
    }]
});
```

So we need to declare a panel and declare each chart we created as an item. So we can declare the Pie chart (`#1`), the Column chart (`#2`), and the Bar chart (`#3`) as items of this **Sales by Film Category** chart panel. By default, the item 0 (which is the first item: Pie chart) is going to be the default item to be displayed when the chart panel is rendered.

Next, we can declare the toolbar that will contain the **Menu** button, so the user can choose the chart type and the download type. So the following code will be placed at the `#4` of the preceding code:

```
{
    text: 'Change Chart Type',
    iconCls: 'menu_reports',
    menu: {
        xtype: 'menu',
        itemId: 'changeType',
        items: [
            {
                xtype: 'menuitem',
                text: 'Pie',
                itemId: 'pie',
                iconCls: 'chart_pie'
            },
            {
                xtype: 'menuitem',
                text: 'Column',
                itemId: 'column',
                iconCls: 'chart_bar'
            },
            {
                xtype: 'menuitem',
                text: 'Bar',
                itemId: 'bar',
                iconCls: 'chart_column'
            }
        ]
    }
}
```

The first button we declared with **Menu** is the **Change Chart Type** button as shown in the following screenshot:

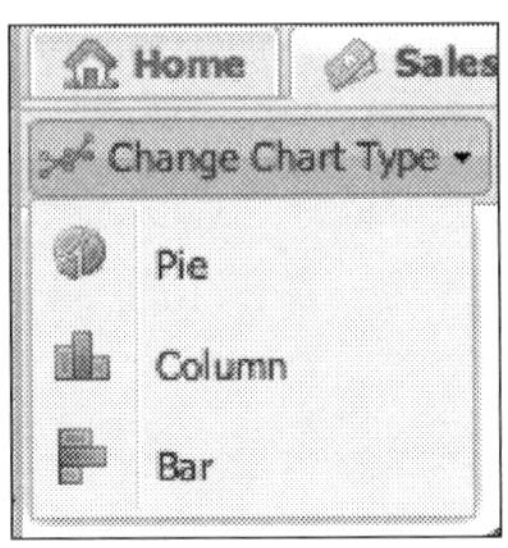

We have the **Change Chart Type** button as item of the toolbar (remember that the button is the default `xtype` of toolbar items). This button has a menu that has three menu items, one for each chart type.

As the second item of the toolbar we have the **Download Chart** button. Following the same behavior as the **Change Chart Type** button, the **Download Chart** button also has a menu with three menu items in it: one for each download type:

```
{
    text: 'Download Chart',
    iconCls: 'download',
    menu: {
        xtype: 'menu',
        itemId: 'download',
        items: [
            {
                xtype: 'menuitem',
                text: 'Download as Image',
                itemId: 'png',
                iconCls: 'image'
            },
            {
                xtype: 'menuitem',
                text: 'Download as SVG',
                itemId: 'svg',
                iconCls: 'svg'
            },
            {
                xtype: 'menuitem',
                text: 'Download as PDF',
                itemId: 'pdf',
                iconCls: 'pdf'
            }
        ]
    }
}
```

The output for the **Download Chart** button is shown in the following screenshot:

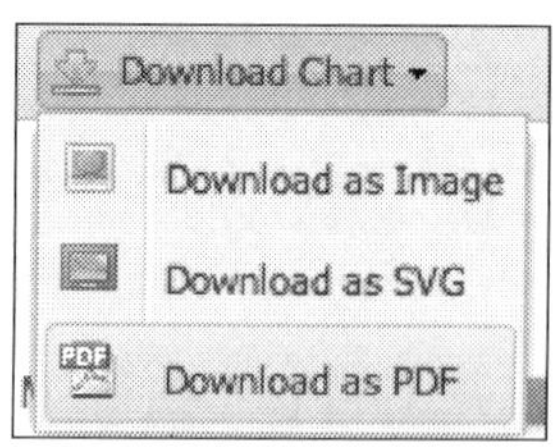

Changing the chart type

As the user has the capability to change the chart type by choosing an option from the **Menu** button, we first need to listen to the click event from `menuitem`:

```
"salesfilmcategory menu#changeType menuitem": {
    click: this.onChangeChart
}
```

The `menuitem` click event is similar to the button click event; the difference is that the menu item we are looking for is inside the menu in which `itemId` is `changeType`. When the user clicks on a menu item, the Films Controller will execute the following method:

```
onChangeChart: function(item, e, options) {
    var panel = item.up('salesfilmcategory'); // #1

    if (item.itemId == 'pie'){
        panel.getLayout().setActiveItem(0); // #2
    } else if (item.itemId == 'column'){
        panel.getLayout().setActiveItem(1); // #3
    } else if (item.itemId == 'bar'){
        panel.getLayout().setActiveItem(2); // #4
    }
}
```

First, we need to get the panel so we can change the active item (`#1`). Then, we can compare which `itemId` the user clicks on and we set the active item according (`#2`, `#3`, and `#4`) to the option the user chose.

Exporting charts to images (PNG and SVG)

Likewise the **Change Chart Type** menu, we will follow the same logic on the controller to listen to the event, the difference is that the menu items we are listening to are from the menu whose `itemId` is set as `download`:

```
"salesfilmcategory menu#download menuitem": {
    click: this.onChartDownload
}
```

On the `onChartDownload` method we will follow the same logic as we did for the **Change Chart Type** menu items. But in this case, we want to save the chart as an image (PNG) or SVG file.

```
onChartDownload: function(item, e, options) {
    var chartPanel = item.up('salesfilmcategory');
    var chart = chartPanel.getLayout().getActiveItem(); // #1

    if (item.itemId == 'png'){
        Ext.MessageBox.confirm('Confirm Download',
'Would you like to download the chart as Image?', function(choice){
            if(choice == 'yes'){
                chart.save({  // #2
                    type: 'image/png'
                });
            }
        });
    } else if (item.itemId == 'svg'){
        Ext.MessageBox.confirm('Confirm Download',
'Would you like to download the chart as SVG + XML?', function(choice)
{
            if(choice == 'yes'){        // #3
                chart.save({
                    type: 'image/svg+xml'
                });
            }
        });
    }
    // download PDF code - next topic
}
```

The `chart` class already has a method named `save`, which we can use to download the chart in an image format. And this is a native feature from Ext JS.

So first, we need to get a reference of the chart, which we can get through the active item of `chartPanel` (`#1`).

Then, depending on the user choice, we will first ask if the user really wants to download the chart in the specific format, and if yes, we will ask Ext JS to generate the file. So if the user chooses to download in PNG (`#2`) or SVG (`#3`), we simply need to call the method `save` from the chart reference passing the specific type selected by the user. In this case, the application will send a request to `http://svg.sencha.io` and the download will start.

The following screenshot is from an image that was generated by choosing to save the chart as PNG:

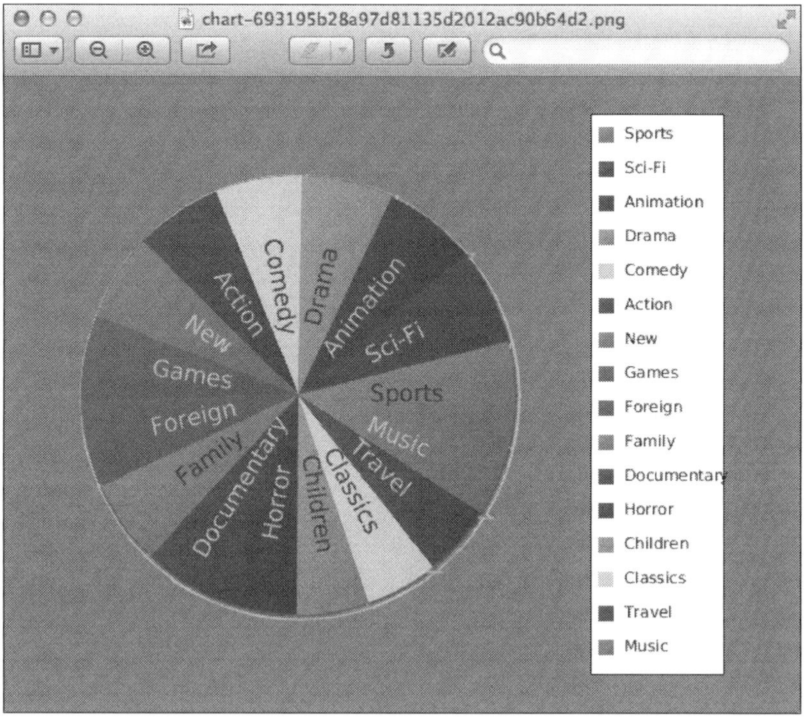

Exporting charts to PDF

Then continuing the code from the last topic, we have:

```
else if (item.itemId == 'pdf'){
    Ext.MessageBox.confirm('Confirm Download',
'Would you like to download the chart as PDF?', function(choice){
        if(choice == 'yes'){
            chart.save({      // #4
                type: 'image/png',
                url: 'php/pdf/exportChartPdf.php'
            });
        }
    });
}
```

As we can see on `#4`, we called the `save` method from the `chart` class and we are also passing a URL to the `save` method.

If we go further in the analysis of the `save` method, we will find that it calls the `generate` method from the `Ext.draw.engine.ImageExporter` class. This class uses `defaultUrl` as the URL where the request will be sent, and we can customize it. If we take a look at the request, we can see that it is sending four parameters to the server: **width**, **height**, **type** and **svg**:

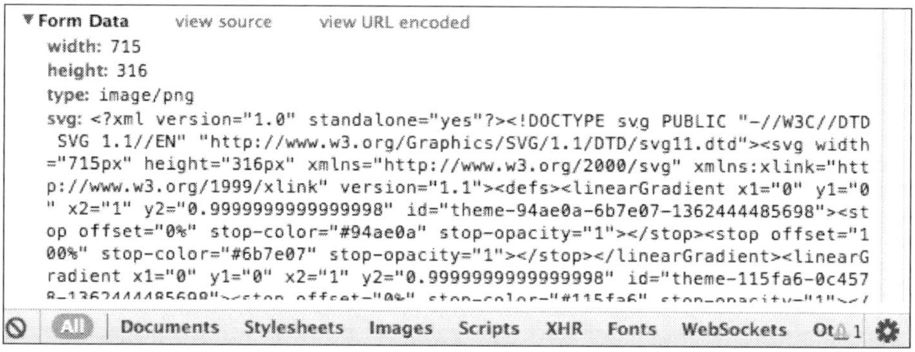

So what we need to do on the server side is to get these items of information that are sent on the POST request:

```
$width = $_POST['width'];
$height = $_POST['height'];
$type = $_POST['type'];
$svg = $_POST['svg'];
```

And using the TCPDF library, we can use the `ImageSVG` method passing these parameters to it:

```
$pdf->ImageSVG($file='@'.$svg, $x=10, $y=10, $w=$width, $h=$height,
$link='', $align='T', $palign='C', $border=0, $fitonpage=true);
```

The magic will happen and a PDF file like the one in the following screenshot will be generated:

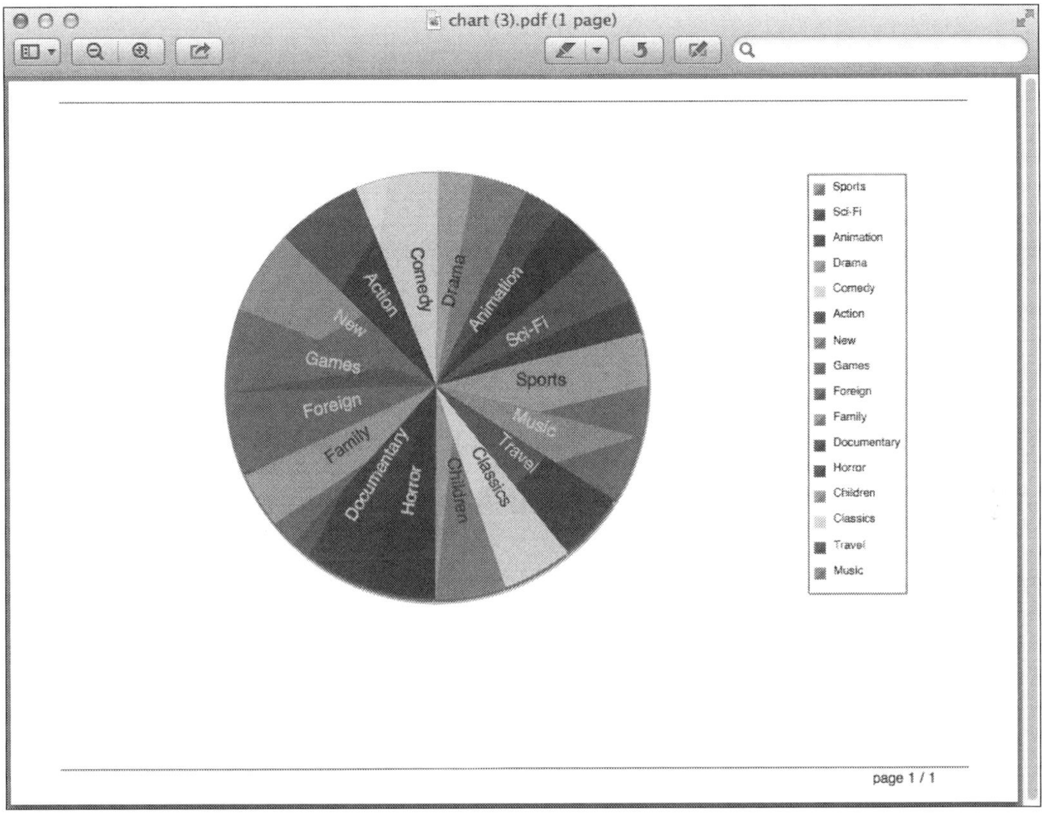

If for some reason the application is going to be deployed on an environment where it cannot make requests outside the domain (`http://svg.sencha.io`), you can use the same approach to generate the PNG, JPEG or SVG files. Ext JS will always send the four parameters to the server; we just need to handle them according to what needs to be done.

Summary

In this chapter we learned how to export the content of a Grid panel to PDF, Excel, and also a page that is printer friendly.

We have also learned how to create different type of charts, use only one component and change its active item, export a chart to an image or SVG using Ext JS native features and also how to export a chart to a PDF file.

So for now, we are done with developing capabilities for our application that are related to the `Sakila` database. In the next chapter, we will learn how to build a client e-mail that looks very similar to Outlook.

9

The E-mail Client Module

In this chapter we will implement the last module of our application. We will develop an e-mail client module based on the look and feel of Outlook, a very popular e-mail client from Microsoft.

So in this chapter we will cover:

- Designing the e-mail client
- Listing e-mails
- Creating the inbox menu (Tree panel menu)
- Drag-and-drop between the e-mails to a new folder (between grid and tree)
- Enhancing the Grid panel

Creating the inbox – list of e-mails

Before we get started, let's take a look at a screenshot of the final result we will have once we finish this chapter:

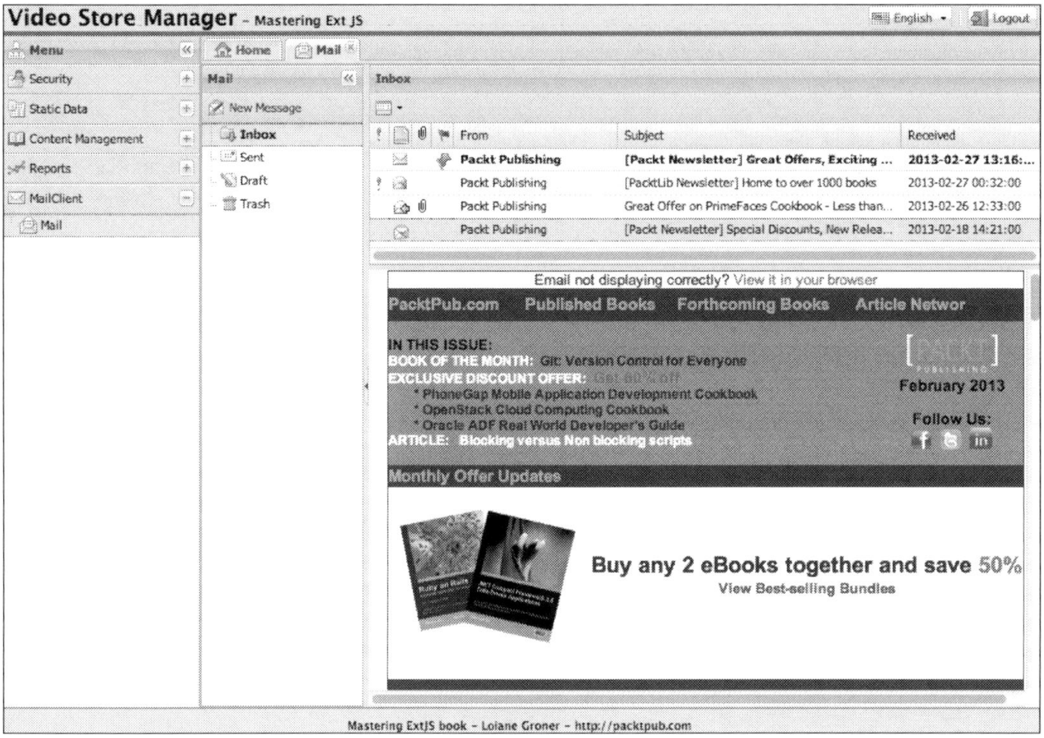

The e-mail client module is composed of four major pieces: the **Mail** menu, the **Inbox** (which is the list of e-mails), the preview mail panel and the **New Message** window. The first thing we are going to implement is **Inbox**, which is a Grid panel with some enhancements. So, following our development workflow, we will first create the model, then the store, then the view, and finally, the controller to listen to the events for which we are interested in taking some action.

The mail message model

So first, we need to create a model to represent an e-mail message that is going to be displayed on the Grid panel. We will create a new model class named `Packt.model.mail.MailMessage`:

```
Ext.define('Packt.model.mail.MailMessage', {
    extend: 'Ext.data.Model',
    fields: [
```

```
            { name: 'importance' },
            { name: 'icon'  },
            { name: 'attachment'  },
            { name: 'from' },
            { name: 'subject' },
            { name: 'received' },
            { name: 'flag' },
            { name: 'folder' },
            { name: 'content' },
            { name: 'id' }
        ]
    });
```

The `importance` field represents the red exclamation mark, which represents that the e-mail has been sent with high importance; `icon` is the icon of the e-mail message (read, unread, forwarded, replied, replied to all); `attachment` represents if the e-mail message has any attachments; the `flag` field is for the status of the flag (for follow-up control on Outlook); and the `folder` field is where the message is located (inbox, draft, trash, and so on).

Basically it is a simple model, nothing different from what we have already implemented in previous chapters.

The mail messages store

Next, we need to create a store to load the e-mail messages. We will create a store named `Packt.store.mail.MailMessages` as follows:

```
Ext.define('Packt.store.mail.MailMessages', {
    extend: 'Ext.data.Store',

    requires: [
        'Packt.model.mail.MailMessage',
        'Packt.proxy.Sakila'
    ],

    model: 'Packt.model.mail.MailMessage',
    autoLoad: true,

    proxy: {
        type: 'sakila',
        api: {
            read: 'php/mail/listInbox.php',
            update: 'php/mail/update.php'
        }
    }
});
```

We will load (read) the e-mail messages from the server (for example purposes, we will not integrate with any e-mail service such as Gmail, Hotmail/Outlook, Yahoo, or any other).

We will also update the e-mail message, in case we change its folder. We will implement the drag-and-drop functionality later.

For this example, we will pull all the model information from the server. If a user has a lot of e-mail messages, the store can take a while to load the information. And as we have learned so far, we can also use two different approaches here: the first one is to implement a paging toolbar and the second one is to load the content field on demand, that is, only when the user clicks on a message from the inbox to read an e-mail.

The mail list view

And finally, we need to implement the view, which is a Grid panel that we are going to name Packt.view.mail.MailList:

```
Ext.define('Packt.view.mail.MailList', {
    extend: 'Ext.grid.Panel',
    alias: 'widget.maillist',

    title: 'Inbox',
    store: 'mail.MailMessages',

    viewConfig: {
        getRowClass: function(record, rowIndex, rowParams, store){
            if (record.get('icon') == 'unread'){ // #1
                return "boldFont";
            }
        }
    },
    columns: [
        // columns here
    ]
});
```

There is a section of code that is brought to our attention in the previous code block, which is the getRowClass function inside viewConfig. Inside this function, we can return a CSS style that is going to be applied to all the cells of a row of the Grid panel. In this case, if an e-mail is unread (#1), we want to make the row's font bold, by applying the boldFont style to it. If it is not, nothing will change.

In our app.css file, we need to declare this style as following:

```
.boldFont .x-grid-cell {
  font-weight:bold; !important;
}
```

Next, we need to declare the columns of the Grid panel. Let's declare them one by one so we can go over the details. First, we will declare the importance column, which is the one that will display the red exclamation mark in case the e-mail message was sent with high importance:

```
{
    xtype: 'gridcolumn',
    cls: 'importance', // #2
    width: 18,
    dataIndex: 'importance',
    menuDisabled: true,
    text: 'Importance',
    renderer: function(value, metaData, record ){
        if (value == 1){
            metaData.css = 'importance'; // #3
        }
        return '';
    }
}
```

There are two important things to notice in this code: if we take a look at the screenshot of the complete e-mail client module, we will notice that in the grid header, there is no text, only an icon. How can we display an icon on the grid header? It is very simple, we just need to apply a CSS to the grid header by declaring the cls attribute inside the column declaration (#2).

The importance CSS needs to be something like the following:

```
.importance {
  background:transparent url('../icons/mail/priority_high.gif') no-
repeat 3px 3px !important;
  text-indent:-250px;
}
```

If the message was sent with high importance, we also want to display an image inside the grid cell instead of a text. To do so, we will also apply the importance CSS to the grid cell inside the renderer function (#3). And we will also return an empty string because we do not want to display any text.

Next, we will declare the `icon` column, which is the column that will display the icon message, in other words, will tell the user if the e-mail is read, unread, replied, forwarded, or replied to all:

```
{
    xtype: 'gridcolumn',
    cls: 'icon-msg', // #4
    width: 21,
    dataIndex: 'icon',
    menuDisabled: true,
    text: 'Icon',
    renderer: function(value, metaData, record ){
        metaData.css = value; // #5
        metaData.tdAttr = 'data-qtip="' + value + '"'; // #6
        return '';
    }
}
```

We will again display an icon on the grid header, so we need to declare the `cls` attribute (`#4`). We will also display an image inside the grid cell, but this time, the CSS will be the column `value` itself that was retrieved from the database (`#5`).

Now, let's say we want to display a tooltip when the user hovers the cursor over the grid cell. We can apply it on the `tdAttr` attribute of the `metadata` as well (`#6`). In this case, we will also display the `value` that comes from the database. The result will be as follows:

For the `attachment` column, the code will be very similar to the previous columns:

```
{
    xtype: 'gridcolumn',
    cls: 'attach', // #7
    width: 18,
    dataIndex: 'attachment',
    menuDisabled: true,
```

```
        text: 'Attachment',
        renderer: function(value, metaData, record ){
            if (value == 1){
                metaData.css = 'attach'; // #8
            }
            return '';
        }
    }
```

We want to display an image on the grid header (`#7`) and also on the grid cell (`#8`).

Likewise for the `flagged` column:

```
    {
        xtype: 'gridcolumn',
        cls: 'flagged', // #9
        width: 20,
        dataIndex: 'flag',
        menuDisabled: true,
        text: 'Flag',
        renderer: function(value, metaData, record ){
            if (value == 1){
                metaData.css = 'flag-e-mail'; // #10
            }
            return '';
        }
    }
```

We want to display an image on the grid header (`#9`) and also on the grid cell (`#10`).

Next, we will declare the remaining columns, that will display a `text` on the grid header (as usual) and also `text` on the grid cell content:

```
    {
        xtype: 'gridcolumn',
        dataIndex: 'from',
        menuDisabled: true,
        width: 150,
        text: 'From'
    },
    {
        xtype: 'gridcolumn',
        dataIndex: 'subject',
        menuDisabled: true,
        flex: 1,
        text: 'Subject'
```

```
},
{
    xtype: 'gridcolumn',
    dataIndex: 'received',
    menuDisabled: true,
    width: 130,
    text: 'Received'
}
```

The output of the code so far will be something like the following screenshot, a Grid panel with some customizations on the grid header, grid cell, and also a custom CSS applied to the grid row. All these features are native; no third-party plugin is necessary:

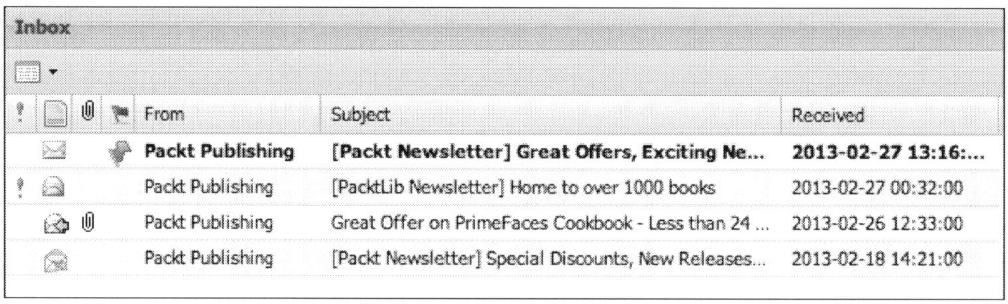

The preview mail panel

There is only one detail left to be implemented, which is the button with a menu that we can see in the previous screenshot:

```
dockedItems: [
    {
        xtype: 'toolbar',
        dock: 'top',
        items: [
            {
                xtype: 'button',
                iconCls: 'preview-hide',
                menu: {
                    xtype: 'menu',
                    itemId: 'preview',
```

```
                        width: 120,
                        items: [
                            {
                                xtype: 'menuitem',
                                itemId: 'hide',
                                iconCls: 'preview-hide',
                                text: 'Hide Preview'
                            },
                            {
                                xtype: 'menuitem',
                                itemId: 'bottom',
                                iconCls: 'preview-bottom',
                                text: 'Preview Bottom'
                            },
                            {
                                xtype: 'menuitem',
                                itemId: 'right',
                                iconCls: 'preview-right',
                                text: 'Preview Right'
                            }
                        ]
                    }
                }
            ]
        }
    ]
```

This menu will allow the user to change the preview tab from right to bottom or even hide it (**Hide Preview**) as follows:

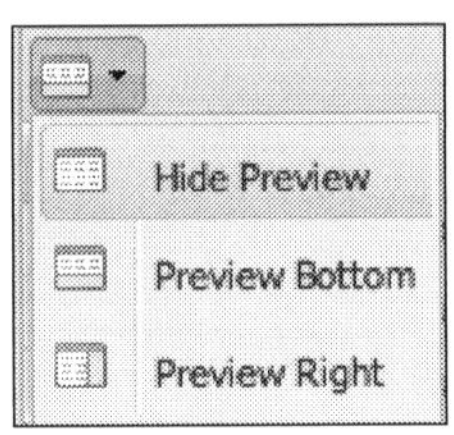

The mail menu (tree menu)

Next, we will create the menu that is going to list the folders of **Inbox**, as demonstrated in the following screenshot:

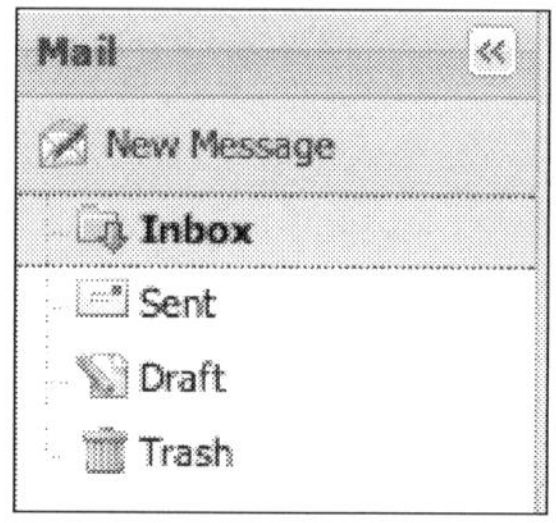

The mail menu tree store

As usual, we will start with the model and store. As we will use the `NodeInterface` class to represent each `node` (which is the default class), we will not need any customization—we do not need to declare the model; we can skip directly to the tree store:

```
Ext.define('Packt.store.mail.MailMenu', {
    extend: 'Ext.data.TreeStore',

    clearOnLoad: true,

    proxy: {
        type: 'ajax',
        url: 'php/mail/mailMenu.php',
    }
});
```

We will be loading the JSON from the server. The PHP code is very simple and it returns the JSON we need, which is already hardcoded in a string:

```
<?php
echo '[{
    "text": "Inbox",
    "iconCls": "folder-inbox",
    "leaf": true
},{
    "text": "Sent",
    "iconCls": "folder-sent",
    "leaf": true
},{
```

```
        "text": "Draft",
        "iconCls": "folder-drafts",
        "leaf": true
    },{
        "text": "Trash",
        "iconCls": "folder-trash",
        "leaf": true
    }]';
    ?>
```

Creating the mail menu view

The next step is to create the tree panel that is going to represent our mail menu. It is a very simple tree panel:

```
Ext.define('Packt.view.mail.MailMenu', {
    extend: 'Ext.tree.Panel',
    alias: 'widget.mailMenu',

    cls: 'selected-node', // #1
    autoScroll: true,
    store: 'mail.MailMenu',
    rootVisible: false,
    split: true,
    width: 150,
    collapsible: true,
    title: 'Mail',

    dockedItems: [
        {
            xtype: 'toolbar', // #2
            dock: 'top',
            items: [
                {
                    xtype: 'button',
                    iconCls: 'new-mail',
                    text: 'New Message',
                    itemId: 'newMail'
                }
            ]
        }
    ]
});
```

There are two things that we need to pay attention to. The first one is: when the user selects a node from the tree panel, we want it to be bold, so we can apply a CSS (#1) to make it happen as follows:

```
.selected-node .x-grid-row-selected .x-grid-cell {
    font-weight: bold;
}
```

The second item is the toolbar with the `New Message` button (#2), in case the user wants to send a new e-mail.

The mail container – organizing the e-mail client

So far, we have two main pieces of the client e-mail module. We need to organize them so that it looks like the first screenshot we demonstrated in this chapter. To do so, we are going to use a container and apply the border layout to it.

> Why are we using a container instead of a panel? The container is a lighter component than the panel. We are not looking at using the panel's capabilities, such as panel header and `DockedItem`; we only want to use something to wrap some components and organize them using a specific layout. So in this case, the container is a better choice.

So, let's take a look at the `MailContainer` component:

```
Ext.define('Packt.view.mail.MailContainer', {
    extend: 'Ext.container.Container',
    alias: 'widget.mailcontainer',

    requires: [ // #1
        'Packt.view.mail.MailList',
        'Packt.view.mail.MailPreview',
        'Packt.view.mail.MailMenu'
    ],

    layout: {
        type: 'border' // #2
    },

    initComponent: function() {
        var me = this;
```

```
        var mailPreview = { // #3
            xtype: 'mailpreview',
            autoScroll: true
        };

        me.items = [
            {
                xtype: 'container', // #4
                region: 'center',
                itemId: 'mailpanel',
                layout: {
                    type: 'border'
                },
                items: [
                    {
                        xtype: 'maillist',
                        collapsible: false, // #5
                        region: 'center'
                    },
                    {
                        xtype: 'container',
                        itemId: 'previewSouth', // #6
                        height: 300,
                        hidden: true,
                        collapsible: false,
                        region: 'south',
                        split: true,
                        layout: 'fit',
                        items: [mailPreview]
                    },
                    {
                        xtype: 'container',
                        width: 400,
                        itemId: 'previewEast', // #7
                        hidden: true,
                        collapsible: false,
                        region: 'east',
                        split: true,
                        layout: 'fit',
                        items: [mailPreview]
                    }
                ]
            },
            {
```

```
                xtype: 'mailMenu', // #8
                region: 'west',

            }
        ];

        me.callParent(arguments);
    }
});
```

We always need to remember to declare the classes we created (not native classes) in the `requires` declaration that we are going to instantiate using their `xtype` (`#1`).

We are also going to use the `border` layout (`#2`). The idea is to have the mail menu on the `west` side of the container and the mail list and preview in the `center`.

As we want to have a mail preview container on the `south` and `right` of the e-mail list and to avoid duplicating code, let's declare it once (`#3`) and reuse it on `#6` and `#7`.

Next, we have the mail panel, which is going to organize the control e-mail list and the mail preview container. The mail panel (`#4`) will also use the border layout and will have items in the `center` (center region is mandatory), `south` and `east` (mail preview container).

The mail list (`#5`) will be the `center` item of the mail panel. The mail preview container will be in the `south` (`#6`) and `east` (`#7`) regions. We will control which one will be `hidden` and which one will be shown by the button with a menu declared on the mail list. And finally, we have the mail menu that we developed (`#8`).

Now, the only missing piece is the mail preview, which is also a container that is going to use the `fit` layout (we want the mail content to occupy all the available space on this container):

```
Ext.define('Packt.view.mail.MailPreview', {
    extend: 'Ext.container.Container',
    alias: 'widget.mailpreview',

    layout: 'fit'
});
```

The controller

Now that we have everything we need in place, let's implement the functionality that allows the user to change the position of the mail preview. The user can choose to see the preview panel on the right-hand side, on the south, or to hide it.

So the first thing we need to do is to create a new controller for the e-mail client module:

```
Ext.define('Packt.controller.mail.Mail', {
    extend: 'Ext.app.Controller',

    views: [ // #1
        'mail.MailContainer',
        'mail.MailList',
        'mail.MailPreview'
    ],

    stores: [// #2
        'mail.MailMessages',
        'mail.MailMenu'
    ],

    refs: [// #3
        {
            ref: 'south', // #4
            selector: 'mailcontainer container#previewSouth'
        },
        {
            ref: 'east', // #5
            selector: 'mailcontainer container#previewEast'
        }
    ]
});
```

First, we must not forget to declare the `views` we created for this module (`#1`). Then, we have the `stores` (`#2`). And finally, we need to declare some `references` (`#3`). We will declare references for the mail preview containers that are located in `south` (`#4`) and `east` (`#5`) of the mail container.

Just remember, references create shortcuts to components throughout selectors. Instead of using `Ext.ComponentQuery.query('mailcontainer container#previewSouth)[0]` every time we need to get this reference, we can declare the reference and simply call `this.getSouth`. And it is easier to do maintenance in case we need to change the selector in the future, because with references, we only need to change the selector in a single place!

Previewing an e-mail

Next, we need to listen to the click event of the `menuitem` as follows:

```
"menu#preview menuitem": {
    click: this.onMenuitemClick
}
```

We will use the same approach that we used in the previous chapter to listen to the click event of `menuitem`. Instead of listening to them sequentially (one by one) for each item, we can listen to any `menuitem` of a specific menu and then, inside the method that is going to be executed, we can use `itemId` to know exactly which `menuitem` was clicked on:

```
onMenuitemClick: function(item, e, options) {

    var button = item.up('button'); // #1
    var east = this.getEast();      // #2
    var south = this.getSouth();    // #3

    switch (item.itemId) {
        case 'bottom': // #4
            east.hide();
            south.show();
            button.setIconCls('preview-bottom');
            break;
        case 'right': // #5
            south.hide();
            east.show();
            button.setIconCls('preview-right');
            break;
        default:      // #6
            south.hide();
            east.hide();
            button.setIconCls('preview-hide');
            break;
    }
}
```

The idea is to update the icon of the button that contains the menu with the icon used by the `menuitem` selected. And depending on the user's choice, we will show or hide the south and east mail preview containers.

So first we need to get the reference of the `button` that contains the menu (`#1`) so we can change its `iconCls`. Then, we need to get the reference of the `south` (`#3`) and `east` (`#2`) mail preview containers.

If the user chooses to display the preview on the `bottom` (`#4`), the `east` container must be hidden and the south container must be shown. If the user chooses to display the preview on the `right` (`#5`), the `east` container must be shown and the `south` container must be hidden. If the user chooses to `hide` the preview (`#6`), both containers (`south` and `east`) must be hidden.

For example, if the user chooses to see the preview on the `right`, this is going to be the output:

Organizing e-mails – drag-and-drop

As on Outlook, we can select a message and drag-and-drop it onto another folder. We will also implement this functionality in our e-mail client module. But there is one important detail: first, we need to do a drag-and-drop between a Grid panel (list of e-mails) and a Tree panel (mail menu). And second, we do not want to move a record from the Grid panel to the Tree panel. We simply want to be able to drop an e-mail message into a node of the Tree Panel and not actually add it to the Tree panel as a new node (meaning it will be added to the tree store). So let's keep this in mind when we implement this functionality. This example is very good because it demonstrates that we can customize some actions of the drag-and-drop capability.

So first, we need to add the drag-and-drop capability to the Grid panel and the Tree panel.

In the `Packt.view.mail.MailList` class, inside the `viewConfig` method, we need to add the following code (before or after the `getRowClass` function; it's your call):

```
plugins: {
    ptype: 'gridviewdragdrop',
    ddGroup: 'mailDD'
}
```

We are adding the drag-and-drop plugin (Ext JS SDK native) and we are giving a name to `ddGroup`, which represents the drag-and-drop zones this plugin is able to interact with. If we implement another drag-and-drop within the application and it has a different name, we will not be able to drag from this Grid panel and drag to a different drag-and-drop zone.

Next, inside the `Packt.view.mail.MailMenu` class we will add the following code:

```
viewConfig: {
    plugins: {
        ptype: 'treeviewdragdrop',
        ddGroup: 'mailDD',
        enableDrag: false
    }
}
```

We are also going to use the drag-and-drop plugin that is specific for the Tree panel. We will not enable the drag action, only the drop action, and notice that the `ddGroup` attribute is the same as in the Grid panel, meaning the Grid panel will be able to interact with this Tree panel regarding the drag-and-drop actions.

So far, nothing will happen. Let's go back to the controller so we can implement the required programming logic.

First, we need to listen to the `beforedrop` event from the `treeview` of the Tree panel.

As Form has the `FormBasic` class, the Tree panel has the `treeview` class and the Grid panel has the `gridview` class. The view is actually the component that is responsible for the content and the grid or tree is the component that contains the view and provides other capabilities.

```
"mailMenu treeview": {
    beforedrop: this.onBeforeDrop
}
```

The following snippet shows how to implement the `onBeforeDrop` method:

```
onBeforeDrop: function(node, data, overModel, dropPosition,
dropHandler, options) {
    Ext.each(data.records, function(rec){ // #1
        rec.set('folder',overModel.get('text')); // #2
```

```
        });
        dropHandler.cancelDrop();// #3

        var grid = Ext.ComponentQuery.query('maillist')[0];
        var store = grid.getStore();
        store.sync();         // #4
    }
```

Inside the `data` parameters, we can find the `records` attribute, which contains the `records` that were dropped into the tree node. So we need to loop over all the `records` (`#1`) to do something with them.

This "do something with them" is changing the `folder` field of the model. Remember, we do not want to remove the `record` from the Grid panel; we simply want to change the e-mail message from one `folder` to another `folder` (`#2`). To get the name of the node where the record was dropped, we can use the `overModel` parameter and retrieve the field we need.

And finally, remember we do not want to append a new node on the Tree panel; we simply want to change the `folder` field of the dropped model. For this reason, we can cancel the drop event from being fired (`#3`). To do it, we can use the `dropHandler` parameter, which contains methods to complete or cancel the data transfer operation and either move or copy model instances from the source view's store to the destination view's store.

After that, we can call the `sync` method of the store of the Grid panel so we can save the name of the new `folder` on the database (`#4`).

We can see how the drag-and-drop from the Grid panel to the Tree panel will look like in the following screenshot:

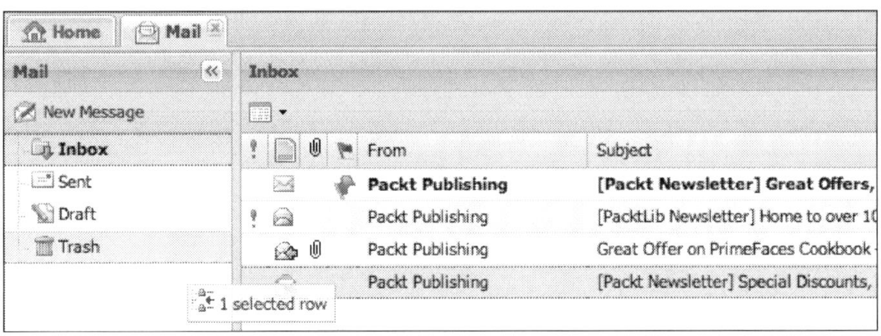

Creating a new message

Now comes the final part of the window where the user can write a new e-mail that is to be sent. Before we start coding, let's take a look at the output of the code that we will implement in this topic:

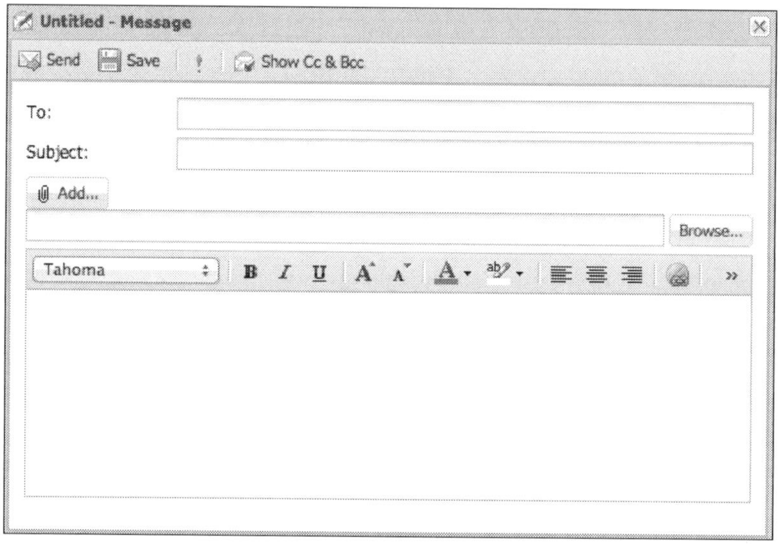

First, we need to create the window that is going to wrap the new message form:

```
Ext.define('Packt.view.mail.NewMail', {
    extend: 'Ext.window.Window',
    alias: 'widget.newmail',

    height: 410,
    width: 670,
    autoShow: true,
    layout: {
        type: 'fit'
    },
    title: 'Untitled - Message',
    iconCls: 'new-mail'
});
```

So far we are OK. Let's declare the `dockedItems`, in which we will declare a toolbar with **Send**, **Save**, **Importance**, and **Show Cc & Bcc** buttons:

```
dockedItems: [
    {
        xtype: 'toolbar',
        dock: 'top',
        items: [
            {
                xtype: 'button',
                text: 'Send',
                iconCls: 'send-mail',
                itemId: 'send'
            },
            {
                xtype: 'button',
                text: 'Save',
                iconCls: 'save'
            },
            {
                xtype: 'tbseparator'
            },
            {
                xtype: 'button',
                iconCls: 'importance'
            },
            {
                xtype: 'tbseparator'
            },
            {
                xtype: 'button',
                text: 'Show Cc & Bcc',
                iconCls: 'bcc',
                itemId: 'bcc'
            }
        ]
    }
]
```

Note that the `importance` button has no text property. The `text` property is optional. As we want to display only the icon, we will use the `iconCls` property only.

Now let's go to the form and its `items`:

```
items: [
    {
        xtype: 'form',
        frame: false,
        bodyPadding: 10,
        autoScroll: true,
        defaults: {
          anchor: '100%',
          xtype: 'textfield'
        }
        items: [
            {
                fieldLabel: 'To',
                name: 'to'
            },
            {
                fieldLabel: 'Cc', // #1
                hidden: true,
                name: 'cc'
            },
            {
                fieldLabel: 'Bcc', // #2
                hidden: true,
                name: 'bcc'
            },
            {
                fieldLabel: 'Subject',
                name: 'subject'
            },
            {
                xtype: 'button', // #3
                text: 'Add...',
                iconCls: 'attach',
                itemId: 'attach'
            },
            {
                xtype: 'filefield',
                name: 'file'
            },
            {
                xtype: 'htmleditor',
```

```
                height: 168,
                style: 'background-color: white;',
                name: 'content'
            }
        ]
    }
]
```

The Cc (#1) and Bcc (#2) fields will be hidden because we will display them only when the user clicks on the **Show Cc** and **Bcc** button.

We also have an Add button (#3) in case the user wants to attach a new file to the e-mail message.

Dynamically displaying Cc and Bcc fields

As we created a button to display the **Cc** and **Bcc** fields, we need to listen to its click event on the controller. When the user clicks on this button, the following method will be executed:

```
onShowBcc: function(button, e, options){
    Ext.ComponentQuery.query('textfield[name=cc]')[0].show();
    Ext.ComponentQuery.query('textfield[name=bcc]')[0].show();
}
```

The only thing we need to do is to retrieve the reference of both fields and call the show method.

The output will be as follows:

Adding the file upload fields dynamically

We have also added the `Add` button so the user can add new attachments to the e-mail message.

So when the user clicks on this button, what we want to do is to add a new `File Upload` class after the existing `File Upload` field and we will implement this message in the following method of the controller:

```
onNewAttach: function(button, e, options){
    var form = button.up('window').down('form');

    var fileUpload = {
        xtype: 'filefield',
        name: 'file' + this.attachPosition // #1
    };

    form.insert(this.attachPosition++, fileUpload); // #2
}
```

There are two important points in the preceding code. The first one is the name of the new `File Upload` field. The existing `File Upload` field already has the name `file` so we cannot use the same name. Just to refresh our memory, the name attribute is going to be the name of the parameter that is going to be sent to the server. And the user can add as many new attachments as desired. So we need to come up with a way to create a unique name for each `File Upload` component (`#1`). We need to create a new attribute inside the controller and we will give the value of the position that the new field needs to be inserted (`#2`). If we count, the new field should be inserted after the original `File Upload` field and before the `HTML Editor` field, so it should be position `6`:

```
attachPosition: 6
```

Also, every time the user adds a new field, we need to increment this value (`this.attachPosition++`).

And when the user closes the new message window and opens it again, we need to reset its value back to `6`:

```
onNewMessage: function(button, e, options){
    Ext.create('Packt.view.mail.NewMail');
    this.attachPosition = 6;
}
```

If we execute the code and click on the **Add** button, new fields will be inserted into the new message form and the user will be able to add new attachments as shown in the following screenshot (three new fields were added):

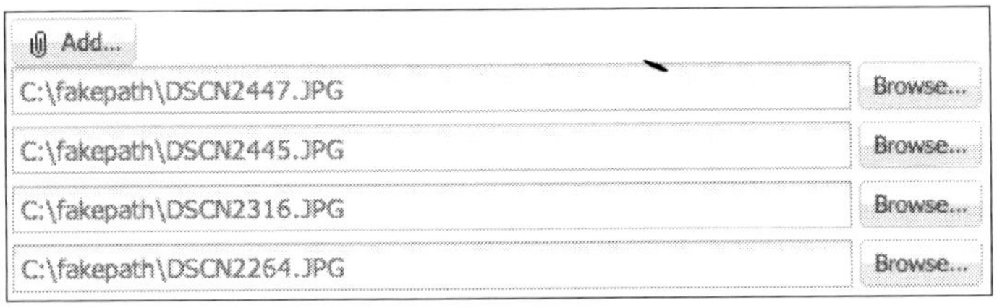

Summary

In this chapter, we implemented an e-mail client module, trying to make it look very similar to the Outlook e-mail client software. This shows us that we can do pretty much anything with Ext JS (it is very flexible); we just need to pay attention to some details.

We have also implemented a drag-and-drop between a Grid panel and a Tree panel, and we also did some customizations.

In this chapter, we finished implementing our application. In the next chapter, we will learn how to customize its look (creating a new theme) and also how to optimize and prepare it so that it is ready to go to production.

10

Preparing for Production

We finished our application in the last chapter. Now it is time to create a nice theme to put a personal touch to the application and also prepare to deploy it on production. After all, we have been working on the development environment and when we want to go live, we cannot simply deploy all the files, we need to do some preparation first. So in this chapter we will cover:

- Creating custom themes
- Packaging the application for production
- Using a desktop packager

Before we start

The main tool we are going to use in this chapter is Sencha Cmd. With Sencha Cmd we will be able to create custom themes and make the production build. As we are using Ext JS 4.2, we are going to use Sencha Cmd 3.1.1, which is compatible with Ext JS 4.2. We need to always make sure that the Sencha Cmd version we are using is compatible with the Ext JS version we are using.

So far, this is what we have developed throughout this book:

All the code we created is inside `app`, `index.html`, `php`, `resources` (CSS and custom image icons), `translations`, and `ux` (third-party plugins we used on our project). The other folders and files were created by Sencha Cmd as we learned in the first chapter.

Customizing a theme

The first task we will perform in this chapter is customizing a theme for our project. To do so, we will use Sencha Cmd and the terminal application of the operating system.

Ext JS 4.2 introduces new ways of customizing themes compared to previous Ext JS 4 versions. Sencha Cmd now has the capability to generate the complete file structure we need to create a brand new theme. We will do an overview of this new way of customizing themes.

So let's create a new theme step by step. First, with the terminal opened, change the directory to the project's root folder. Then, we will use the following command:

```
sencha generate theme masteringextjs-theme
```

The name of our theme is `masteringextjs-theme`. This command will create a new directory with the name of our theme inside the `packages` folder as shown in the following screenshot:

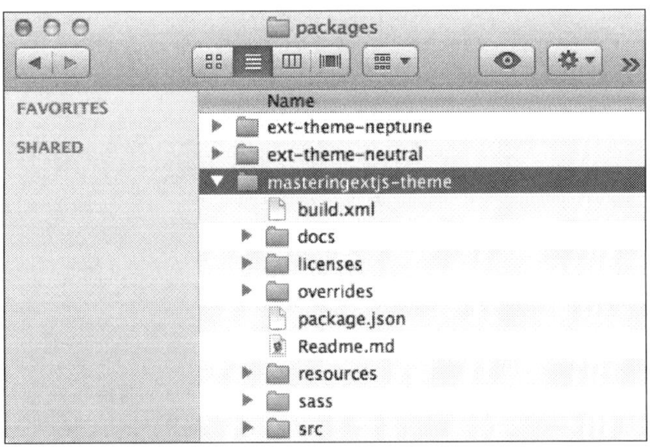

The `package.json` file contains some configurations of the theme used by Sencha Cmd, such as theme name, version, and dependencies.

The `sass` directory contains all the Sass files of our theme. Inside this directory we will find another three main directories:

- `var`: Contains Sass variables.
- `src`: Contains Sass rules and mixins. These rules and mixins use variables declared in files inside the `sass/var` directory.
- `etc`: Contains additional utility functions and mixins.

All the files that we create must match the class path of the component we are styling. For example, if we would like to style the Button component, we need to create the styles inside the `sass/var/button/Button.scss` file; if we would like to style the Component panel, we need to create styles inside the `sass/var/panel.scss` file.

The `resources` folder contains images and other static resources that will be used by our theme.

The `overrides` folder contains all the JavaScript overrides to components that may be required for theming these components.

Spend some time exploring the contents of the following directories that we can find inside the `packages` folder to get more familiar with this way of organizing the Sass files: `ext-theme-classic`, `ext-theme-gray`, and `ext-theme-neptune`.

By default, any theme that we create is going to use the `ext-theme-classic` file as a base (the classic Ext JS blue theme). To try something new let's use the new Ext JS 4.2 theme called **Neptune**. To change the base theme, open the `package.json` file and locate the `extend` property. Change its value from `ext-theme-classic` to `ext-theme-neptune`. The contents of `package.json` will be something similar to the following:

```
{
    "name": "masteringextjs-theme",
    "type": "theme",
    "creator": "anonymous",
    "version": "1.0.0",
    "compatVersion": "1.0.0",
    "local": true,
    "requires": [],
    "extend": "ext-theme-neptune"
}
```

After the theme structure is created and we have changed the base theme, let's build it. To build it, we are going to use the terminal and Sencha Cmd again. Change the directory to `packages/masteringextjs-theme` and type the following command:

```
sencha package build
```

The result will be something like the following:

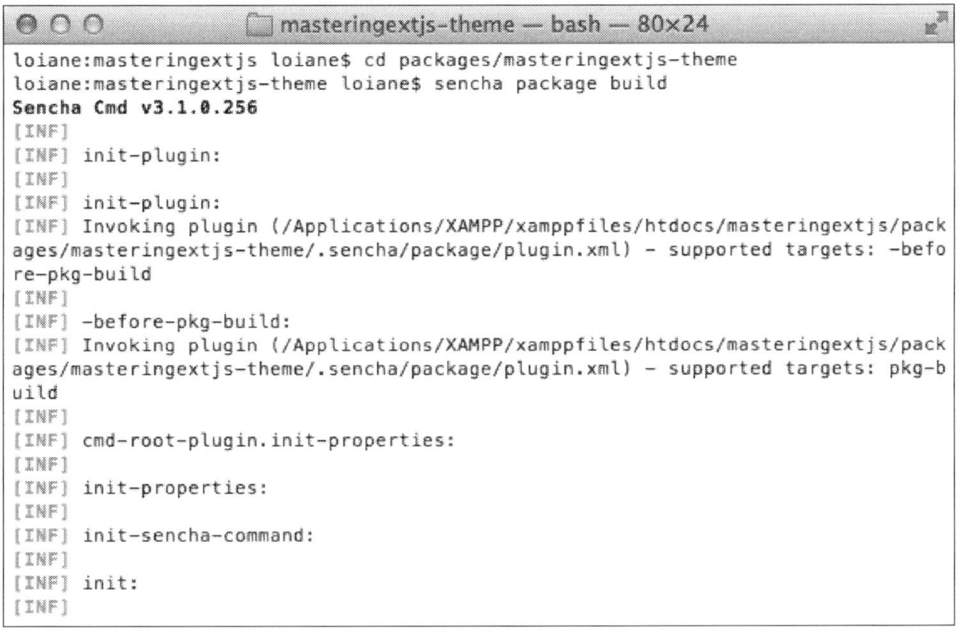

The result of this command will be the creation of the `build` directory inside the `packages/masteringextjs-theme` folder as follows:

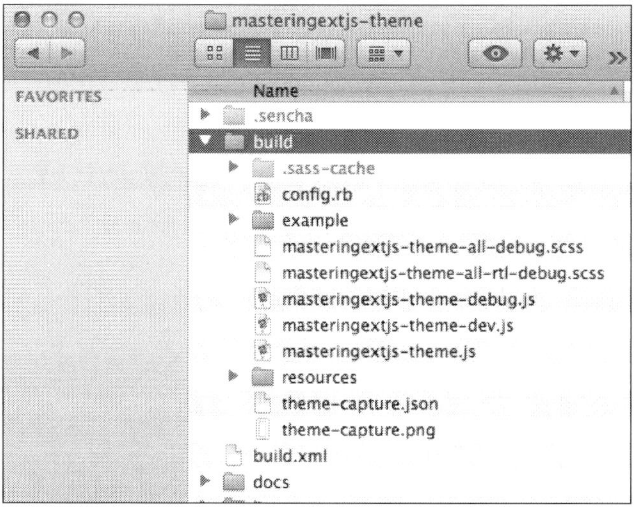

Inside this `build` folder we can find the `resources` folder and inside the `resources` folder we can find a file named `masteringextjs-theme-all.css`, which contains all the styles for all the components we styled in our theme (which is none so far, but we will get there). Even though we create a complete theme (style all components), it is not 100 percent certain that we will use all the components in our application. Sencha Cmd has the ability to filter and create a CSS file with only the components we are going to use in our project. For this reason, we do not need to include the `masteringextjs-theme-all.css` manually in our application.

So let's set up our project so it can use our theme. Inside our project's folder, there is a hidden folder named `.sencha`. Inside this folder, there is a directory named `app` and a file named `sencha.cfg` as follows:

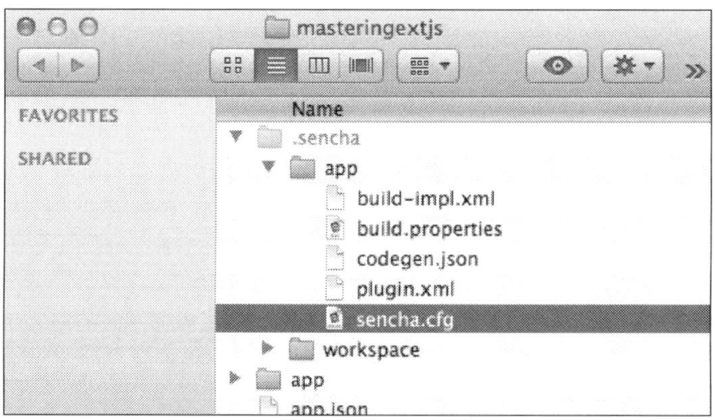

This file contains properties and configurations of the project used by Sencha Cmd, so we need to be careful when changing it. Locate the property `app.theme` and change its value to the name of the theme we just created (`masteringextjs-theme`) as follows:

```
# The name of the package containing the theme scss for the app
app.theme=masteringextjs-theme
```

Now we need to apply the changes to our project. With the terminal opened, change the directory to our application's root folder and type the following two commands:

```
sencha ant clean
sencha app build
```

If we try the application on the browser, we will see that the Neptune theme was applied:

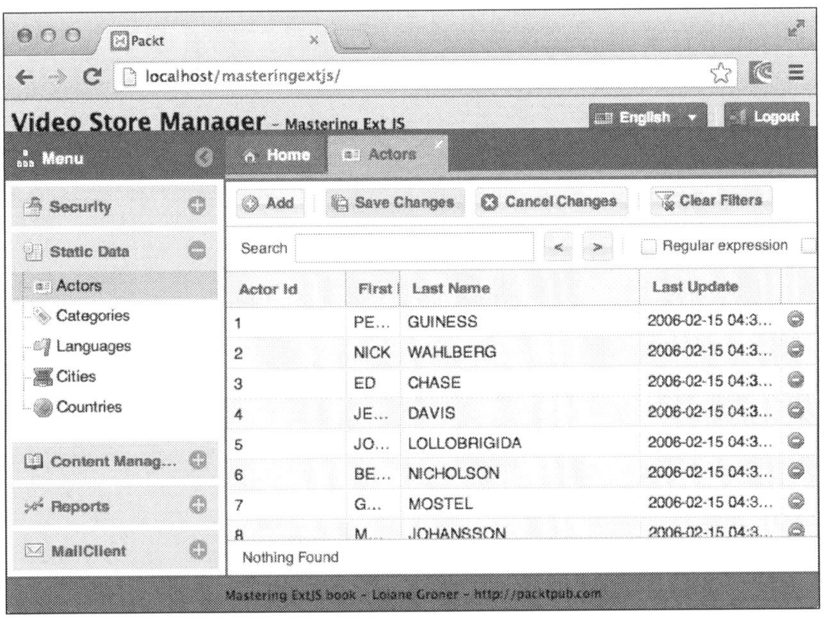

Still, no changes were made so far. Let's start customizing the theme right now! Let's go back to the `packages/masteringextjs-theme` folder. Inside the `sass/var` folder create a new file named `Component.scss`. Let's add the following content to it:

```
$base-color: #317040 !default;
```

With this code, we are declaring a Sass variable named `$base-color` with a greenish value. This will change the base color of the theme from blue to green. Let's apply the changes to our theme and see the difference.

With the terminal opened, change the directory to `packages/masteringextjs-theme` and type the following command:

```
sencha package build
```

Then, change the directory to the project's root folder and type the following command:

```
sencha app build
```

Open the browser and we will have something like the following screenshot:

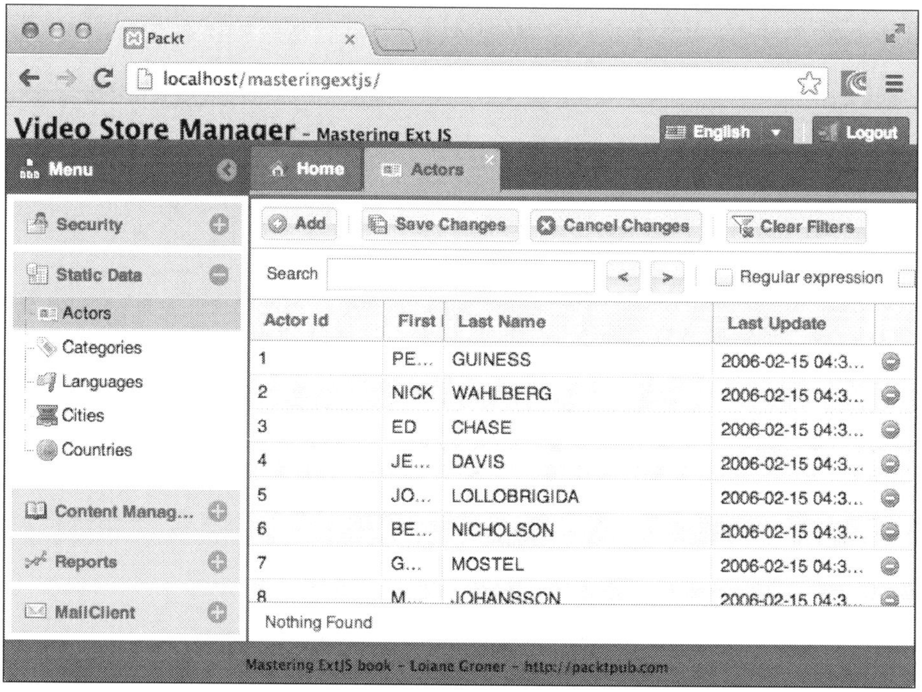

We can continue to add more styles to our custom theme. Whenever we make a change and want to see how it looks like, we need to use the `sencha package build` and `sencha app build` commands as we just did.

This is a big difference from building custom themes from Ext JS 4.2 to earlier versions of Ext JS 4. Before, we would use `compass compile` and do all the creation and compilation of files manually. Now Sencha Cmd is capable of doing it for us, and we only need to focus on the Sass code for the style we want to create. However, the new approach is more time consuming than the old one.

Ext JS documentation is also very complete. If you are looking to customize a specific component, you can find all the Sass CSS variables and CSS mixins that this component uses:

> For more information about theming Ext JS application, visit `http://docs.sencha.com/extjs/4.2.0/#!/guide/theming`. It is highly recommended to learn Sass (`http://sass-lang.com/`) and Compass (`http://compass-style.org/`) as well.

Packaging the application for production

Our theme is created, so now the only thing left is to make the production build and deploy the code on the production web server. Again, we will use Sencha Cmd to do it for us.

To do a production build we need to have a terminal opened. We also need to change the directory to the application's root directory and type the following command:

```
sencha app build
```

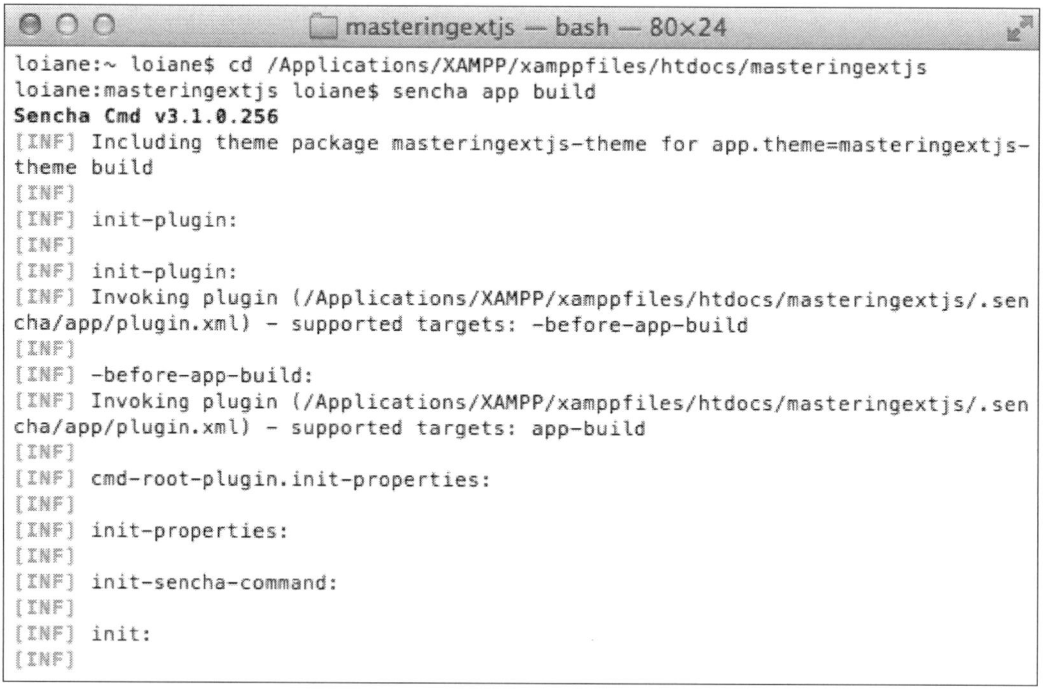

Once the command execution is completed, it will create a new directory called `build/NameofTheApp/production`. As our application namespace is Packt, it created the `build/Packt/production` directory as follows:

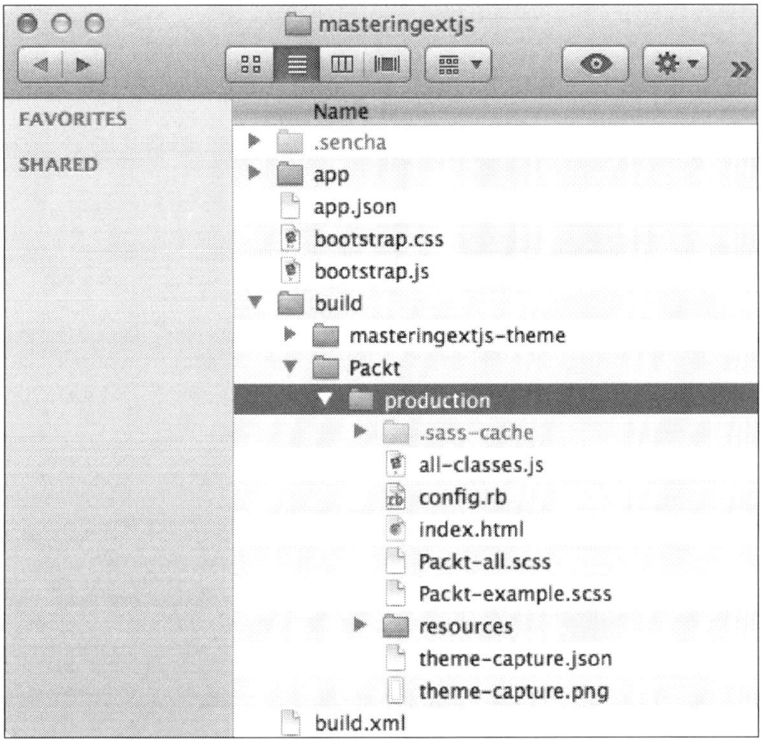

What this command does is to get all the code we developed (inside the `app` folder) along with the Ext JS code we need to run the application and put it inside the `all-classes.js` file. Then, using YUI Compressor, Sencha Cmd will minimize the code and obfuscate the JavaScript code; this way we will have a very small JavaScript file that the user will need to load. Also, Sencha Cmd will evaluate all the components our application is using and will filter the CSS that is not needed and will put it inside the `resources/Packt-all.css` file. All our custom images (icon images) will also be copied from the development environment to the `production` folder (inside the `resources` folder as well).

The next step now is to make sure that the production build is working as expected. To access the development environment we are using `http://localhost/masteringextjs`. To test the production build, we need to access `http://localhost/masteringextjs/build/Packt/production`. When we test it, we will see that it does not work as expected. We will get errors, as shown in the following screenshot:

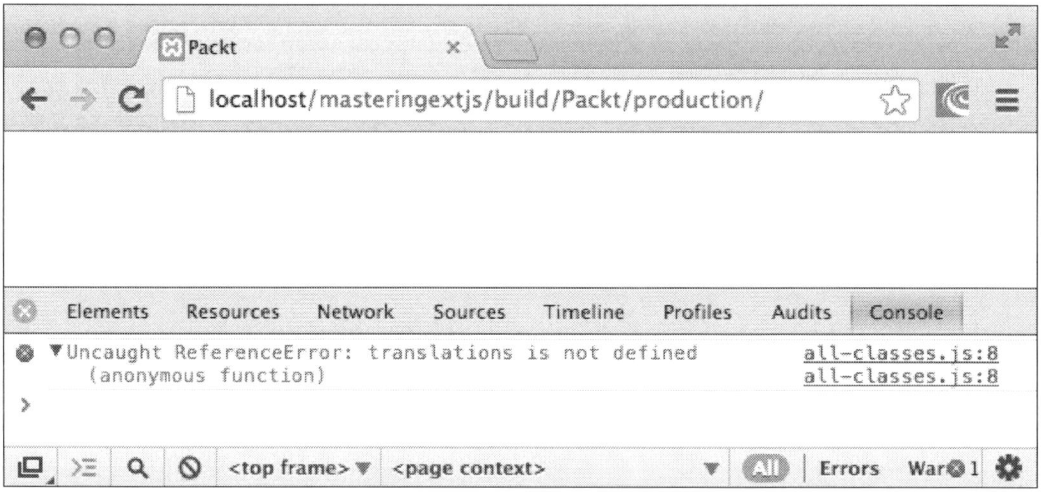

So the first thing we need to do is to make some changes on the `build/Packt/production/index.html` file. We need to add the translations file and also the `app.css` file (that we created with the image icons). The final version will be something like the following:

```
<!DOCTYPE HTML>
<html>
<head>
    <meta charset="UTF-8">
    <title>Packt</title>
<link rel="stylesheet" href="resources/Packt-all.css"/>
<link rel="stylesheet" href="resources/css/app.css">
<script src="translations/locale.js"></script>
<script type="text/javascript" src="all-classes.js"></script>
</head>
<body></body>
</html>
```

Next, we need to copy the `translations` and `php` folders to the `production` folder as well, as shown in the following screenshot:

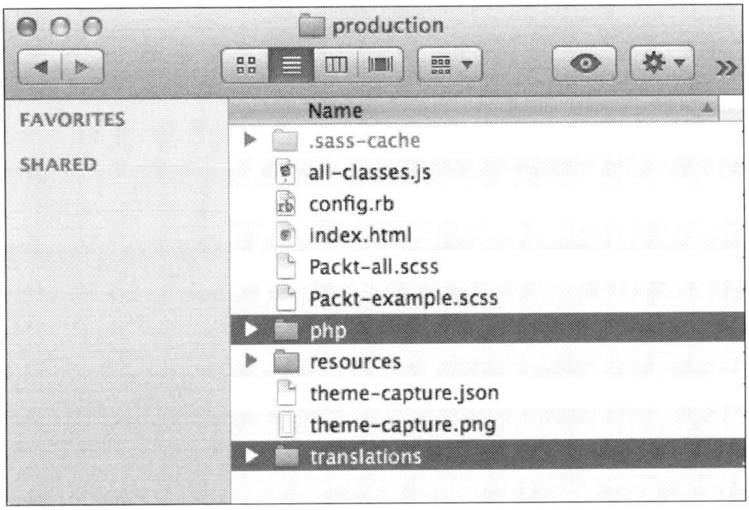

We can now test the application again. It should work as expected.

What to deploy in production

Always remember that we have the `app` folder and all the code developed as our development environment. Inside the `production` folder we have all the code that should be deployed in production.

So let's say we want to deploy this application right now. Simply transfer all the content from `masteringextjs/build/Packt/production` to the desired folder on your web server as follows:

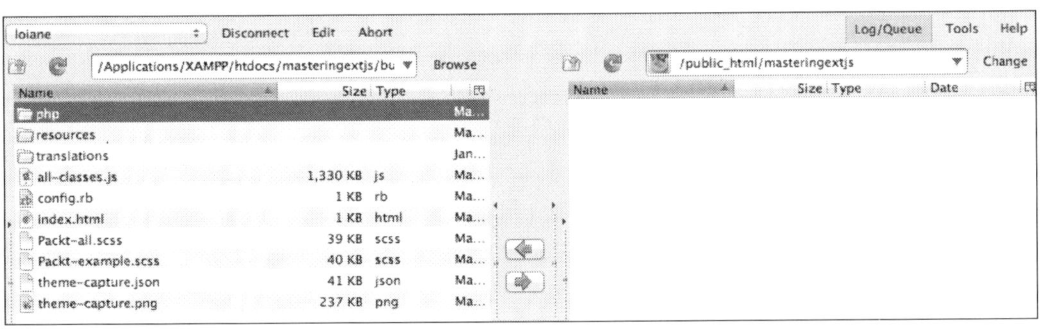

Happy production code!

Benefits

What are the benefits of the production build? Can we just deploy the development code? We can deploy the development code as is in production, but it is not recommended. With the production build we boost the performance while loading the files and the file size is minimized.

For example, let's do the following test: open the application on the browser, log in, and open the **Actors** screen from the static data module.

Using the development code we will have the following result from Google Developer Tools (or Firebug):

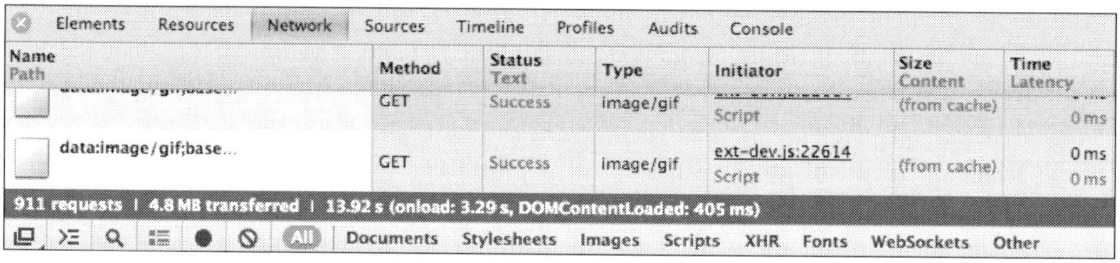

The application made 911 requests, resulting in 4.8 MB of data transferred to the user and it took 13.92 seconds to complete it. This is a lot, and talking about 4.8 MB to be transferred to the user is unacceptable!

Let's see the results using the production build:

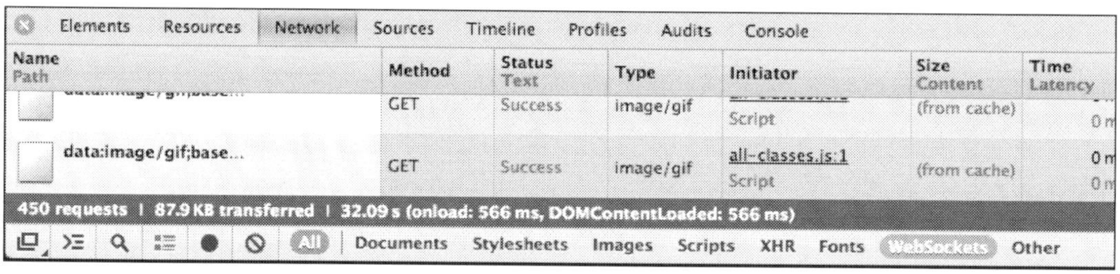

450 requests (still a big number) and 87.9 KB transferred. 450 is still a big number of requests. This is also because we have a lot of image icons to be displayed. In *Chapter 12, Debugging and Testing* we will learn how we can decrease this number even more with the help of other tools. But the most important change is the size of the data transferred: from 4.8 MB to 87.6 KB. It is a great improvement!

Another thing to notice is the files that are being loaded. On the development environment, we can see each Ext JS class being loaded by the browser:

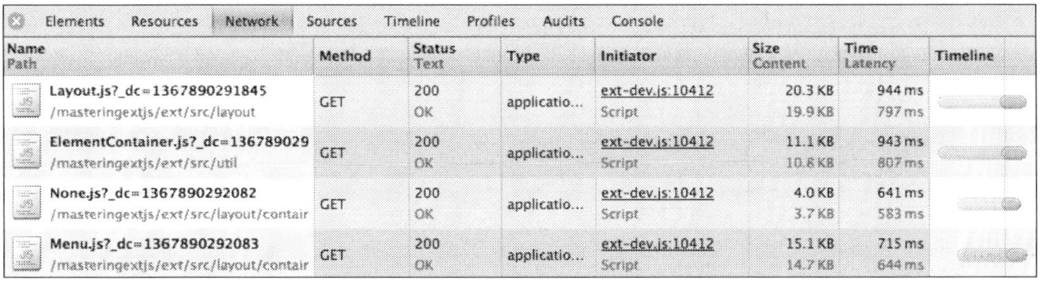

At the end it is going to be more than 400 JavaScript files being loaded just to render the login screen.

If we try the production build, we will get a screen similar to the following screenshot:

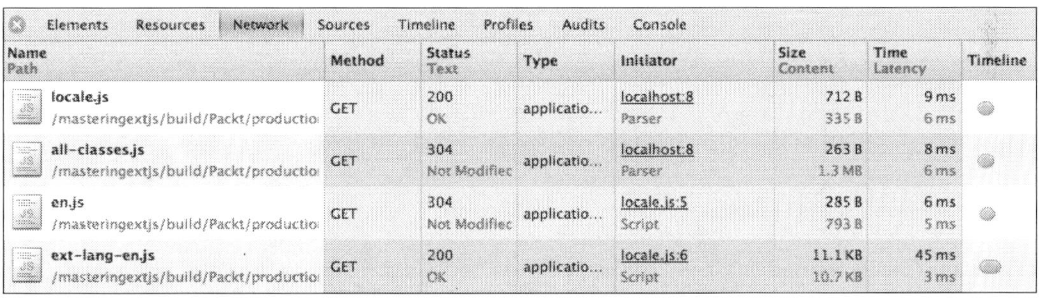

Only four JavaScript files are being loaded. There is a big difference.

So, for performance purposes, always deploy the production build. Use the development code only for development purposes. It is also possible to do a testing build—for testing purposes. We will talk more about it in *Chapter 12, Debugging and Testing*.

From web to desktop – Sencha Desktop Packager

If you are an experienced Ext JS developer, going to production always meant deploying the Ext JS code to a web server and the server code as well; it does not matter if you use PHP, Java, .NET, Ruby, or any other language. Both code, frontend (Ext JS) and backend are deployed on a web server.

But there is another way to distribute the Ext JS code to the users: going desktop! We are not talking about developing a project using Java desktop (such as Swing) or using C or C++, we are talking about having a native application (for Mac OS, Linux, and Windows) made with HTML, CSS, and JavaScript code, and of course, using our favorite framework, which is Ext JS.

There are a few tools in the market that can do it for us, but in this book we will explore another Sencha tool that is called Sencha Desktop Packager. Sencha Desktop Packager is a paid tool from Sencha, but we can download a trial version to test it and see if we like it. To download it, go to `http://www.sencha.com/products/desktop-packager/`.

So let's try to have our application native to Mac OS, Linux, and Windows. We also need to understand if it is enough just to package our code using Sencha Desktop Packager or if we need to do something else. Again, let's do it step by step.

Installation

Once we have downloaded Sencha Desktop Packager, we can unzip it to a directory of our choice.

The next step is adding the Sencha Desktop Packager to the PATH of our OS.

Mac OS and Linux

For Mac OS and Linux, we can do it using the terminal. For example, let's use `/Users/loiane/bin/Sencha/SenchaDesktopPackager` as the directory of Sencha Desktop Packager.

To set the PATH, we simply need to use the following command:

```
export PATH=$PATH:/Users/loiane/bin/Sencha/SenchaDesktopPackager
```

Then, we can print the `PATH` variable (`echo $PATH`) to make sure it was set and at last, test the `ionpackage` command to make sure it is working as expected:

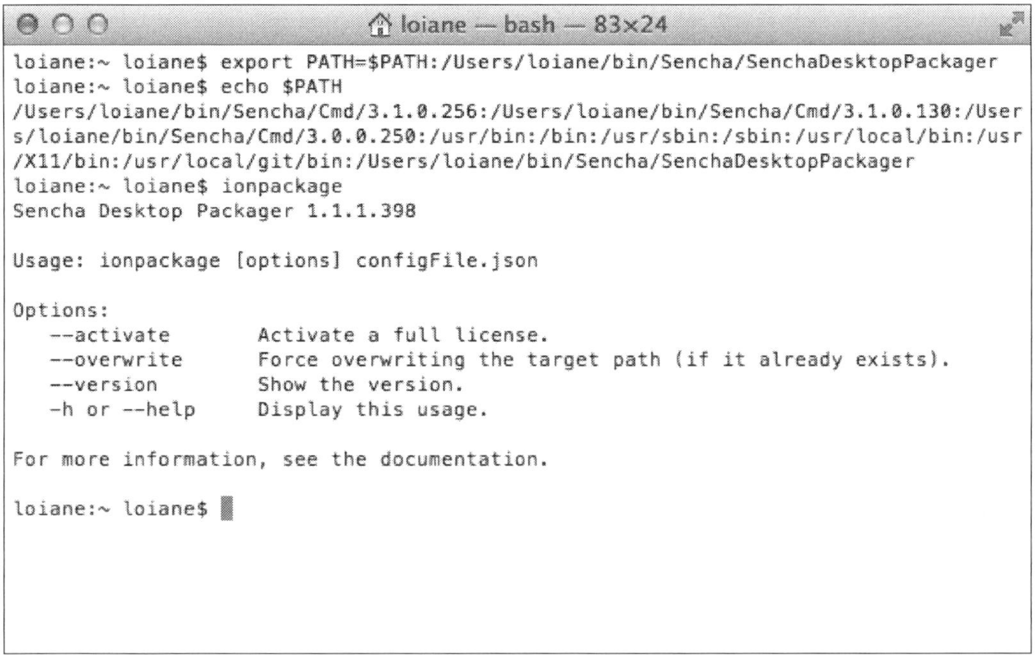

Windows

If you use Windows, we need to set up a new environment variable. Let's use `C:/SenchaDesktopPackager` as the directory for the Sencha Desktop Packager. The following screenshots were taken using Windows 8, but the steps are the same for Windows 7 and very similar for Windows XP as well.

Locate the My Computer icon, right-click on it, and select **Properties**:

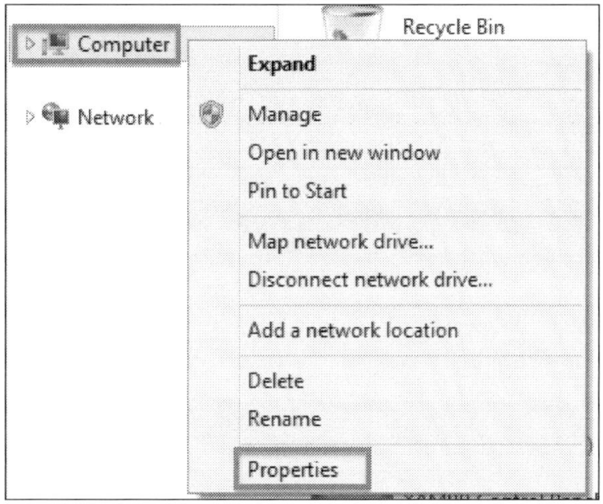

Click on **Advanced system settings**:

Click on **Environment Variables...**:

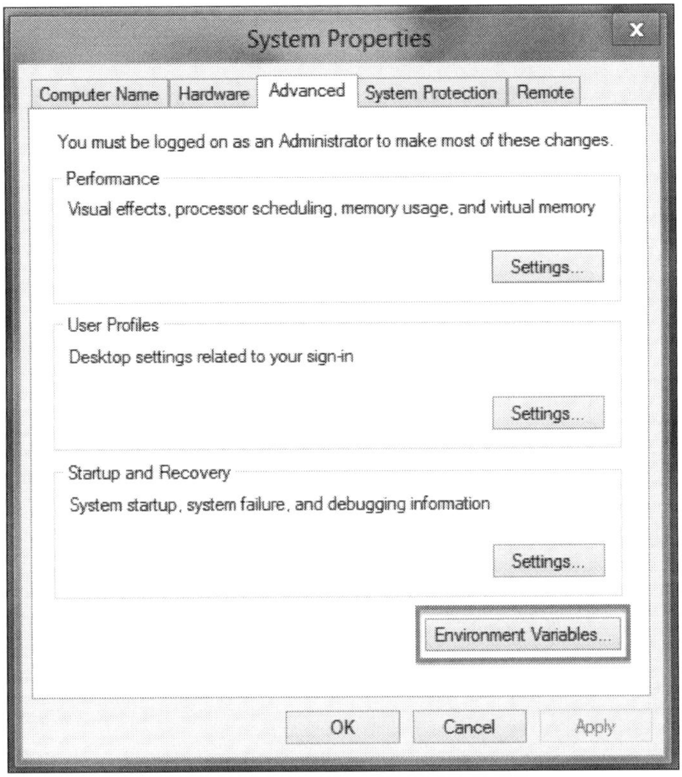

In the **System variables** frame, locate the **Path** one and click on **Edit...**:

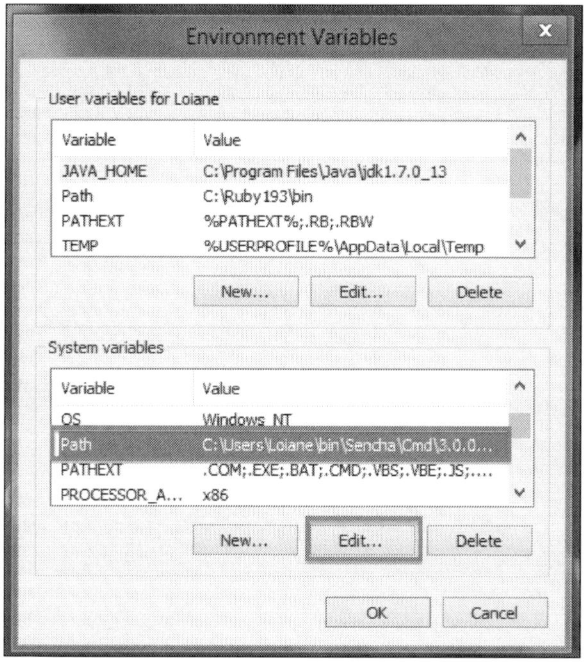

Add `;C:\SenchaDesktopPackager` at the end of it and click on **OK** and save it:

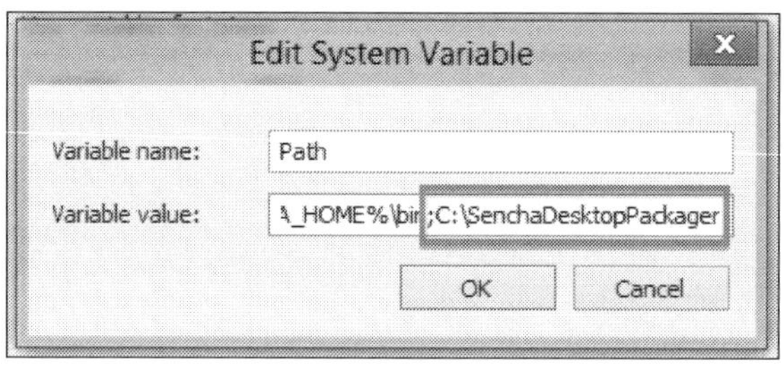

Open the terminal and test it by typing the ionpackage command as follows:

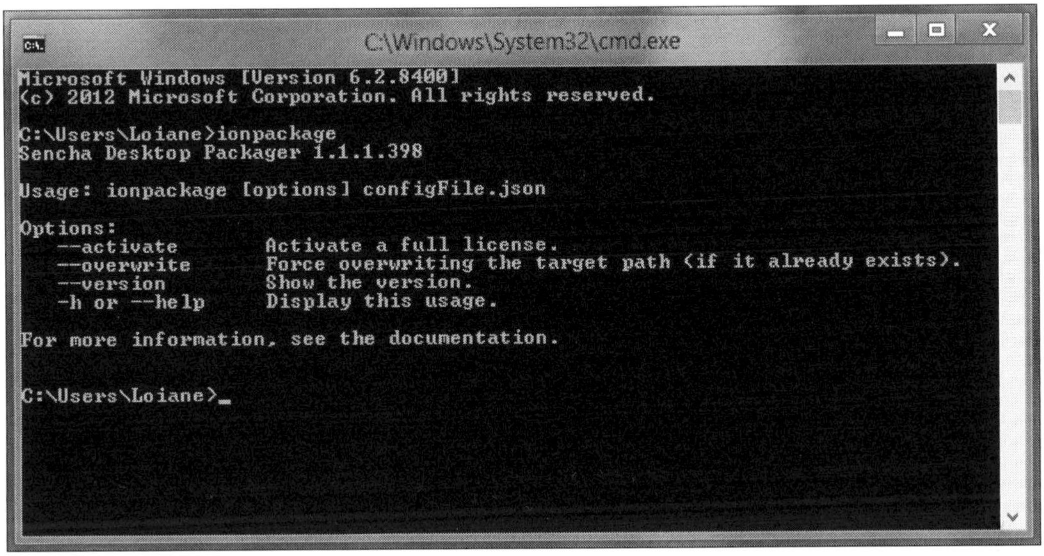

We are now good to go!

Packaging the application

One of the requirements is to have the production build ready, which we have already done in the last topic.

Inside the project's folder, we need to create a JSON file with some configurations. We will create a new file named `desktoppackager.json` with the following content:

```
{
    "applicationName"      : "Mastering Ext JS",
    "applicationIconPaths" : ["HelloWorld.ico", "HelloWorld.icns"],
    "versionString"        : "1.0",
    "outputPath"           : "build/Packt/package/",
    "webAppPath"           : "build/Packt/production/",
    "settings"             : {
        "mainWindow" : {
            "autoShow" : true
        }
    }
}
```

We also need an icon to represent our application. We will use the **HelloWorld.icns** and **HelloWorld.ico** icons from the *HelloWorld* example we can find inside the examples folder of Sencha Desktop Packager.

The structure of our application with these three new files will be as shown in the following screenshot:

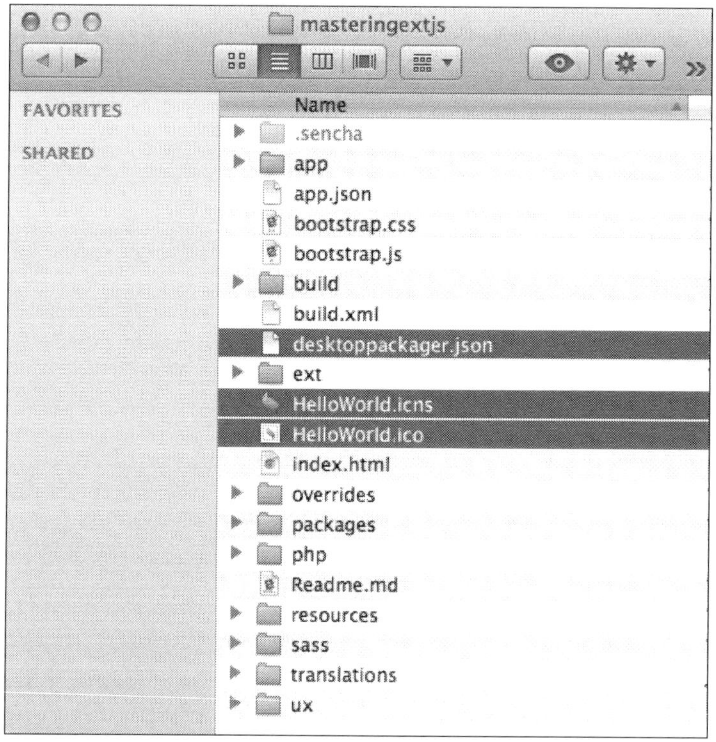

Then, using the terminal, change the directory to the application's directory and type the following command:

```
ionpackage desktoppackager.json
```

The output should be something like the following:

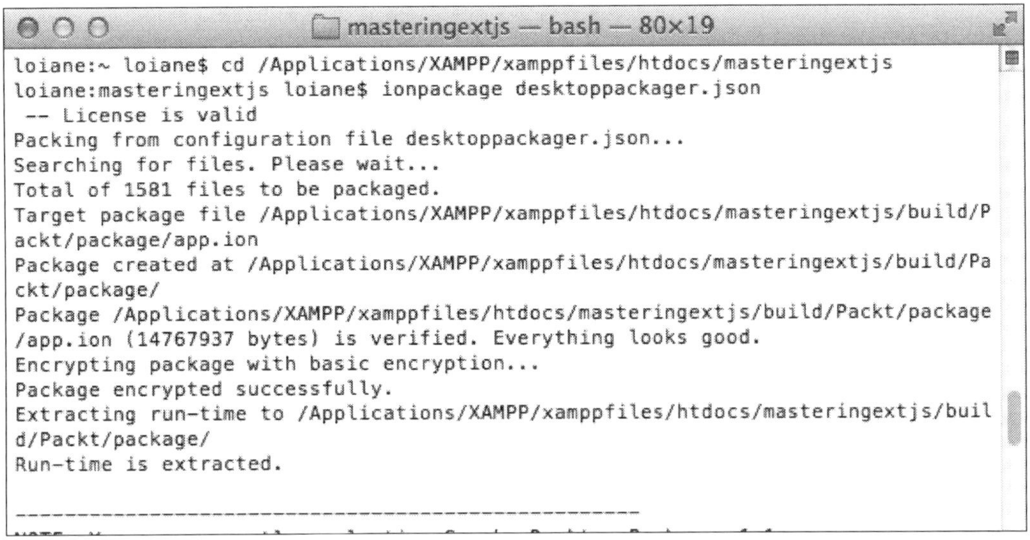

If this is the first time you are using Sencha Desktop Packager, it is going to prompt you to enter your Sencha user ID and password. This user ID and password are the same that you use on Sencha forums.

After the command is completed, open the `build` directory. You should see a new directory that was created (`Packt/package`), and inside it, a native application (`.app` for Mac OS and `.exe` for Windows) named Mastering Ext JS:

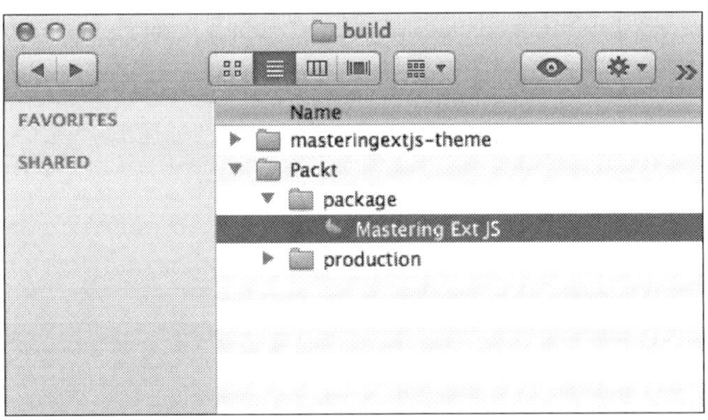

If we execute this application, we will get some errors, but we will be able to see the login screen as follows (and notice that the theme is the one we created):

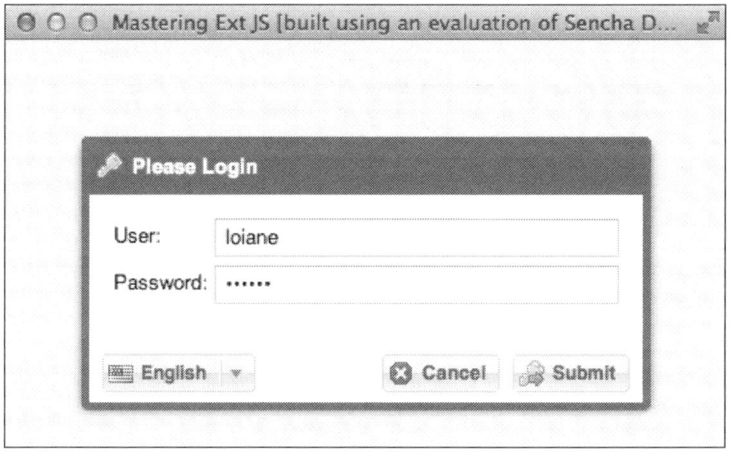

Sencha Desktop Packager will generate the native application for the OS that we are using. For example, if we execute the `ionpackage` command from a Mac OS, it will generate a native application for Mac OS. If we execute it from Linux, it will generate a native application for Linux, and if we execute the command from Windows, it will generate a native application for Windows.

Required changes on the server side

Why did we get an error? How can we know if something is wrong, since it is a native app? It is possible to debug as if we were running in a normal browser. To do it, we need to add the following configuration inside the `settings` property on `desktoppackager.json`:

```
"remoteDebuggingPort": 9100
```

Then, run the `ionpackage desktoppackager.json` command again and wait until a new executable file is created. Open it and also open a Webkit browser (Chrome) using the following address: `http://localhost:9100`. The name of the application should be listed and when we click on it, all the **Developer Tools** options should be available:

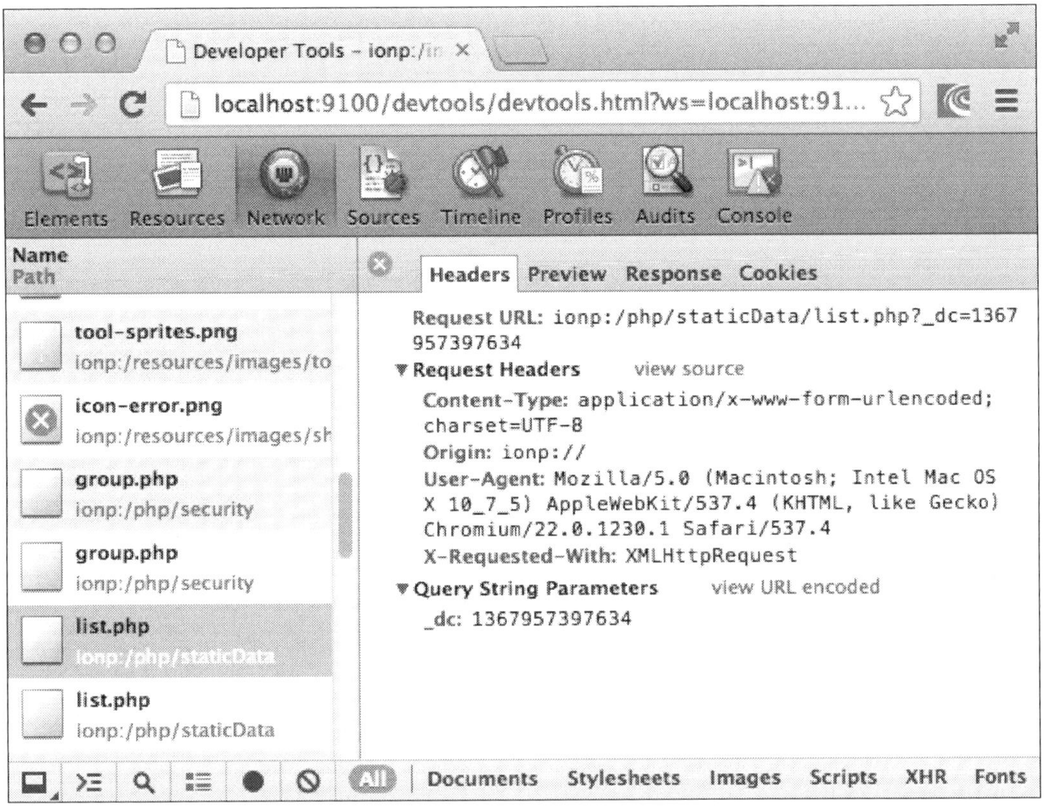

If we take a look, we will notice that Sencha Desktop Packager packaged the PHP code as well, and it is trying to access it, as it it is a JavaScript file. As Sencha Desktop Packager does not support PHP code, only HTML, CSS, and JavaScript code, it will not work.

Our server-side code, independently of the language used (PHP, Java, .NET) must be deployed in a web server, and our desktop application will access it.

So for a first test, we need to add the complete URL in all stores, proxies, and Ajax requests in our code.

For example, let's use the Menu Store as an example. Simply add `http://localhost/masteringextjs` before the original URL. The result will be:

```
url: 'http://localhost/masteringextjs/php/menu.php'
```

Now search all the stores, proxies, and Ajax requests (inside the controllers) and do the same thing. All URLs must be completed as we did for the Menu store.

After making all the changes, do the production build again (do not forget to apply the changes to the `index.html` file inside the `build/Packt/production` directory again—or simply the current production `index.html` file somewhere and after the new production build replace it—every time we make a new production build, the `index.html` file will be replaced). To make sure it is working, remove the `php` folder from the production build as well and test it (`http://localhost/masteringextjs/build/Packt/production/`). It should be working and we should not get any errors.

The production build for the Sencha Desktop Packager should look like this (all the same files from the previous build, with the exception of the `php` folder):

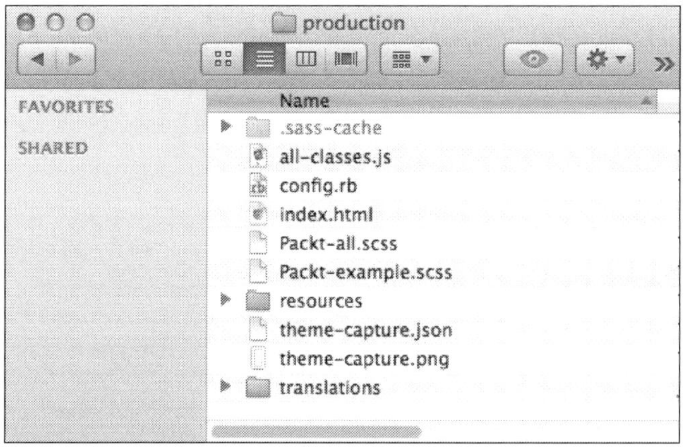

Now we need to run the `ionpackage desktoppackager.json` command again. Then, let's test our native application again. The result should be the same as that we would get accessing the application on a browser, but the difference is that it is a native application:

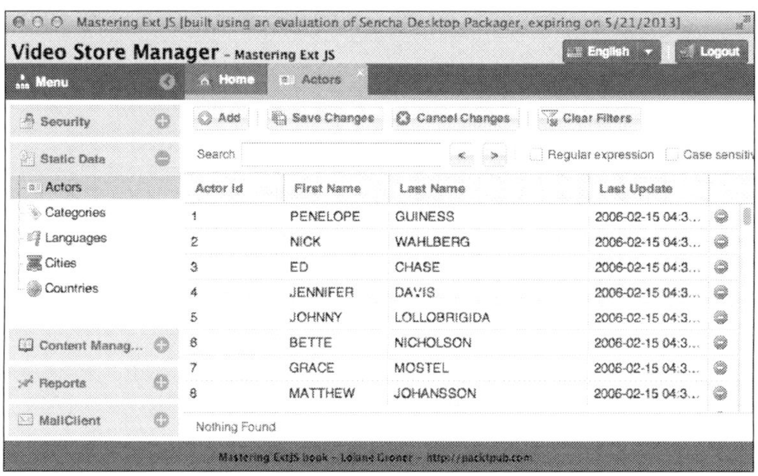

If we package for Windows, we will have the same application, but running a `.exe` file and looking like a Windows program. The same will apply to Linux.

Ajax versus JSONP versus CORS

One thing that is very important to know: our server code is deployed locally (*localhost*) and our application is also running locally.

It is also very important to remember that we are using Ajax requests all over the application and Ajax only allows requests from one domain to the same domain, it does not allow requests from domain1 to domain2 (cross-domain requests).

What if we decide to distribute our application to users that are in several different domains (domainA, domainB, domainC, and so on) and our server-side code is deployed on `packt.com`? We will get errors because Ajax does not allow requests like these.

We can use JSONP, but then we will need to change our server-side code to send back the JSONP callback parameter, and JSONP is only good to `GET` requests, meaning we can only retrieve information; we cannot use `POST`, `PUT`, and `DELETE` requests.

Thankfully, there is a third alternative, which is **Cross-Origin Resource Sharing (CORS)**. If we enable CORS on the server-side code, we will be able to make Ajax requests from domainA to `packt.com`, for example. The change on the server side is minimum.

For example, in PHP, we simply need to add the following code in all PHP files (at the beginning of each file):

```
<?php  header("Access-Control-Allow-Origin: *");
```

Problem solved!

We also need to make some changes in the `desktoppackager.json` file, such as adding a special configuration to allow cross-site access.

```
{
    "applicationName"       : "Mastering Ext JS",
    "applicationIconPaths"  : ["HelloWorld.ico", "HelloWorld.icns"],
    "versionString"         : "1.0",
    "outputPath"            : "build/Packt/package/",
    "webAppPath"            : "build/Packt/production/",
    "settings"              : {
        "remoteDebuggingPort": 9100,
            "security": {
                "allowCrossSite": true
```

```
                },
            "mainWindow" : {
                "autoShow" : true
            }
        }
    }
```

> To learn more about the Sencha Desktop Packager configurations and everything that is possible to do, go to `http://docs.sencha.com/desktop-packager/1.1`.

So, if we want to distribute our native application to different users, we will need to enable CORS in our code. The same applies in case we want to deploy the Ext JS code in one server and the server-side code in another server (different domain).

> To learn more about CORS, how to enable it on server side (different languages), browser support and other information, please access `http://enable-cors.org/`.

Summary

In this chapter we have learned how to create a new theme using the new theming engine of Ext JS 4.2, we learned why it is important to make a production build and how to do it, including the difference between the files from the development environment those for the production environment.

We have also learned about Sencha Desktop Packager and how to natively package our Ext JS application to be executed as a native application on Mac OS, Linux, and Windows. We learned that it is not simply a matter of packaging the application and that some changes are required. In case we want to distribute the application to be accessed from different domains, there are alternatives we can use.

In the next chapter, we will learn how to build a complete WordPress theme using Ext JS.

11
Building a WordPress Theme

There is no doubt that Ext JS is a great JavaScript framework and its use is not only for CRUD applications. You can implement a real-time application such as an application to follow the price for market stocks as well. Also, you can use Ext JS to do what your imagination is up to. In this chapter, Ext JS will be used to build a theme for WordPress. If you are not familiar with WordPress, it is a web software you can use to create a beautiful website or blog. In other words, it is a content management tool for blogging. You will notice that the approach we will use is completely different from the approach we have used so far to develop our applications in the previous chapters.

So in this chapter, we will cover:

- Structuring the theme
- Building the Header and Footer
- Building the Main page
- Building the Sidebar
- Building the single post page
- Building the single page

Before we start

Before we start the step-by-step tutorial for this chapter, you need to have WordPress installed. You can use the one you use for your blog (for example, `http://loiane.com` and `http://loianegroner.com` uses WordPress) or you can use a local installation.

If you do not know how to install WordPress, you can follow this tutorial: `http://codex.wordpress.org/Installing_WordPress`.

For testing purposes, in this chapter we will use a local installation. The WordPress installation used in this chapter was installed inside the `masteringextjs` folder inside the `htdocs` folder from XAMPP as shown in the following screenshot:

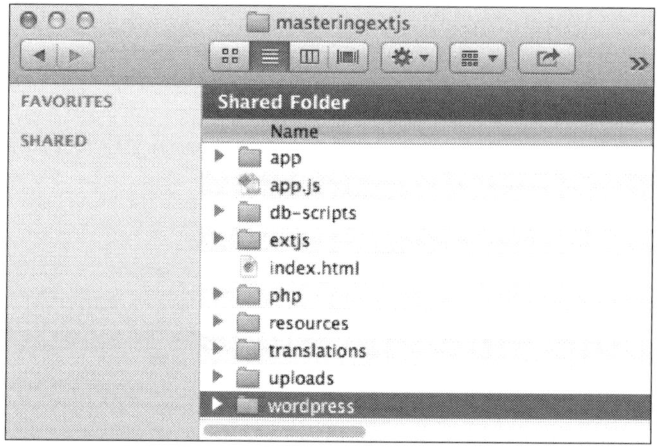

The preceding screenshot shows the WordPress installation with some posts for testing purposes. We will build our theme based on this installation.

After you install WordPress, you will have something like the following screenshot (using the default theme that is active when we install WordPress):

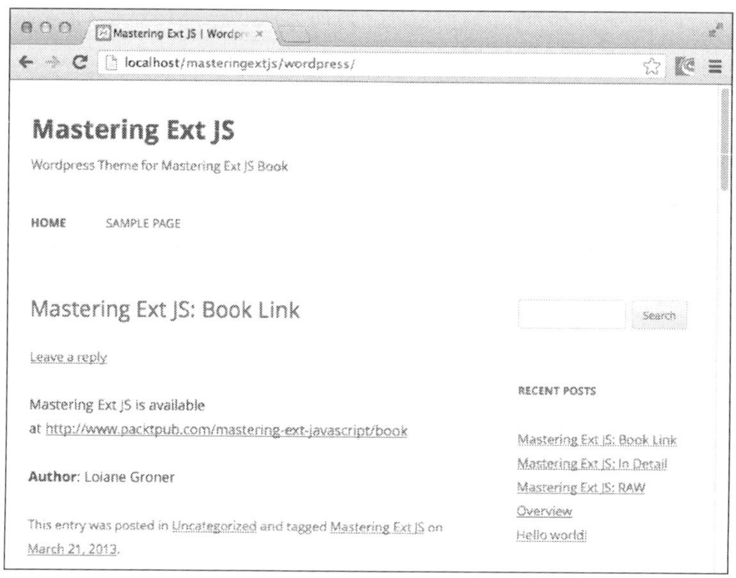

And by the time we finish implementing the Ext JS theme for WordPress, we will have something like the following screenshot:

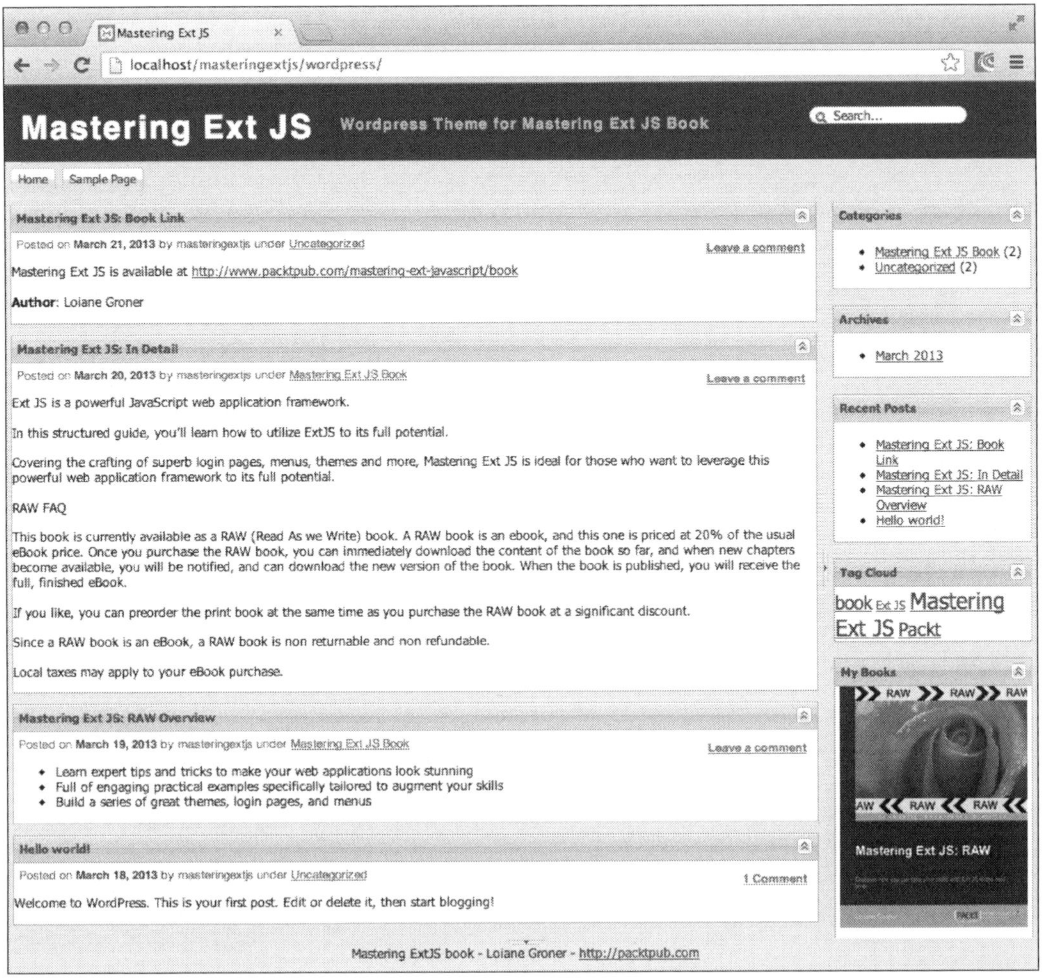

A brief introduction to WordPress themes

WordPress themes are part of what makes WordPress so popular. Before we start coding we need to understand a little bit of how WordPress themes work. When we are creating a new WordPress theme, we need to create some files that will be recognized automatically by WordPress. Most of the files are self-explanatory, but let's take a look at them:

- `header.php`: When we load a blog, WordPress transforms it into a single HTML page so that the browser can render it. The `header.php` file contains the theme code until the `</head>` tag.
- `sidebar.php`: This is an optional file that can be called by using the WordPress `get_sidebar()` function. This is where we can add the code to render widgets and also render the Sidebar of the theme, in case it has one.
- `footer.php`: This is where we will end our HTML code to wrap up the theme. You can also display widgets here if you would like.
- `page.php`: This is used to display a single page. Examples of single pages are about page and press page.
- `single.php`: This is used to display a single blog post. It is very similar to `page.php` regarding the source code.
- `index.php`: The `index.php` page is called when the blog is rendered. This displays posts, search results, the Header, Footer, Sidebar, error messages, and so on.
- `functions.php`: This is where we can put extra theme functions if we need to.
- `comments.php`: This displays the comments, trackbacks, and comment forms.

A WordPress theme can use as many files as desired, but these are the files that are most commonly used to build a theme.

Structuring our theme

Well, let's get started. Navigate to the `themes` directory to create our theme. The `themes` directory can be found at `masteringextjs/wordpress/wp-content/themes` (and the `masteringextjs` folder is inside the `htdocs` folder of the XAMPP application). Create a new folder named `ext-theme` as follows:

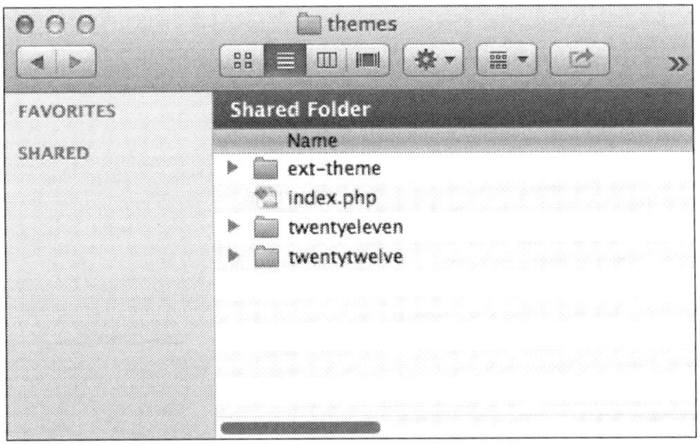

Create the following files: `comments.php`, `footer.php`, `functions.php`, `header.php`, `index.php`, `page.php`, `sidebar.php`, `single.php`, and `style.css` as follows (the files can be empty, we just need to create them):

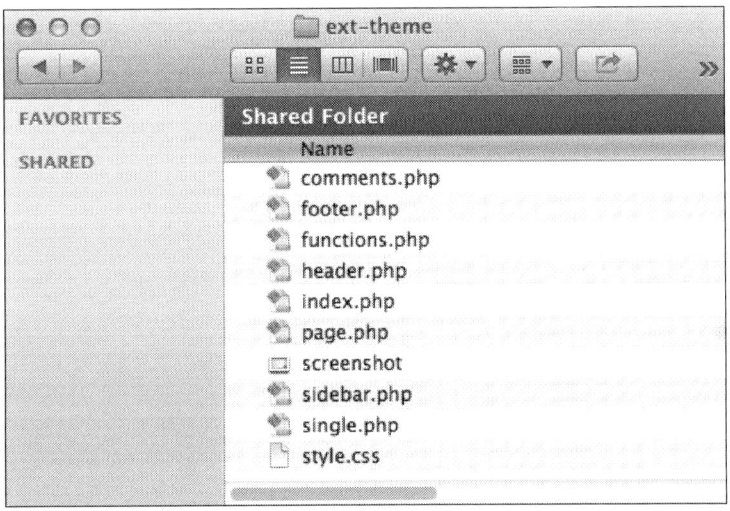

Also create (or paste) a file named `screenshot.png` inside the `ext-theme` folder with the screenshot that will be used to represent the theme.

Now that we have the theme skeleton, we need to make our theme to appear on the WordPress dashboard. To do so, we need to modify the `style.css` file. Add the following content to the `style.css` file:

```
/*
Theme Name: Mastering Ext JS
Theme URI: http://packtpub.com
Description: Wordpress theme example for Mastering Ext JS Book -
http://packtpub.com

Author: Loiane Groner
Version: 1.0
Tags: minimalistic, simple, extjs, sidebar, elegant, masteringextjs
*/
```

Here, WordPress will try to find the `style.css` file inside the `theme` directory to extract information about the theme. If we open the WordPress dashboard on the Appearance menu, we can see our theme as a theme available to be activated:

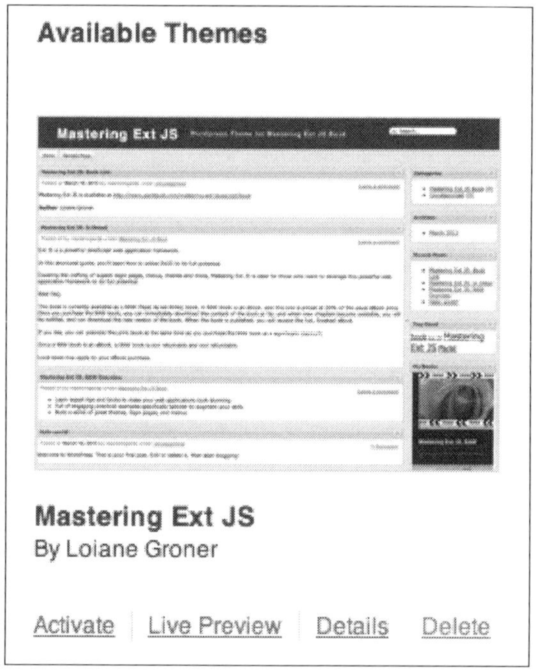

When we activate it and try to visualize the blog, it will be blank. But do not worry because it is a good thing; it means that we can now start building our theme.

Let's take a look again at our theme screenshot, but now, with the most important theme parts highlighted:

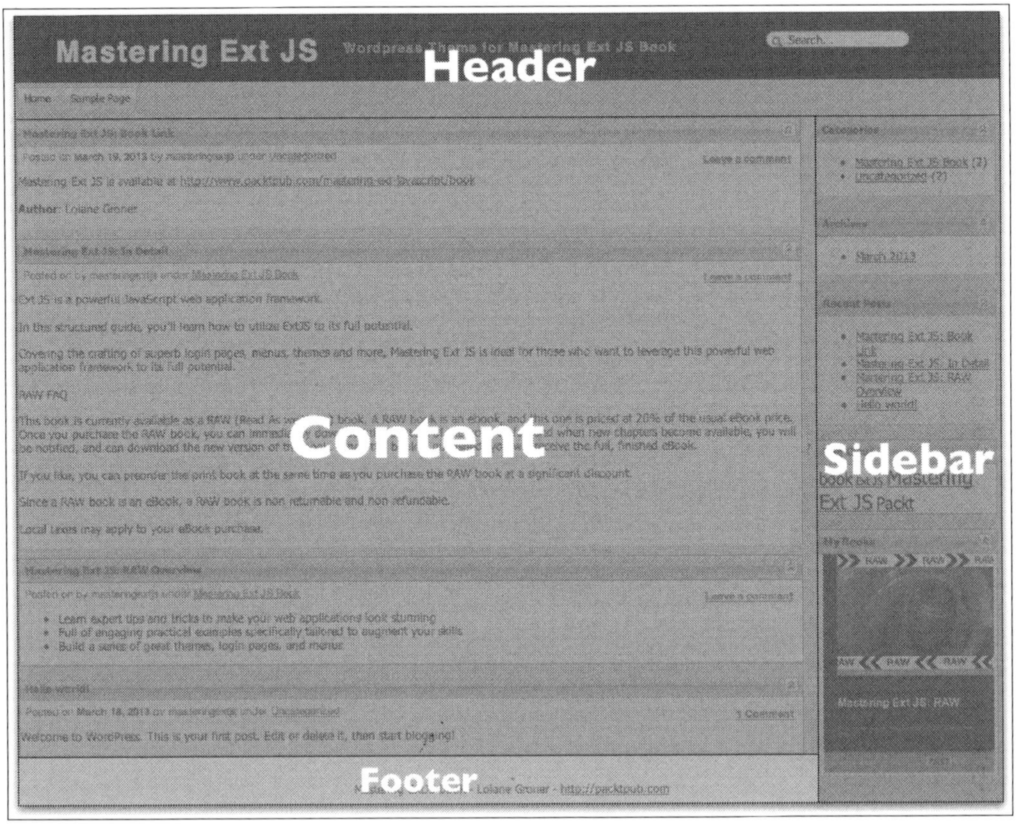

The Header contains the blog title, description, and also a search field. Below it, we have the navigation links so that the reader can navigate between the blog pages. The Sidebar contains widgets to display **Categories**, **Archives**, **Recent Posts**, **Tag Cloud**, and a custom widget (**My Books**). The Footer contains a copyright message and the content area contains the list of the latest posts.

So let's have some fun and start coding.

Building the Header

As we are building a WordPress theme with Ext JS, we need to have Ext JS library installed in our theme's directory and also create a `js` file where we will add all the Ext JS code we need. So let's go ahead and do it. Copy the Ext JS SDK into the `ext-theme` folder and also create a new file called `app.js`:

Now, inside the `header.php` file add the following code:

```
<html>
<head>
<title><?php bloginfo('name'); ?> <?php wp_title(); ?></title>   // #1
<link rel="stylesheet" href="<?php bloginfo('stylesheet_directory');
?>/extjs/resources/css/ext-all.css" type="text/css"/> // #2
<link rel="stylesheet" href="<?php bloginfo('stylesheet_url'); ?>"/>
// #3
<script src="<?php bloginfo('stylesheet_directory'); ?>/extjs/ext-all.
js"></script> // #4
<script src="<?php bloginfo('stylesheet_directory'); ?>/app.js"></
script> // #5
</head>
```

WordPress has a function called `bloginfo` that allows us to get all sorts of information about the blog, such as blog name, description, theme directory, stylesheet URL, site URL, and much more. As you can see, we are using this function in five different places in the preceding code. To know more about this function, please visit `http://codex.wordpress.org/Function_Reference/bloginfo`.

The `title` tag will display the name of the blog, `bloginfo('name')`, and will also display the name of the page we are currently accessing using the `wp_title` function (`#1`). For example, if we open the **Hello world!** post, the title will display **Mastering Ext JS >> Hello world!**.

Next, we need to import the Ext JS files: `ext-all.css` (`#2`), `ext-all.js` (`#4`), and `app.js` (`#5`). To do so, we can use the `bloginfo('stylesheet_directory')` function to get the current theme's directory, and then complete the path with each file's correct path.

> `ext-all.js` contains the entire Ext JS framework source code within it. So this is a different approach than the one we have been using in the previous chapters of this book.

And finally, we also need to import the `style.css` file. To do it, we will use the `bloginfo('stylesheet_url')` function (`#3`).

Next, let's add some more code to the `header.php` file:

```
<body>
<div id="headerCont" style="display:none;">
  <!-- content here #6 -->
</div><!-- headerCont -->
```

Inside this `headerCont` div we will add the code that will display the blog title and description, the search field, and also the blog navigation links. The style is displayed as `none` because we do not want to display it as a simple HTML, but we want an Ext JS component to display it.

We will replace `#6` with the following content:

```
<div id="top-bar-tile">
<div id="top-bar-content">
  <h1><a href="<?php bloginfo('url'); ?>">
    <?php bloginfo('name'); ?> <!-- #7 -->
  </a></h1>
  <span class="slogan">
    <?php bloginfo('description'); ?> <!-- #8 -->
  </span>
  <div id="search-box"> <!-- #9 -->
    <form method="get" id="searchform" action="" >
      <input type="text" value="Search..."
      onfocus="if(this.value == this.defaultValue) this.value = ''"
      name="s" id="s" />
    </form>
  </div><!-- search-box -->
</div><!-- top-bar-content -->
</div><!-- top-bar-tile -->
```

We will display `name` of the blog (`#7`) and its `description` (`#8`) along with `search-box` (`#9`).

Then, we will display the navigation bar where we will dynamically display all the blog pages using the `wp_nav_menu` function (`http://codex.wordpress.org/Function_Reference/wp_nav_menu`) as follows:

```
<div id="links" style="display:none;">
   <?php wp_nav_menu(array(
   'menu' => 'mainnav',
   'menu_class' => 'nav-bar-content',
   'menu_id' => 'navigation',
   'container' => false,
   'theme_location' => 'primary-menu',
   'show_home' => '1')); ?>
</div><!-- links -->
```

Finally, open the `index.php` file and add the following code to it:

```
<?php get_header(); ?>
```

From the PHP side this is enough to display the Header.

Creating the Ext JS code

Now we need to create the Ext JS code. To create a simple theme, as demonstrated earlier in this chapter, does not require a large amount of Ext JS code. The Ext JS side is simpler; most of the work relies on the PHP and WordPress functions.

So the basic idea is to create a viewport that uses a Border Layout. On the North region we will have the Header, on the South region we will have the Footer, on the East region we will have the Sidebar, and on the Center region we will have the Content. We do not need to create a MVC application for this; we can go with the old style and put our code inside the `Ext.onReady` function. All the creation of posts, widgets, and navigation buttons will be done dynamically using the good old DOM manipulation. Of course, you can use any other approach that you desire, but this is the one we will follow in this chapter.

Inside the `app.js` file, add the following code:

```
Ext.onReady(function() {
    Ext.create('Ext.container.Viewport', {
        layout: 'border',
        items: [{
            region: 'north',
            html: Ext.getDom('headerCont').innerHTML, // #1
            border: false,
            margins: '0 0 5 0',
            height: 100,
            dockedItems: [{
                xtype: 'toolbar',
                itemId: 'navToolbar', // #2
                dock: 'bottom',
                ui: 'footer'
            }]
        }, {
            region: 'center',
            xtype: 'container',  // #3
            autoScroll: true,
            styleHtmlContent: true,
            defaults: {
                xtype: 'panel', // #4
                padding: '5px',
                margins: '0 0 5 0',
                collapsible: true,
                styleHtmlContent: true,
                autoScroll: true
            }
        }]
    });
  // #5
});
```

On the North region, we will have a panel that will use the HTML content of the `headerCont` div; that is why we used `style="display:none;"` (#1). To display the navigation links, we will add them to `navToolbar` (#2). We will create this code in a minute.

As the Center region is mandatory when we create a container that uses a Border Layout, we need to create it right away. For this reason, we will create a `Container` (`#3`) and it will have children panels (`#4`) to display the blog posts (each blog post will be inside a panel).

Right after the definition of the viewport (`#5`) we need to declare the following code:

```
var buttons = Ext.get(Ext.getDom('links')).dom.children[0]; // #1
var list = Ext.get(buttons).child('ul').dom.children; // #2
var toolbar = Ext.ComponentQuery.query('toolbar#navToolbar')[0];
Ext.Array.each(list, function(li) { // #3
    toolbar.add({// #4
        text: Ext.get(li).dom.children[0].firstChild.data, // #5
        href: Ext.get(li).dom.children[0].href, // #6
        hrefTarget: '_self' // #7
    });
});
```

The preceding code will retrieve the `links` div first child (which is the nav-bar-content div: `#1`). Then, it will retrieve the list of children of the first `ul` child (`#2`). Then we need a reference to the Header toolbar. With everything we need on hands, we can iterate (`#3`) the list of `li` children and create buttons for the toolbar from its content (`#4`). The text can be retrieved from the `data` attribute (`#5`), the HREF can be retrieved from the `href` attribute (`#6`). By default, a **Link** button will open the HREF in a new browser window. As we want to open it on the same page, we simply need to change `hrefTarget` to `_self` (`#7`).

How can we get to this code? Opening the Firebug or Google Chrome developer tools and analyzing the HTML created for the links div, we will have the following HTML code:

```
▼<div id="links" style="display:none;">
  ▼<div class="nav-bar-content">
    ▼<ul>
      ▶<li class="current_page_item">…</li>
      ▶<li class="page_item page-item-2">…</li>
     </ul>
   </div>
 </div>
 <!-- links -->
```

And we are good for our first test now. Refresh the blog page and we will have the following output:

Building the Footer

The next step is to build the Footer. In the `footer.php` file add the following content:

```
<div id="footer" style="display:none;">
  <center>Mastering ExtJS book - Loiane Groner -
    <a href="http://packtpub.com">http://packtpub.com
  </a></center>
</div>
<?php wp_footer(); ?>
<?php get_sidebar(); ?>
</body>
</html>
```

Following the same behavior as the Header, we have a div, `footer`, that is not going to be displayed. This content will be displayed on a container later. This `div` contains a simple copyright message and you can also add anything you like, even a widget.

Next, we are calling the `wp_footer` function. On a WordPress template, we always need to call the `wp_footer` function before closing the `</body>` tag. If we do not use this function, it can break some plugins. This function fires the `wp_footer` action; it is not going to make any difference in our theme.

Then, we have the `get_sidebar` function. This function is going to call the `sidebar.php` file; it is the same as `require("sidebar.php")`. Since we are always going to require the `sidebar.php` file after the Footer, we need to call it at the end of `footer.php`, but before closing the `</body>` and `</html>` tag.

This is it for the `footer.php` file. In the `index.php` file we also need to call `footer.php`, so after calling the Header add the following content:

```
<?php get_footer(); ?>
```

And the last part is to implement the code on the `app.js` file. Inside the viewport, we will add a new item as follows:

```
{
    region: 'south',
    xtype: 'container',
    collapsible: true,
    html: Ext.getDom('footer').innerHTML,
    split: true,
    height: 25
}
```

The Footer will be located at the bottom of the page, so we need to add a new container on the South region of the viewport. And as HTML content, we will use the `footer` div. After these changes, if we refresh our WordPress blog, this will be the output:

Building the Main page

Our next step is to create the Main page, which is the `index.php` file. We have already added the call to get the Header and the Footer, but inside the `index.php` file we also need to add the code to display the list of posts of the blog. So our `index.php` file will look like this:

```
<?php get_header(); ?>

<div id="main">
<div id="content">
  <div id="contentCont" style="display:none;">  <!-- #1 -->
  <?php while ( have_posts() ) : the_post(); ?>

    <div id='post' class="post"> <!-- #2 -->
      <div id="title" style="display:none;"><?php the_title(); ?></
div> <!-- #3 -->
```

```
        <div class="post-details"> <!-- #4 -->
          <div class="post-details-left">
          Posted on <strong><?php the_date(); ?></strong> by
  <span class="author"><?php the_author(); ?></span> under <span
  class="author"><?php the_category(', '); ?></span>
          </div>
          <div class="post-details-right">
          <?php edit_post_link('Edit', '<span class="comment-
  count">  ' , '</span>'); ?><span class="comment-count"><?php
  comments_popup_link('Leave a comment', '1 Comment', '% Comments');
  ?></span>
          </div>
        </div>

        <?php if ( is_archive() || is_search() ) : // Only display
  excerpts for archives and search. ?>
            <?php the_excerpt(); ?>
        <?php else : ?>
            <?php the_content('Read More'); ?>
        <?php endif; ?>

      </div><!-- post -->
    <?php endwhile; ?>
    </div><!-- contentCont -->
  </div><!-- content -->
  </div><!-- main -->

  <?php get_footer(); ?>
```

So to help us organize the code better, the content area is represented by the `main` div. Inside this div we have a child `div` with ID `contentCont`, which is also using `style="display:none;"` (`#1`). This means this content will not be visible on the screen. What we will do once again is to get this content and use it as the HTML content of an Ext JS container. If we take a look again at the code we will notice that there is a loop, `while ( have_posts() )`. In WordPress themes we call it "The Loop". This will retrieve all the posts from the `WordPress` database and display them on the screen so that the user can read them.

So for each post, we will display its content on a div whose `id` is `post` (`#2`). This way we will be able to manipulate the DOM later. And also we will know how many posts we have to create one panel for each post. Then we have a div in which content is the post `title` (`#3`). We will use this information to set the panel title. Next, we have the `post-details` div that contains the post content (`#4`). This information will be used to render the HTML content of the panel that will represent a post.

So let's take a look at the Ext JS code. We simply need to add the following content after the viewport code:

```
var posts = Ext.get(Ext.getDom('contentCont')).dom.children;
var panel = Ext.ComponentQuery.query('container[region=center]')[0];
Ext.Array.each(posts, function(post) {
    panel.add({
        title: Ext.get(post).child('div#title').getHTML(),
        html: post.innerHTML
    });
});
```

The `posts` variable contains the array of children of the `contentCont` div, which is a collection of the `post` div. Then, we need to get the reference of the container that was created on the Center region so that we can add panels as items. Next, for each post, we will retrieve the div with the `title` ID, so that we can get the title of the post and we will use the `post` div as content of the panel.

If we refresh our blog, we will see the following output:

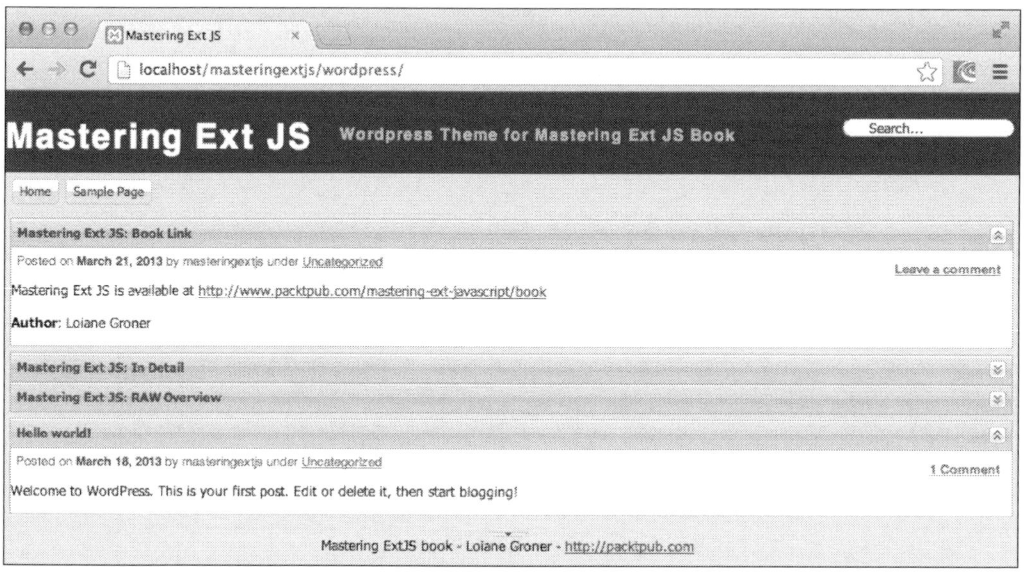

The Center region container will wrap all the single posts inside it, and a panel represents each single post.

Building the Sidebar

The next step is to create the Sidebar. We have already added its call in the code (in the `footer.php` file), now we need to implement some code inside the `sidebar.php` file. Let's go step by step.

First, we will add a div with the `sidebar` ID as follows:

```
<div id="sidebar" style="display:none;">
<!-- #1 -->
</div>
```

Note that the `div` in the preceding code has `style="display:none;"`. Again, we will do some DOM manipulation so that we can display its children inside Ext JS components. Inside `#1`, which is inside the div, we will add some other divs, each one representing a widget on the Sidebar.

The first widget we will add to the Sidebar is the **Categories** list with their respective post count:

```
<div id="categoriesCont">
  <ul>
    <?php wp_list_cats('sort_column=name&optioncount=1&hierarchic
al=0'); ?>
  </ul>
</div>
```

> The `wp_list_cats` function is a WordPress function that will retrieve the list of categories for us. To learn more about this function, please go to `https://codex.wordpress.org/Function_Reference/wp_list_cats`.

The final result for the `categoriesCont` div is:

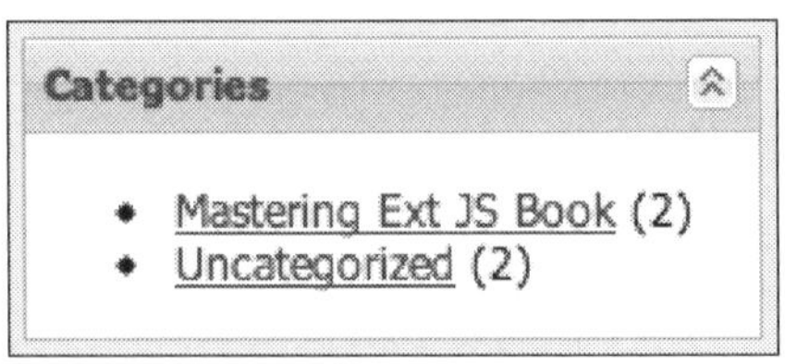

Next we will declare the **Archives** widget:

```
<div id="archivesCont">
  <ul class="list-archives">
    <?php wp_get_archives('type=monthly'); ?>
  </ul>
</div>
```

> We can use the `wp_get_archives` WordPress function to get the list of archives. To learn more about this function, please go to: `http://codex.wordpress.org/Function_Reference/wp_get_archives`.

The final result for the `archivesCont` div is:

Next we will implement a **Tag Cloud** widget:

```
<div id="tagsCont">
  <?php
    $args = array(
      'smallest'  => 8,
      'largest'  => 16
     );

    wp_tag_cloud($args);
  ?>
</div>
```

> The `wp_tag_cloud` function is a WordPress function that will retrieve the list of tags for us. To learn more about this function, please go to `http://codex.wordpress.org/Function_Reference/wp_tag_cloud`.

The final result for the `tagsCont` div is:

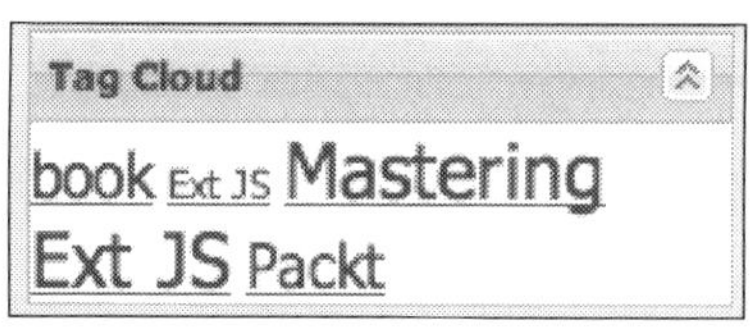

Next we will implement a **Recent Posts** widget:

```
<div id="recentCont">
  <ul class="list-archives">
    <?php
      $args = array( 'numberposts' => '5' );
      $recent_posts = wp_get_recent_posts( $args );
      foreach( $recent_posts as $recent ){
        echo '<li><a href="' .
        get_permalink($recent["ID"]) .
        '" title="Look '.
        esc_attr($recent["post_title"]).'" >' .
        $recent["post_title"].'</a> </li> ';
      }
    ?>
  </ul>
</div>
```

> The `wp_get_recent_posts` function is a WordPress function that will retrieve the list of recent posts for us. To learn more about this function, please go to `http://codex.wordpress.org/Function_Reference/wp_get_recent_posts`.

The final result for the `recentCont` div is:

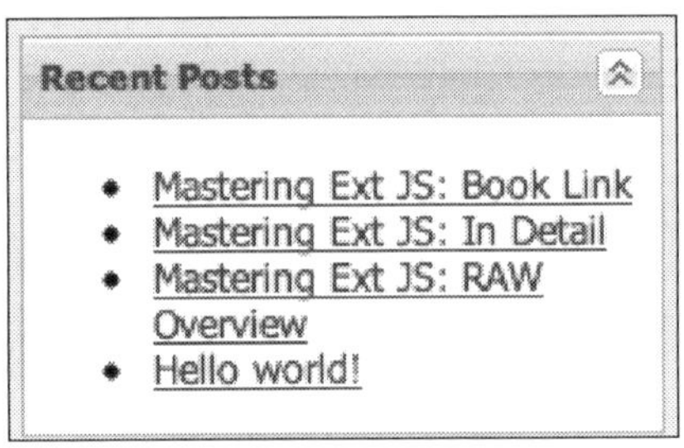

You can also create a custom widget with any HTML code inside it. For example, we can display an image in the following widget.

```
<div id="booksCont">
  <!-- random HTML code -->
</div>
```

The final result for the booksCont div is:

And this is it for the sidebar.php file. If we go back to the app.js file, we need to add a new container on the East region to represent the Sidebar as follows:

```
{
    region: 'east',
    xtype: 'container',
    collapsible: true,
    autoScroll: true,
    styleHtmlContent: true,
    layout: {
        type: 'vbox',
        align: 'stretch'
    },
    split: true,
    width: 200,
    defaults: {
        xtype: 'panel',
        padding: '5px',
        margins: '0 0 5 0',
        collapsible: true,
        styleHtmlContent: true,
        autoScroll: true
    },
    items: [{
```

```
            title: 'Categories',
            html: Ext.getDom('categoriesCont').innerHTML
        },{
            title: 'Archives',
            html: Ext.getDom('archivesCont').innerHTML
        },{
            title: 'Recent Posts',
            html: Ext.getDom('recentCont').innerHTML
        },{
            title: 'Tag Cloud',
            html: Ext.getDom('tagsCont').innerHTML
        },{
            title: 'My Books',
            html: Ext.getDom('booksCont').innerHTML
        }]
    }
```

And each item of the east container will represent the HTML of each div we just created.

If we refresh the blog, we will get the following output:

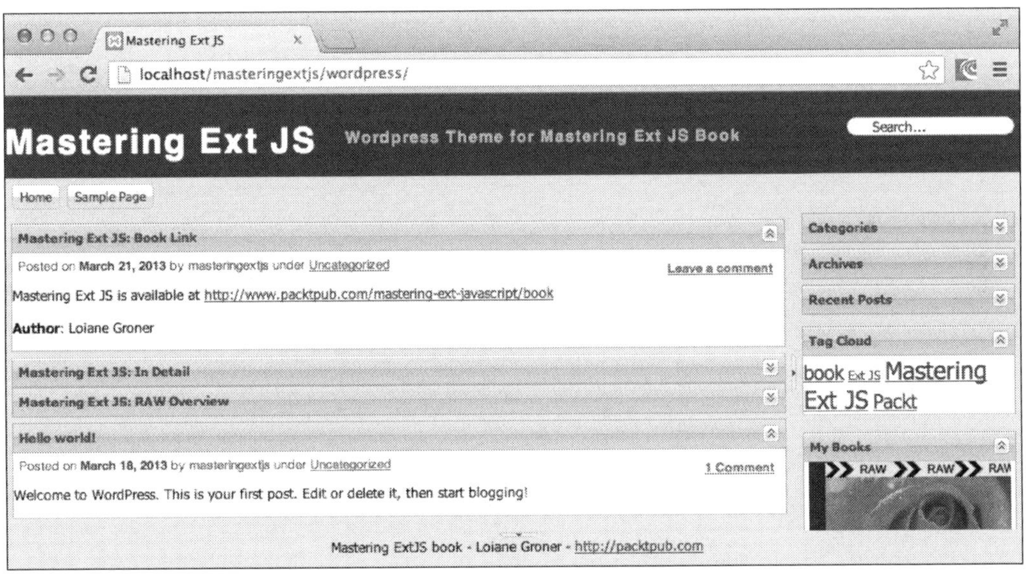

Building the single post page

We are getting to our final stage to build our first WordPress theme with Ext JS. There are two steps left: build the `page.php` and `single.php` files. In this topic we will build `single.php` as follows:

```
<?php get_header(); ?>

<?php /* If there are no posts to display, such as an empty archive
page */ ?>
<?php if ( ! have_posts() ) : ?>
    <h1>Not Found</h1>
      <p>Apologies, but no results were found for the requested
archive. Perhaps searching will help find a related post</p>
<?php endif; ?>
<div id="contentCont" style="display:none;">
<?php while ( have_posts() ) : the_post(); ?>

<div id='post' class="post">
  <div id="title" style="display:none;"><?php the_title(); ?></div>
  <div class="post-details">
    <div class="post-details-left">
    Posted on <strong><?php the_date(); ?></strong> by <span
class="author"><?php the_author(); ?></span> under <span
class="author"><?php the_category(', '); ?></span>
    </div>
    <div class="post-details-right">
    <?php edit_post_link('Edit', '<span class="comment-
count">  ' , '</span>'); ?><span class="comment-count"><?php
comments_popup_link('Leave a comment', '1 Comment', '% Comments');
?></span>
    </div>
  </div>

  <?php if ( is_archive() || is_search() ) : // Only display excerpts
for archives and search. ?>
      <?php the_excerpt(); ?>
```

```
    <?php else : ?>
        <?php the_content('Read More'); ?>
    <?php endif; ?>

  </div><!-- post -->
  </div>
  <div class="spacer"></div>

  <?php endwhile; ?>

  <div class="spacer"></div>
  <?php get_footer(); ?>
```

If we compare this file to the `index.php` file, you will see that it is very similar. But instead of displaying the list of all posts, WordPress will retrieve only one post. And as we already have the Ext JS for it (the same used to list all the posts), we do not need to do anything else.

The result of the `single.php` file will be the following when we click on the single post:

Building the single page

The `single.php` file will have the same content as the `page.php` file. So we only need to copy and paste its content into the `page.php` file. Pages and posts are treated the same way by WordPress. If we open a page in our blog, we will have something like the following screenshot:

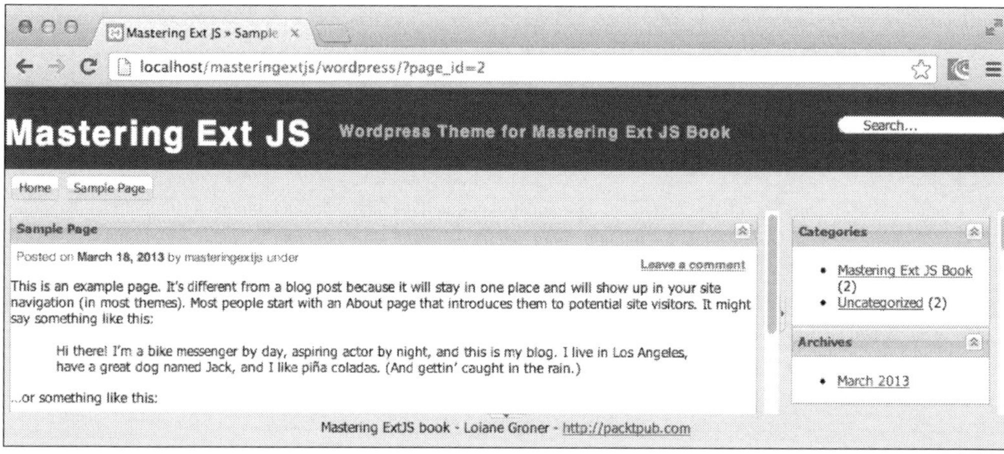

And this is it. We have completed our first WordPress theme with Ext JS. The next step is to enhance the theme as you desire.

Summary

In this chapter we learned how to build a complete WordPress theme using Ext JS. We learned that to build the simplest theme requires very little Ext JS code. WordPress has a lot of functions we can reuse to make our job easier.

In the next chapter, we will learn how to test an Ext JS application, re-use the code to build a mobile app, and also where we can get more resources to enhance our Ext JS application even more.

12
Debugging and Testing

We will cover much more than debugging and testing in this chapter. But before we bring up other topics, let's talk a little bit about debugging first. The art of debugging is much important as the art of programming. We usually write code that we think is going to work as soon as we execute it, but this is not true sometimes. We write the code, and then we get an exception or JavaScript error, and we need to dive into the code again to see what went wrong. It's part of being a developer and it is also part of life. The second topic we will discuss in this chapter is testing. How do you test an Ext JS application? You code and then you open your browser and do the test yourself without using any book. But is there a better way of doing this? Of course, there is and we will see it in this chapter as well. Going a little bit further, we know we love the text editor (and we are sure that you have the one you like the most, such as Sublime Text, Text Mate, Notepad++, Eclipse, Aptana, Visual Studio, Vim, and others). But there are also other tools that can help us to be more productive when coding with Ext JS. We will also talk about them. And we already know that Sencha API is amazing, but there are great developers around the world who share their work to help us as well. We will see how we can find other functionalities that Ext JS does not provide us, so that we can use them and make our projects even better. And as a last topic, we will talk about mobile. Ext JS is a framework used to build web desktop applications, not mobile applications. How can we have the same application running on a desktop and also on a mobile device? We will also talk about it in this chapter.

So in this chapter, we will cover:

- Debugging Ext JS applications
- Testing Ext JS applications
- Helpful tools
- Transforming Ext JS projects into mobile applications
- Where to find extra and open source plugins

Debugging Ext JS applications

Throughout this book, we learned that debugging is important, especially when we were learning an easier way to figure out the correct ComponentQuery selector. When developing applications with Ext JS, it is mandatory to use a debug tool. Not only for debugging, but you will also be able to learn more about the framework, and it is a great learning exercise.

A few things we always need to remember while creating Ext JS applications (not only Ext JS, but JavaScript in general) are: case sensitive matters, the class `LoginScreen` is different from Login screen. Be careful with reserved words (`http://mattsnider.com/reserved-words-in-javascript/`): you cannot use them as namespace, name of classes, and packages nor as variable names. Check spelling, this is very important, sometimes when we are typing, we can type an extra character (fat finger syndrome).

If you were programming in JavaScript almost 10 years ago, our only friend was the dear alert. We used to put several alerts in the code and then execute it, and see which alert was not executed so we could find where the error was. Now we have our dear friend console. Use the console for logging and to see warnings and errors as much as you like.

We also have great tools to debug. The two most important are Google developer tools and Firebug for Firefox, learn to use at least one of them (they are very similar).

For example, let's use Firebug for Firefox. It comes with a few tabs: on the **Console** tab, we can see any console messages and also the files that were loaded as shown in the following screenshot:

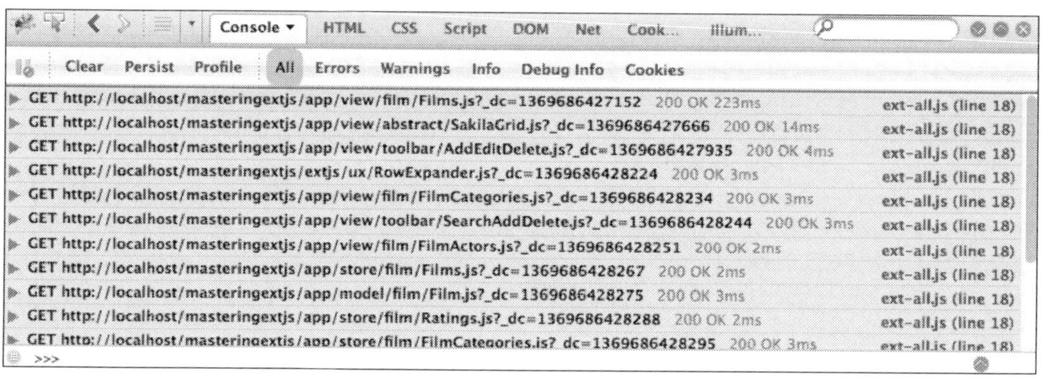

And speaking of files that are being loaded or not, this is a very huge deal. Simple mistakes as name of the class (using MVC), path of CSS, and JS in the `index.html` file. All these common errors can be verified using the **Console** or the **Net** tab.

On the **HTML** tab we can see details, the HTML code that was generated by Ext JS code:

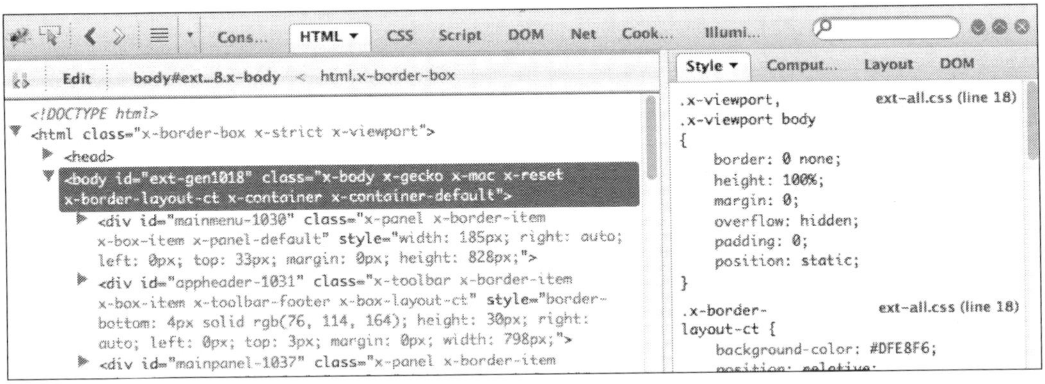

When we mouse over, the portion related to that HTML code is highlighted on the screen. We also have the **CSS** and **Script** tabs. We can change the CSS and script in real time and see the changes applied in real time. This is simply amazing. So it is very important to learn how to use a debug tool.

> To learn more about Firebug, please visit: `http://getfirebug.com/`. And to learn more about Google developer tools, please visit: `https://developers.google.com/chrome-developer-tools/`.

And of course, there is a very special tool if you are looking for taking Ext JS debugging to the next level. There is this tool called Illuminations for developers (`http://www.illuminations-for-developers.com/`) that is specific for Ext JS debugging. It is a paid tool, but the cost-benefit is great. This tool is an add-on for Firebug/Firefox.

For example, let's take a look at the **Data** tab:

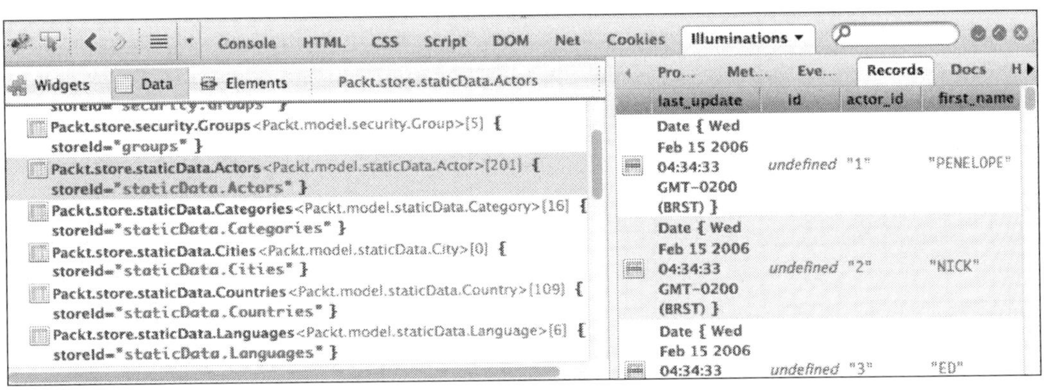

We can see all the stores, the data that was loaded, and what methods are available so that we can call them (if needed). We can also see all the widgets and the events that were fired, along with the widgets hierarchy.

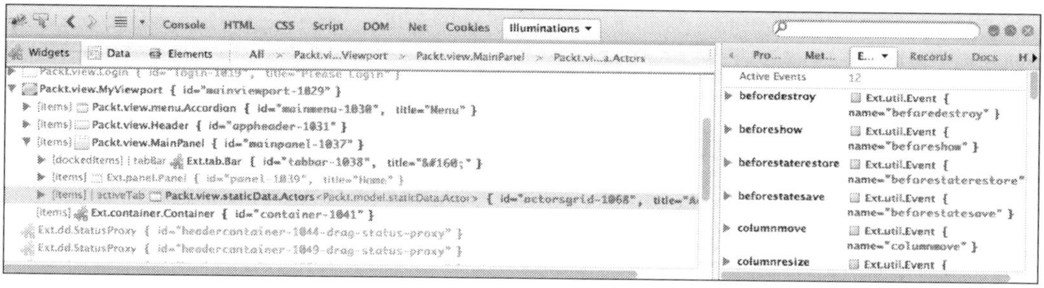

Mastering one debugging tool is important as mastering the art of programming in Ext JS. Choose your favorite weapon and have fun coding and debugging.

Testing Ext JS applications

Testing is a very important part when developing applications or performing maintenance. When we do not write tests, we need to verify each use case manually, and if we change anything in the code, we will need to perform all the testing manually again. The same happens when we need to maintain the code; developers usually test only what has been changed, but the correct way would be to do regression tests to see if the change did not break anything else. So spending some time to write tests can be a win at the end. You will spend a little bit more time, but then you will be able to run all the tests with a single click and then verify what is broken and what is still working.

We are also very used to do unit tests on the server-side code. Java, PHP, Ruby, C# communities offer a lot of options to perform unit tests on the server-side code, and sometimes we can forget to test the front-end code (in this case, Ext JS). But do not worry; there are few tools we can use to include Ext JS in the tests as well.

One tool that is very popular for JavaScript testing in general is Jasmine (`http://pivotal.github.io/jasmine/`). Jasmine is a testing tool that is used for BDD (Behavior-driven development: `http://en.wikipedia.org/wiki/Behavior-driven_development`). In Ext JS documentation you can find two guides explaining how to test Ext JS applications with Jasmine: `http://docs.sencha.com/extjs/4.2.0/#!/guide/testing` and `http://docs.sencha.com/extjs/4.2.0/#!/guide/testing_controllers`.

We will present examples using another testing tool, called Siesta (`http://www.bryntum.com/products/siesta/`). Siesta can also be used to test JavaScript code in general, but the cool side of Siesta is that it provides a special API so we can test Ext JS applications.

Before we begin, here is a list of steps we need to perform so we can test Ext JS applications:

1. Generate the test build using Sencha command.
2. Test the "test" build.
3. Install Siesta.
4. Create a Harness.
5. Create test cases.

So let's get it started.

Generating the "test" build with Sencha command

The first step is to generate the test build of our project using Sencha command. As we already learned how to do it in *Chapter 10, Preparing for Production*, we need to open the terminal application, change the directory to our application's directory and execute the command `sencha app build testing` as shown in the following screenshot:

Sencha command will create a folder inside `masteringextjs/build/Packt/testing` with the code compiled for testing. We also cannot forget to copy the `php` and `translations` folders to the `testing` folder; otherwise, the test build will not be executed successfully:

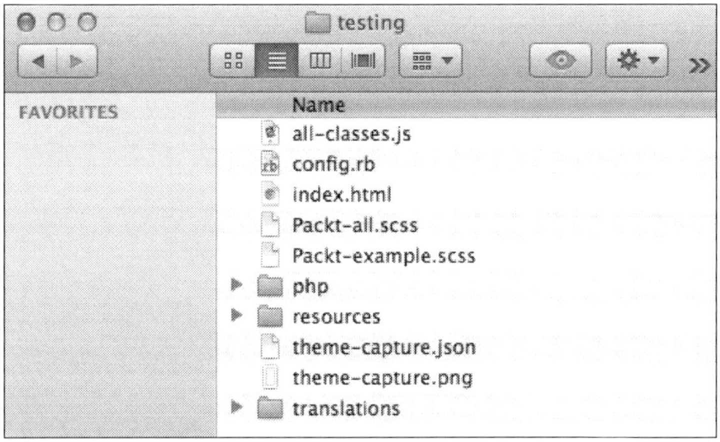

And the next step is to test the "test" build. To do so, we need to execute the following URL: `http://localhost/masteringextjs/build/Packt/testing` as shown in the following screenshot:

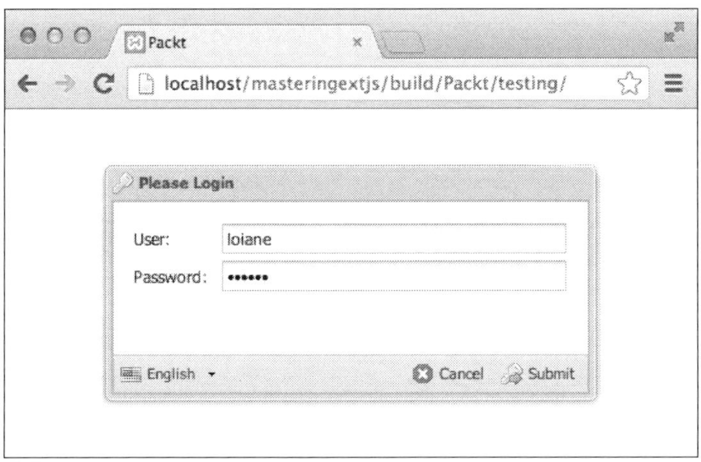

Everything should be working normally.

Installing Siesta and creating test cases

The next step is to install Siesta in our project so that we can use this really nice tool to create our test cases.

But first, we need to download it from `http://www.bryntum.com/products/siesta/`. For these examples, we will be using the Lite version, which is free. The paid version includes support and also automated integration with Selenium and Phantom JS, and also Cross page testing.

After downloading Siesta, unzip it inside our project folder. Now we need to start coding the tests. Before we start, here is an overview of what needs to be done:

1. Create the `tests` folder.
2. Create the `Harness` file.
3. Create the `index.html` file.
4. Create each desired test case.

So the first step is creating a new folder called `tests` inside our project's folder. At the end of this topic, we will have something like the following screenshot:

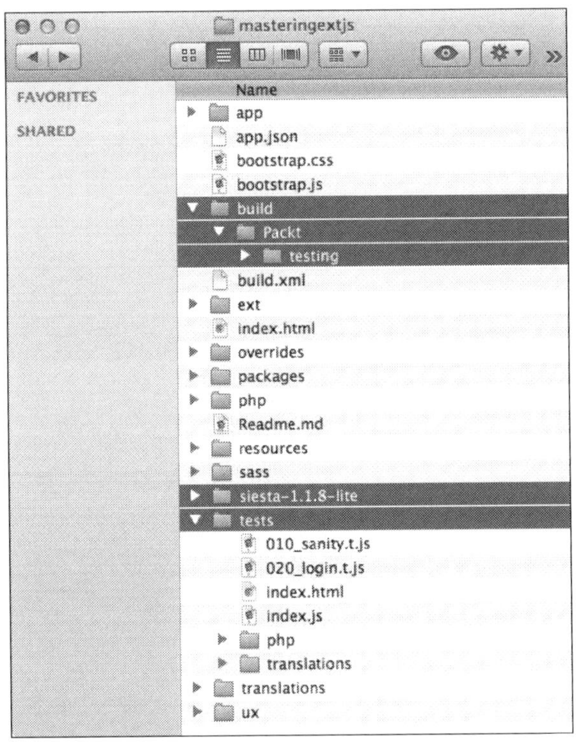

The next step is to create the `Harness` file. The `Harness` file is where we will declare all the test cases we want to be part of our project. So we will name it `index.js` and we will create it inside the `tests` folder with the following content:

```
var Harness = Siesta.Harness.Browser.ExtJS;

Harness.configure({
    title       : 'Mastering Ext JS Test Suite',

    preload     : [
        '../build/Packt/testing/resources/Packt-all.css',
        '../build/Packt/testing/resources/css/app.css',

        '../build/Packt/testing/translations/locale.js',
        '../build/Packt/testing/all-classes.js'
    ]
});

Harness.start(
    '010_sanity.t.js',
    '020_login.t.js'
);
```

We are configuring `Harness` to run two test cases that we will create in a bit: `010_sanity.t` and `020_login.t`. We also need to add our `css` and the application's `js` files to the `preload`; after all, we need to have our code available for testing. So we are asking Siesta to preload our application's CSS files and also the JS files.

Next step is to create the `tests/index.html` file as follows:

```
<!DOCTYPE html>
<html>
    <head>
        <link rel="stylesheet" type="text/css" href="../bootstrap.
css">
        <link rel="stylesheet" type="text/css" href="../siesta-1.1.8-
lite/resources/css/siesta-all.css">

        <script type="text/javascript" src="../ext/ext-all.js"></
script>
        <script type="text/javascript" src="../siesta-1.1.8-lite/
siesta-all.js"></script>
```

```
        <script type="text/javascript" src="translations/locale.
js"></script>
        <script type="text/javascript" src="index.js"></script>
    </head>

    <body>
    </body>
</html>
```

In this HTML code, we are including Siesta's `JS` and `CSS` files, as long with Ext JS CSS and the `Harness` file we created.

The next step now is to start creating all the test cases we want to include on our project. The first one we will create is the `010_sanity.t.js` file inside the `tests` folder with the following content:

```
StartTest(function(t) {
    t.diag("Sanity");

    t.ok(Ext, 'ExtJS is here');
    t.ok(Ext.Window, 'Ext.Window as well');


    t.ok(Packt, 'Packt namespace is here');
    t.ok(Packt.view.Login, 'Packt.view.Login as well');

    t.done();
});
```

Let's try to understand the preceding code. All test code implemented with Siesta must be wrapped inside the `StartTest(function(t)` constructor.

Then, inside the constructor we have a few assertions. For this first example, we will use a very simple one, which is to make sure that some classes are loaded, such as the Ext namespace and our application namespace as well. Then, we can make sure any arbitrary class from Ext JS framework and any arbitrary class from our project is also present, meaning we can start any more complex testing.

Now we can try to execute the first test case. To do so, simply access `http://localhost/masteringextjs/tests` on your local browser. The tests should pass as shown in the following screenshot:

Now let's create our second test case. We will also create it inside the `tests` folder with the name `020_login.t.js` with the following content:

```
StartTest(function(t) {
    t.diag("Sanity test, loading classes on demand and verifying they
were indeed loaded.");

    t.ok(Ext, 'ExtJS is here'); // #1
    t.ok(Packt, 'Packt namespace is here'); // #2

    t.requireOk('Packt.view.Login'); // #3

    t.waitForComponent('Packt.view.Login', true, function(){// #4

        var submitButton = Ext.ComponentQuery.query('login
button#submit')[0];

        t.chain(
          { action : 'click', target : submitButton } // #5
        );
```

```
            t.waitForComponent('Packt.view.MyViewport', true, function()
{  // #6
                t.ok(Packt.view.MyViewport, "Packt.view.MyViewport
was rendered."); // #7
             t.done();
            });
      });
});
```

If we take a look, this test case is a little bit more complex. As an overview, this test case makes sure `Ext` (`#1`) and `Packt` (`#2`) namespace are loaded, then requires to have the `Packt.view.Login` (`#3`) class loaded, and then will wait until this component is rendered on the screen (`#4`: will wait for the Splash screen to fade out). Once the Login screen is rendered, it will press the **Submit** button (`#5`: for test purposes, the name and password are already set as text in each TextField component). Once the **Submit** button is clicked, the test suite will wait until the viewport is rendered (`#6`), and then will assert the class has been loaded (`#7`).

One of the best qualities of the Siesta testing framework is that it has specific test cases for Ext JS framework, making the tests a lot easier than with any other tool. And an advantage is to use the test build as well, meaning our code will be in our application, and we do not need to write it again in the test cases, we simply need to call it as we just did on the previous test cases we implemented.

For further knowledge of Siesta assertions and test possibilities, please visit `http://www.bryntum.com/docs/siesta/` or access the `docs` folder from a Siesta installation.

Helpful tools

In this topic we will present some tools that can help developers a lot while implementing Ext JS applications. You can find all the links of the tools mentioned here at the end of this topic.

The first tool is JSLint. JSLint is a tool that can help you to find JavaScript errors and can also help you to clean your code.

The second tool is YSlow. YSlow analyzes web pages and tells you why they're slow based on the rules for high performance websites. YSlow is a Firefox add-on integrated with the popular Firebug web development tool.

Ext JS is a JavaScript framework and JavaScript performance is a topic that is a concern for a lot of companies. The minimum the user needs to load on the browser, the better. That is why it is very important to make a production build using Sencha command and not simply deploy all the application files on production.

Sencha command is also going to minify the Ext JS CSS file to a smaller CSS and we can also include only the CSS for the components that we are going to really use (in case, we create a custom theme). But we usually also have an application CSS with icons and custom styles we apply on our application. So we have three very useful tips. For the custom CSS, you can use a pre-processor such as Sass or Less. In case, you use Sass or Less to create the `app.css`, always remember to compile the CSS output to be minified. The second tip is even you do not use Sass or Less to compile your custom CSS, always deploy on production a minified version of it. Some tools that can help are YUI compressor and CSS minifier. And a third tip: usually, it is normal to have multiple CSS custom files to help organizing the styles better. One CSS for icons, another one for general styles, and others for a very specific reason. But for production, always remember to combine all these CSS into a single one. This will be better for the user to load on the browser. A tool that can help us with this is grunt-contrib-concat.

CSS Sprites. This is another very important topic. Remember that we have several icons that we are using in lot of places in the application? button icons, panel, and tab icons? We can create a CSS Sprite, which is creating a single image with all the icons. And in the CSS, we simply have one single image, and pass the background-position of the icon we want to display such as this:

```
.icon-message {
  background-image: url('mySprite.png');
  background-position: -10px -10px;
}

.icon-envolope {
  background-image: url('mySprite.png');
  background-position: -15px -15px;
}
```

There are a few tools that can also help us to create CSS Sprites such as SpritePad, SpriteMe, and Compass Sprite Generator.

All the links for the tools mentioned in this topic are as follows:

- JSLint: `http://www.jslint.com/`
- YSlow: `http://developer.yahoo.com/yslow/`
- Sass: `http://sass-lang.com/`
- Less: `http://lesscss.org/`
- YUI Compressor: `http://developer.yahoo.com/yui/compressor/`

- CSS Minifier: `http://www.cssminifier.com/`
- grunt-contrib-concat: `https://npmjs.org/package/grunt-contrib-concat`
- SpritePad: `http://wearekiss.com/spritepad`
- SpriteMe: `http://www.spriteme.org/`
- Compass Sprite Generator: `http://compass-style.org/help/tutorials/spriting/`

Always remember that Ext JS is JavaScript, so we need to care about performance as well. With all these little tips posted on this topic, an Ext JS application can improve its performance as well.

And at last but not least, two tools from Sencha: Sencha Architect and Sencha Eclipse plugin. Sencha Architect is a visual designer tool that is very similar to Visual Studio: you drag and drop and you can see how the application looks like, and all the configuration that you need to do is done using the config panel. Only methods, functions, and templates are free to enter whatever code you like. The good thing about Sencha Architect is that it helps us to follow all the best practices and the code is very well organized. You can also develop all the Ext JS code using Sencha Architect, and on the server side, you can continue using the IDE you like the most (Eclipse, Aptana, Visual Studio, and others).

And Sencha Eclipse Plugin is a plugin for Eclipse IDE that has the auto-completion feature enabled. Both Sencha Architect and Sencha Eclipse plugin are paid tools. But you can download a trial version for testing at: `http://www.sencha.com/products/complete/` or `http://www.sencha.com/products/architect/`.

From Ext JS to mobile

Mobile applications are very popular nowadays. And if we have a really nice application implemented with Ext JS, it is normal that we want to have the same app available on a mobile device. What a lot of people think is that just because Ext JS is cross browser, we just need to deploy the application in a domain on the Internet, give the link to the mobile users and that is okay, the job is done. But it is not. Although Ext JS is compatible to mobile browsers as well, Ext JS does not offer the best user experience to mobile users. If we really want to offer a great mobile experience, we need to transform our Ext JS application into a mobile application. But, how can we do that? Learning Objective-C, Java API for Android, and other languages can be time consuming, and we do not always have that much time to spend.

So we would like to introduce Sencha Touch, the Ext JS cousin. Sencha Touch was the first HTML 5 mobile framework in the market. And more good news: you do not need to rewrite all of your code to have the same application also available to mobile devices.

Sencha Touch and Ext JS share the API. The data package, such as Models, Stores, and the core of the framework is same. Sencha Touch also uses MVC. The Controllers and Views (components) work in a very similar way as Ext JS controller and Views do. Of course the biggest difference is in the Views, since a Web component is different from a Mobile component. However, Sencha Touch also offers forms, lists, and we can find even Grid components customized for mobile devices.

If we do an analysis of how much code we can reuse of using Sencha Touch, take a look at the following diagram:

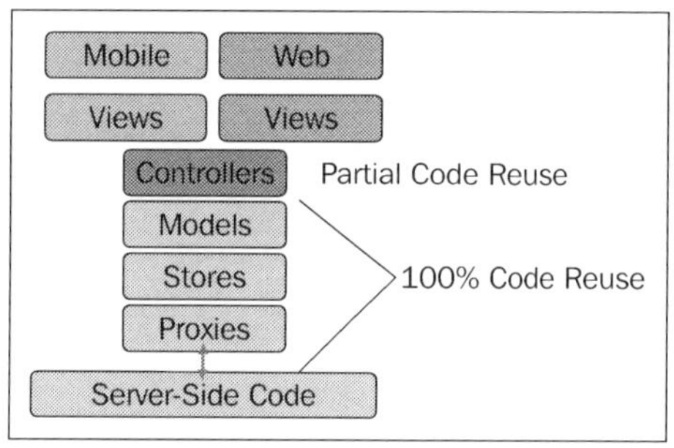

The amount of code we can reuse is huge. And we also have two ways of implementing it: the first one is to have a mobile application, where the user will access a URL pointing to a Sencha Touch deploy (Sencha Touch and server-side code at the same domain). And the second option is to have the Sencha Touch code running on the user's device (Sencha Touch offers native packaging to iOS and Android, but we can also have native Blackberry 10 and Windows Phone 8 native applications with Sencha Touch) and the server-side code running on a server on the Web. In this case, we can use CORS to make the Ajax communication between the application and the server-side code (as we already discussed in *Chapter 10, Preparing for Production*).

> To learn more about Sencha Touch, please go to `http://www.sencha.com/products/touch/`.

Third-party components and plugins

Although Ext JS provides great components, we usually will also want to develop our own components or maybe use other developer's components. And the Ext JS community is great regarding this subject. A lot of developers share their own components, extensions, and plugins with the community. There are two main places where you can find them:

- Sencha market: `https://market.sencha.com/`
- Sencha forum: `http://www.sencha.com/forum/forumdisplay.php?82-Ext-User-Extensions-and-Plugins`

Summary

In this chapter we learned the importance of knowing how to debug Ext JS application and some tools that can help us with this task. We have also learned how to create test cases for Ext JS application using Siesta, an open source tool available in Lite and paid versions. We have also learned that performance is really important and we can do a lot more to improve the performance of our Ext JS application with the help of some free tools. And finally, we learned some tips of how to migrate an Ext JS application to a mobile platform and also where to find great plugins, extensions, and new components that we can use in our projects.

Now, it is time to let the creativity flow and create really awesome projects with Ext JS.

Index

A

abstract Grid panel
- action column, handling 161
- creating 156-160
- iconCls, setting 161, 162
- Live Search plugin, versus Filter plugin 162, 163
- specific Grid panels, creating 164, 165

Accordion panel
- dynamic menu, creating with 106

ACK (acknowledgment) 150
action column 161
Activity Monitor plugin
- URL 82

Actor model 145
Actors table 179
AddEditDelete toolbar 187
Ajax requests
- using 291

Apache Ant
- URL 22

app.js, dynamic menu
- changing 112

B

Business module 175

C

Caps Lock warning message
- about 66
- implementing 66-70

Categories table 178
central container, dynamic menu
- replacing 107

CheckBox group 198
click event listener 78
client e-mail module 16
client-side activity monitor 82
Column chart, Sales by Film Category chart
- creating 227

Compass Sprite Generator
- about 328
- URL 329

content management
- Film data grid, displaying 180
- Film data grid panel, editing 192
- information, managing 175

content management control 14
controller, user identification
- about 131
- add button, listening to 131
- cancel button, listening to 135
- edit button, listening to 132
- user, saving 133, 134

controller, e-mail client module
- about 252, 253
- e-mail, previewing 254

controller, MySQL table management
- about 166
- action column, handling 170
- autoSync configuration 172
- changes, canceling 172
- changes, saving 171
- existing record, editing 169
- filter, clearing 173
- grid panel store, loading 167
- record, adding on grid panel 168, 169
- store events, listening 173, 174

Create Read Update Destroy (CRUD) operation 138

Cross-Origin Resource Sharing (CORS)
enabling 291
CSS minifier
about 328
URL 329
CSS Sprites 328
Customer Data module 175
custom event 170
custom themes
creating 265, 266
custom VType
creating 40

D

DAO (Data Access Object) pattern 17
database model, dynamic menu
about 97
groups 97
menus 97
permissions 98
dataIndex 120
debugging
Ext JS applications 318-320
Document Object Model (DOM) 128
DoS attack
about 172
URL 172
dynamic menu
app.js, changing 112
central container, replacing on viewport 107
creating 95, 96
creating, with Accordion panel 106
creating, with Tree panel 106
database model 97
handling, on server 102-105
menu controllerside, creating 108, 109
menu models, creating 99
store, creating 102

E

edit view
creating 125-129
e-mail client module
about 239
Bcc field, displaying 261
Cc field, displaying 261
controller 252
e-mails, organizing 255-257
file upload fields, adding 262, 263
inbox, creating 240
mail container 250
mail menu 248
new message, creating 258-261
organizing 250, 252
e-mails, e-mail client module
organizing 255-257
ER (Entity Relationship) 142
Ext JS
content management 175
failure, handling 61
logout capability, implementing 73
multilingual capability, implementing 73
required software, installing 8
success, handling 61
WordPress Theme 293
Ext JS application
capabilities 10
client e-mail module 16
content management control 14, 15
debugging 318-320
deploying, in production 277
dynamic menu, creating 95
login screen 11
main screen 11
mobile applications 329
MySQL table management 13, 14
packaging, for production 273-277
presenting 10
production build, benefits 278, 279
Siesta, installing 323-327
splash screen 10
test build, generating with Sencha 321, 322
test cases, creating 323-327
testing 320
third party components 331
third party plugins 331
tools 327
user control management 13
Ext JS code, WordPress theme
creating 302-304

Ext JS MVC application
base 74-77
capabilities, adding 217
creating 17-20, 23
edit view, creating 125-129
e-mail client module 239
file, previewing 135
Grid panel content, printing with Grid printer plugin 221
Grid panel, exporting 217, 218
Grid panel, exporting to Excel 221
Grid panel, exporting to PDF 219, 220
group model, creating 129
groups store, creating 130
Groups table, creating 56
loading page, creating 25-31
login controller, creating 44
login page, handling 57
login screen 33
login screen, creating 34-38
login screen, enhancing 64
logout capability 78
multilingual capability 84
Sales by Film Category chart, creating 223
simple Grid panel, implementing 117
user, adding 124
user, deleting 138
user, editing 124
users, managing 115
User table, creating 56

F

failure function 62
file preview, before upload 135, 137
files, WordPress themes
comments.php 296
footer.php 296
functions.php 296
header.php 296
index.php 296
page.php 296
sidebar.php 296
single.php 296
Film actors
about 206
Edit view 207
live search combobox 208
searching 208
store 206
Film categories
about 200
Edit view 201, 202
Packt.view.sakila.SearchWindow 204, 205
Search Add Delete toolbar 202
search categories 203, 204
store 200
Film data grid
controller, creating 191
creating 183-188
Film model 180
Films store 181-183
paging, handling on server side 188, 189
paging queries, on Microsoft SQL Server 190
paging queries, on MySQL 190
paging queries, on Oracle 190
Film data grid panel
editing 192-196
Film actors 206
Film categories 200
films controller 212
Film model 180
films controller
about 212
film info, loading within Edit form 212, 213
MultiSelect values, getting 214
selected actor, getting from live search 215
Films store 181, 182
Film table
about 176
description field 193
film_id field 193
language_id field 194
length field 194
original_language_id field 194
rating field 194
release_year field 193
rental_duration field 194
rental_rate field 194
replacement_cost field 194
special_features field 194
title field 193

Firebug
URL 319
footer, WordPress theme
building 305, 306
Form panel 14

G

GET HTTP method 151
Grid panel
about 14
content, printing with printer plugin 221, 222
exporting 217-219
exporting, to Excel 221
exporting, to PDF 219, 220
PDF file, generating on PHP server 221
Grid printer plugin
URL 222
group model
creating 129
groups store
about 130
creating 130, 131
Group table
creating 56, 57
grunt-contrib-concat
about 328
URL 329

H

handleActionColumn method 170
header, WordPress theme
building 300-302
HTML5 local storage 89
URL 89

I

inbox, e-mail client module
creating 240
mail list view 242-246
mail message model 240, 241
mail messages store 241, 242
preview mail panel 246, 247
inheritance 144
initComponent method 158
Internet Information Services (IIS) 137
Inventory module
about 175
Actors table 179
Actor table 176
Categories table 178
Category table 176
Film table 176
Language table 176
ionpackage command 281
ionpackage desktoppackager.json command 290
iText
URL 221
iTextSharp
URL 221

J

Jasmine
about 320
URL 320
JSLint
about 327
URL 328
JSON file 285
JSON (JavaScript Object Notation) format 60

L

Less
about 328
URL 328
live search combobox
about 209-211
model 208
store 208, 209
Live Search plugin
versus, Filter plugin 162, 163
Local Storage 89
login controller
adding, on app.js 45, 46
button click event, listening to 46-50
button listener implementation, canceling 51, 52
button listener implementation, submitting 52-55

creating 44, 45
login page
database, connecting to 57, 58
handling, on server 57
login.php 58, 59
login screen
about 11, 33
client-side validations 38, 39
code, running 42
creating 34-38
custom VTypes, creating 40
itemId, using 43
toolbar, adding with buttons 40-42
login screen, enhancing
Caps Lock warning message 66-70
form submit on Enter, implementing 65, 66
loading mask, applying on form 65
logout capability
about 78, 79
client-side activity monitor 82, 83
handling, on server 82
login code, refactoring 79, 80
logout code, refactoring 79, 80

M

mail list view 242
mail menu, e-mail client module
about 248
mail menu tree store 248
mail menu view, creating 249, 250
mail menu tree store 248
mail menu view
creating 249
mail message model 240
mail messages store 241
main page, WordPress theme
building 306-308
main screen 11
masteringextjs directory 21
MD5 algorithm 54
menu controllerside, dynamic menu
creating 108, 109
menu item, opening dynamically 111
rendering, from nested JSON 109, 110
menu items, MySQL table management
creating 153-155
menu models, dynamic menu
creating 99-101
hasMany association 99
Menu Module 153
minimizing the payload size 81
mobile applications 329, 330
models, MySQL table management
abstract model 144, 145
creating 143, 144
specific models 145, 146
Model-View-Controller. *See* **MVC**
Model-View-Controller-Store. *See* **MVCS**
multilingual capability
about 84
change language component, creating 84-86
change language, handling in real-time 90-93
Ext JS, translating 93
HTML5 local storage 89, 90
translation, applying 88
translation files, creating 87, 88
MultiSelect component 203, 204
MVC 17, 18
MVC (Model-View-Controller) 7
MVCS 17
MySQL table management
about 13, 14, 141
abstract Grid panel, creating 156
controller 166
menu items, creating 153
models, creating 143
stores, creating 146
tables, presenting 142, 143

N

new message, e-mail client module
creating 258-261

O

onButtonClickCancel method 52, 135
onButtonClickDelete method 138
onButtonClickEdit method 132
onButtonClickLogout method 78
onButtonClickSave method 133

onload event 137
onRender method 123
OOP(Object Oriented Programming) 144

P

Packt.view.Header class 86
Packt.view.sakila.SearchWindow 204, 205
Packt.view.sakila.WindowForm 198, 199
PHPExcel
  URL 221
Pie chart, Sales by Film Category chart
  creating 225
POST method 151
preview mail panel 246

R

renderer function 121
render event 123
RIA (Rich Internet Application) 7
RowExpander plugin 185

S

Sakila database
  about 175
  Business 175
  Customer Data 175
  Inventory 175
  Views 175
Sales by Film Category chart
  chart panel, displaying 230, 231
  chart type, changing 233
  Column chart, implementing 2270229
  creating 223-225
  exporting, to images 233, 234
  exporting, to PDF 235-237
  Pie chart, developing 225, 226
Sass
  about 328
  URL 328
Search Add Delete toolbar 202
Sencha Cmd 265
Sencha Cmd 3.1.1
  about 265
  using 265
Sencha command 328
Sencha Desktop Packager
  about 279
  Ajax, using 291
  application, packaging 285-288
  CORS, enabling 291
  download link 280
  installing 280
  installing, for Mac OS and Linux 280
  installing, for Windows 281-284
  server side changes 288, 289
Sencha Eclipse Plugin 329
Sencha forum
  URL 331
Sencha market
  URL 331
Sencha Touch deploy 330
sidebar, WordPress theme
  building 309-313
Siesta
  about 321
  downloading 323
  installing 323
  URL 321
simple Grid panel
  implementing 117
  user model 117
  users controller 123, 124
  users grid panel 119-122
  users store 118
single page, WordPress theme
  building 316
single post page, WordPress theme
  building 314, 315
specific Grid panels 164
splash screen 10
SpriteMe
  about 328
  URL 329
SpritePad
  about 328
  URL 329
Static Data 153
stores, MySQL table management
  abstract proxy 148-151
  abstract store 147
  creating 146, 147
  specific stores 152, 153

stripslashes function 58
success function 61, 62, 139

T

TCPDF
URL 221
testing
about 320
Ext JS applications 320
theme
customizing 266-273
Tree panel
dynamic menu, creating with 106

U

UI Components 21
user
adding 116
deleting 138, 139
editing 117
user control management 13
user management
about 115
user, adding 116
user, editing 117
user model 117
users controller 123, 124
users grid panel 119, 120
users store 118
User table
creating 56

V

Viewport 23

W

WordPress
Ext JS theme, implementing 295
installing 293, 294
WordPress themes
about 296
files, creating 296
structuring 296-299
WordPress theme, with Ext JS
building 300
Ext JS code, creating 302
footer, building 305, 306
header, building 300-302
main page, building 306-308
sidebar, building 309-313
single page, building 316
single post page, building 314, 315

Y

YSlow
about 327
URL 328
YUI Compress
about 144
URL 328
YUI compressor 328

[PACKT] open source
community experience distilled
PUBLISHING

Thank you for buying
Mastering Ext JS

About Packt Publishing

Packt, pronounced 'packed', published its first book "*Mastering phpMyAdmin for Effective MySQL Management*" in April 2004 and subsequently continued to specialize in publishing highly focused books on specific technologies and solutions.

Our books and publications share the experiences of your fellow IT professionals in adapting and customizing today's systems, applications, and frameworks. Our solution based books give you the knowledge and power to customize the software and technologies you're using to get the job done. Packt books are more specific and less general than the IT books you have seen in the past. Our unique business model allows us to bring you more focused information, giving you more of what you need to know, and less of what you don't.

Packt is a modern, yet unique publishing company, which focuses on producing quality, cutting-edge books for communities of developers, administrators, and newbies alike. For more information, please visit our website: `www.packtpub.com`.

About Packt Open Source

In 2010, Packt launched two new brands, Packt Open Source and Packt Enterprise, in order to continue its focus on specialization. This book is part of the Packt Open Source brand, home to books published on software built around Open Source licences, and offering information to anybody from advanced developers to budding web designers. The Open Source brand also runs Packt's Open Source Royalty Scheme, by which Packt gives a royalty to each Open Source project about whose software a book is sold.

Writing for Packt

We welcome all inquiries from people who are interested in authoring. Book proposals should be sent to author@packtpub.com. If your book idea is still at an early stage and you would like to discuss it first before writing a formal book proposal, contact us; one of our commissioning editors will get in touch with you.

We're not just looking for published authors; if you have strong technical skills but no writing experience, our experienced editors can help you develop a writing career, or simply get some additional reward for your expertise.

Ext JS 4 First Look

ISBN: 978-1-84951-666-2 Paperback: 340 pages

A practical guide including examples of the new features in Ext JS 4 and tips to migrate from Ext JS 3

1. Migrate your Ext JS 3 applications easily to Ext JS 4 based on the examples presented in this guide
2. Full of diagrams, illustrations, and step-by-step instructions to develop real word applications
3. Driven by examples and explanations of how things work

Learning Ext JS 4

ISBN: 978-1-84951-684-6 Paperback: 434 pages

Sencha Ext JS for a beginner

1. Learn the basics and create your first classes
2. Handle data and understand the way it works, create powerful widgets and new components
3. Dig into the new architecture defined by Sencha and work on real-world projects

Learning Ext JS

ISBN: 978-1-84719-514-2 Paperback: 324 pages

Build dynamic, desktop-style user interfaces for your data-driven web applications

1. Learn to build consistent, attractive web interfaces with the framework components
2. Integrate your existing data and web services with Ext JS data support
3. Enhance your JavaScript skills by using Ext's DOM and AJAX helpers
4. Extend Ext JS through custom components

Learning Ext JS 3.2

ISBN: 978-1-84951-120-9 Paperback: 432 pages

Build dynamic, desktop-style user interfaces for our data-driven web applications using Ext JS

1. Learn to build consistent, attractive web interfaces with the framework components
2. Integrate your existing data and web services with Ext JS data support
3. Enhance your JavaScript skills by using Ext's DOM and AJAX helpers

21830543R00193

Made in the USA
Charleston, SC
01 September 2013